Lost over Laos

Lost over Laos

A True Story of Tragedy, Mystery, and Friendship

Richard Pyle

Horst Faas

Foreword by David Halberstam

DA CAPO PRESS
A Member of the Perseus Books Group

Designed by Melodie Wertelet

Cataloging-in-Publication data for this book is available from the Library of Congress.

ISBN 978-0-306-81251-4

Published by Da Capo Press
A Member of the Perseus Books Group
http://www.dacapopress.com

Da Capo Press books are available at special discounts for bulk
purchases in the U.S. by corporations, institutions, and other
organizations. For more information, please contact the Special Markets
Department at the Perseus Books Group, 11 Cambridge Center,
Cambridge, MA 02142, or call (800) 255–1514 or (617) 252–5298,
or e-mail special.markets@perseusbooks.com.

1 2 3 4 5 6 7 8 9—08 07 06 05 04

Contents

Foreword

This is a remarkable book, and long, long overdue. It is modest, poignant, and compelling. Thirty-one years after a South Vietnamese military helicopter was shot down over Laos, taking the lives of four combat photographers and seven Vietnamese, two of our most distinguished—and dogged—journalists, Richard Pyle and Horst Faas, have told not merely the story of what happened that day and the days leading up to it, but also the story of their own journey to discover the remains of their four comrades in the mountains of Laos. In the process, Pyle and Faas have produced a book whose truths are much larger than they seem at first—an eloquent and thoughtful rumination about why men and women in the press corps risk so much in a combat zone for marginal glory, and even more surely, marginal salaries.

Two of the four photojournalists who died that day, Larry Burrows and Henri Huet, were quite well known in the profession; two of them, Kent Potter and Keisaburo Shimamoto, were not so famous. Burrows, who was shooting for *Life* magazine, was the most celebrated photographer of the war, a man considered an artist by both his colleagues and his employers. In the earlier part of the war, before television news became an increasingly important instrument of coverage—the "living room war" in Michael Arlens's phrase—it was Burrows's brilliant, haunting, and strangely artistic photos in *Life* that provided the most important and defining images of the war to millions of Americans. If he had any peer, it was Huet, who was equally well loved by his colleagues, and who was working for the Associated Press. The other two were not as famous: Kent Potter was a young man from Quaker background in Philadelphia who was escaping a difficult situation at home and had followed his star to Vietnam where he was shooting for UPI, and Keisaburo Shimamoto was a Japanese shooting as a freelancer for *Newsweek*.

They died late in the war, in February 1971. It was three years after the Tet offensive, long after interest in America had begun to decline. The assignment that day was an ARVN (or South Vietnamese Army) strike against the NVA in Laos—part of Nixon's Vietnamization, it was an ill-advised use of Vietnamese forces that somewhat predictably ended badly. All four photographers were there voluntarily; in the case of Burrows, having heard of the forthcoming assault in Laos, he had rushed back from the Indian subcontinent to cover it, and had used his seniority to make sure he got a seat on the chopper. He was the senior man among photographers in the journalistic pecking order, the great photographer-as-artist for a still powerful photo magazine that could do long multiphotograph stories that tracked beneath the surface of normal daily photojournalism. This was very much his war; his signature had been on it since 1962, and he had decided much earlier that he was going to see it through.

:: :

The two men who not only wrote this book, but who visited Laos in 1998 in search of the remains of their friends and made sure the book was published, deserve the approbation of their colleagues. It was not an easy course: They went against the grain to do it, in a book market not exactly hospitable to stories about events which took place so long ago, and about men who are largely remembered only by their families and their colleagues. Taking on this project, making sure somehow that the book happened, following the trail of the crash to Laos, and looking for any traces of the men twenty-seven years after it all happened is an act of rare integrity and conscience—and finally love—on the part of Pyle and Faas. It reflects a belief that their four colleagues should be remembered not just for what they did, but why they did it. Knowing Pyle and Faas, I am not surprised by what they have accomplished.

Of the two authors, Horst Faas is the better known, and the word *legendary* is now often attached to his name, quite appropriately. Perhaps no one is more respected and revered by his Vietnam colleagues. Over the thirteen years from the time he first arrived in Saigon in 1962 to the fall of that city in 1975, I don't think anyone stayed longer, took more risks, or showed greater devotion to his work and his colleagues. He has been my friend for forty-one years, and I think of him as nothing less than a genius. Again it was entirely in keeping with Faas's uncommon commitment to his job and his colleagues that he was one of the two driving forces behind *Requiem*, one of the most beautiful and moving books ever published on the Vietnam War, a book which is devoted to the work of the many photographers who were killed in that war, on both sides.

Richard Pyle is not as recognized, but perhaps he should be, because he reflects what is at the heart of this profession: the willingness to do something extremely difficult under exhausting and dangerous conditions, for reasons that you yourself do not always understand at the time, but which seem to leave you at certain junctures in your life with no alternative—in effect, a choice without a choice. He spent five years in Vietnam, arriving there in 1968 just after the Tet offensive when he was thirty-three. At first he thought he had gotten there a little late, but a shrewd colleague named John Wheeler told him—quite prophetically—not to worry, there would be plenty of war left for him to cover. Three of those years were spent as bureau chief, and all of them were dangerous—in Vietnam every mission you went on was dangerous. What he won, if not fame and glamour, was the respect of his colleagues, which in Vietnam was what mattered most. He was the AP bureau chief on the day that members of the press corps learned about the crash of the helicopter, and it was his melancholy duty to write the first news story that told of the deaths of his four colleagues. He has been drawn to that story and that moment ever since.

: :

The book is really something of a search, first a search both physical and metaphysical to find out what happened and why it happened that day, and then a second search decades later to join the extraordinary people from the American military whose difficult duty it has been to look for crash sites in so vast, difficult, and unforgiving a landscape. But there is also an additional search, and that is to try and understand a little better not just why the four men were there that day, but why we were *all* there and why we did what we did. That part—the contemplation on why journalists and photographers do what they do in combat zones—is very low key, forming something of an undertow to the book. Pyle, who did the writing, is listening to many voices here—the voices of the four men he knew, the voices of his colleagues, and perhaps the most important one, his own—in trying to answer that most difficult question.

I suppose in some way what drives *Lost over Laos*, or perhaps more accurately, what compelled the authors to write it, is the age-old question asked by someone who survives a terrifying experience: Why did I survive when people I knew and loved, and who may even have been nobler in spirit and braver in performance of duty, did not? Added to that is the additional question about Vietnam that none of us ever answers satisfactorily: Why was I there voluntarily, what pulled me there, and what made it so important, so central, indeed so defining a part of my life? I think Pyle and Faas have answered the eternal question far better than most, in trying to get at the strange, unrelenting pull that Vietnam had on so many journalists of my generation. None of the four that died, Pyle writes, "would have proclaimed any grand motive for what they did with their lives, yet all were men imbued with purpose larger than themselves. In purest form, this was the reporter's creed—the telling of a story so that others might know it. In their case, it was to invite, even compel, the world to see Vietnam as they saw it, through a camera lens that illuminated, explained, told truths of what the war looked like and how it felt to be there."

With those sentences, I think he has found the answer to the question—the fact that a story of this nature alters and enhances those who struggle to tell it, that what we do (and thus who we are) truly matters. The rewards are thus internal ones. It really is about doing something, for all of the veneer of ego, that is larger than self. Men—and now more and more women as well—who probably thought of themselves as weak and fragile and unsure of themselves when they were young, are surprised to find that covering something so important gives them not merely purpose and focus, but courage as well.

We who survived think after a time that we have become immune to the pulls and emotions of the past—jaded now and filled with newer memories, we feel sufficiently distanced from the bad days to deal effectively with the rest of our lives. And to some degree that is true, we do get on with our lives, and we do have our second acts. And then a book like this comes along, and we are brought back to that other time. We remember, first, where we were when we heard the news of the deaths of the four colleagues, and then a quick flash of memories of some of the four men: an early morning Army breakfast with Burrows at a helicopter base in Soc Trang in 1962, the memory oddly focused on a sense of how weak the Army coffee was—I wanted it stronger—and then seeing the stunning cool of Larry, and realizing how much better a job he had done in immunizing himself from his fears. Then another moment later in the war at the AP office, seeing a strikingly handsome Eurasian man who was uncommonly quiet but who seemed to inspire considerable respect from his friends, and being told that it was Henri Huet and how good he really was.

All of this happened a long time ago, thirty-two years ago as I write now, and men who were young then would be, if they had lived and had dodged the normal obstacles on their actuarial tables, much older in a culture designed increasingly for the young. Larry Burrows would be seventy-six, Henri Huet, who seemed destined to be ageless, would be seventy-five. Kent Potter, so young that his colleagues thought of him—eternally—as being a kid, would be fifty-five, and Keisaburo Shimamoto sixty-five. Yet because of their work during those years, because so many of their photos still mean so much, and because of books like this, what they did—and who they were and why they did it—still has meaning.

David Halberstam
December 2002

Preface

Among all wars in U.S. history, the second Indochina War—known to a generation of Americans as the Vietnam War—was the longest, the least popular, and the most intensively reported. For those in the news profession, it was also the most accessible. In no previous war, and in none since, have reporters, photographers, and camera crews had such ready access to the battlefield as they did in Vietnam. There was no censorship; journalists based in Saigon operated under self-policing rules that posed no serious impediment to coverage and, except in the most egregious cases, carried minimal penalties for violations.

This relatively loose arrangement had a flip side, however. The same freedom afforded journalists to cover and report the war left them open to charges that they were undermining U.S. and/or South Vietnamese policy or effectively helping the enemy—a perception that, though groundless, has endured for decades in some military and official circles. It also exposed the press to dangers on an unprecedented scale; during the fifteen years of the so-called American War (1960–1975), more than seventy accredited journalists were killed.

This book tells one story of the Vietnam War primarily in that journalistic context, in which reporters, photographers, and camera crews strove to tell the story honestly and diligently, sometimes paying the ultimate price. The narrative centers on 1969–1971, a period that involved some of the bloodiest fighting and most significant military decisions— including U.S.-supported offensives into Cambodia and Laos—yet has received less attention in postwar writings than other phases of the war.

At home, Americans were losing interest and confidence in U.S. policy in Southeast Asia; the military was showing signs of corrosion in morale and motivation; and politicians were urging a U.S. withdrawal at whatever cost. After years in which top Vietnam policy makers in Washington had put domestic political expediency ahead of military practicality, President Richard Nixon's administration was seeking ways to extricate U.S. forces from Indochina without simply abandoning South Vietnam to face a determined, politically unrestrained enemy alone.

Perhaps the one constant in all this was that the Saigon-based press was still covering the story as it always had. This did *not* mean that journalists were swarming over the battlefields of Indochina like the fire ants that dropped from the trees. Of more than 5,000 correspondents accredited by U.S. and South Vietnamese officials during the entire conflict, only 200–400 were usually in Vietnam at a given time—the peak was around 600 in early 1968, during and after the Tet Offensive—and only about a third of those actually went into the field. The rest were managers, spouses, technicians, and others with marginal connections to the actual reporting of the war.

For those who did venture afield, getting there was itself a risky undertaking. It was possible to drive Vietnam's roads, although it was important to observe special rules of safety and discretion, such as not going down a deserted highway. Remote areas could be reached only by helicopter, a machine that revolutionized warfare in Vietnam yet was relatively slow and highly vulnerable to ground fire.

: :

When Saigon fell to the North Vietnamese Army (NVA) in 1975, the roster of foreign and local journalists killed or unaccounted for was more than seventy. An unknown number of Cambodians, who had worked for the Western press and would vanish in the Killing Fields, were eventually added to an uncertain final toll.

Reporters and photographers could not know how often death merely came close—the helicopter that was not taken, the bullet that did not whine past the ear. "Today I know that death was often much closer than I was willing to admit to myself in those years," says this book's coauthor Horst Faas, whose respect for the power of luck was assured in 1967, when he was severely wounded in an ambush. He might have bled to death but for the nineteen-year-old U.S. Army medic who pinched off the gushing artery in his upper left leg and would tell him years later, when they met by chance, "You were so gray, I thought you were a goner."

As the longtime chief of Saigon photos for the Associated Press, Horst met most of the photographers who passed through Vietnam. "I never encountered anyone with a 'death wish,' but there were young and inexperienced ones, who tended to be more daring. Some had a tendency to brag and belittle the fears of more cautious colleagues, and some were fooled by the bucolic and peaceful countryside and the seemingly peaceful inhabitants."

A decade earlier, Robert Capa of *Life* magazine had defined the combat photographer's creed by saying, "If your pictures aren't good enough, you're not close enough." As if to underscore the point, Capa had stepped on a landmine while accompanying French troops in 1954. He was the first photojournalist killed in Vietnam, the patron saint of all who came after.

History, in repeating itself, had a way of choosing the exceptional. In 1965, a Viet Cong booby trap killed American reporter Dickey Chapelle, the first woman journalist to die in Indochina. AP's Henri Huet took a memorable photo of a Marine chaplain giving her last rites. In 1967, Bernard Fall, the French-born author of such seminal books on France's war in Vietnam as *Hell in a Very Small Place*, an account of Dien Bien Phu, and *Street Without Joy*, was killed by a mine— on the same coastal road that French Legionnaires had dubbed *La Rue Sans Joie*.

Journalists died in various ways. In the space of two weeks in 1965, AP photographer Bernard Kolenberg perished in a midair collision of two South Vietnamese fighter-bombers, and AP lost its top Viet-

namese staff photographer, Huynh Thanh My, in a Mekong Delta firefight between government troops and the Viet Cong. Sam Castan of
Look magazine, freelancers Charles Chellappah and Ronald Gallagher,
and Agence France Presse reporter Alain St. Paul also died covering
ground combat. In May 1968, four Australian reporters were murdered in their jeep at a Viet Cong roadblock in Saigon, the first multiple deaths involving the press.

In 1955, the little-known but brilliant American photographer
Everette "Dixie" Reese was shot down in a French observation plane
over Saigon, the first journalist killed in an air incident. Ten years later,
U.S. freelancer Jerry Rose died in a crash in the Central Highlands. During the 1968 siege of Khe Sanh, a crash killed freelancer Robert Ellison,
known for his photo coverage of the civil rights revolution in the American South. In 1971, French-born *Newsweek* reporter Francois Sully,
who had covered Vietnam for a decade, died along with Lieutenant
General Do Cao Tri, a flashy officer who was widely considered Saigon's
best combat leader, in a helicopter crash near the Cambodian border.
Sully was the magazine's second combat loss in less than a month.

On August 19, 1969, AP photographer Oliver Noonan and I
slipped out of the Danang Press Center before dawn to cover an as yet
unreported battle that was taking shape near Hiep Duc, in the Son
Chang River valley southwest of Danang. We agreed that to maximize
our coverage we would split up and then rendezvous at the Americal
Division headquarters at Chu Lai later in the day.

While waiting for the division helicopter to pick us up, I asked Ollie why he was carrying a large metal camera case, cumbersome gear
for the field. "It's for protection," he joked. "If they shoot at the helicopter I'll hide behind it."

Predawn fog lay thick as shaving cream across the jungled ridges
as our Huey corkscrewed down to Firebase Center, a hilltop poking
above the mist, where Noonan jumped off, waved, and headed for the
command bunker. I flew on to Firebase West, overlooking the valley
where artillery, mortars, air strikes, and diving Cobra gunships were
blasting communist positions.

In late afternoon, I caught a ride out on an ammo resupply chopper. An hour or so later and three miles away, Noonan climbed aboard
the helicopter of a battalion commander who had landed to check his

troops' tactical situation. As it lifted off, the Huey was hit by .51-caliber antiaircraft fire, spun out of control, and crashed. All aboard were killed, including the commander of the 3rd Battalion, 21st Infantry, his sergeant-major, four crewmen, another GI, and Oliver Noonan.

In one letter home Ollie had written, "Nothing comes easy here. Everything is earned." He had been earning it only a few months when he became the third AP staffer to die in Vietnam combat.

Journalists who flocked to Cambodia after the fighting spread there in 1970 found different rules for coverage and survival. The press fanned out in Mercedes-Benz taxis, which for a time proved more dangerous than helicopters. No-man's-land began at the city limits. Traveling in groups did not guarantee safety; going alone was akin to suicide. During the intense month of April, twelve journalists—Germans, Japanese, Swiss, French, Austrian, and American—disappeared in eastern Cambodia, having naively assumed the Viet Cong, the Khmer Rouge, and local bandits would respect noncombatants.

Dana Stone and Sean Flynn, son of the swashbuckling film actor Errol Flynn, who were freelancing with cameras for CBS News and *Time*, respectively, left Phnom Penh on motorcycles one morning, headed down Highway 1 toward the Vietnam border, and vanished. A last shot of the pair was taken by Terry Khoo, an ABC cameraman who would himself be killed in Vietnam in 1972.

Stone and Flynn became part of the war's mythology; friends speculated that Flynn would one day turn up in style befitting his father—riding the lead tank into Phnom Penh. Years later, their friend Tim Page established with near certainty that they had been captured by Viet Cong, turned over to Khmer Rouge guerrillas, and ultimately executed—perhaps bludgeoned to death with a garden hoe, the agrarian reformers' weapon of choice.

As Highway 1 was a death trap, so were other roads. United Press International photographer Kyoichi Sawada and reporter Frank Frosch were found shot, execution-style, beside Highway 2 south of Phnom Penh. Nine television news crew members were killed in a single episode, among them NBC's well-known Hong Kong–based correspondent, Welles Hangen, CBS producer Gerald Miller, and CBS correspondent George Syvertsen. Ramnik Lekhi and Tomoharu Ishii, of CBS, and Roger Colne of NBC were the first TV cameramen killed in

Indochina, a remarkable fact considering the high risk of physical exposure required of them in combat situations.

In all, twenty-five foreign reporters and photographers had been killed or were missing in Cambodia by the end of 1970. As the new year began, only Laos, among the three embattled states of Indochina, had not witnessed the deaths of journalists.

Richard Pyle

Acknowledgments

For many years after it happened, the 1971 helicopter crash that killed photojournalists Larry Burrows, Henri Huet, Kent Potter, and Keisaburo Shimamoto was a story without an ending. As friends and fellow journalists, we felt fervently that it needed one. That is why we went back to Laos twenty-seven years later, and that is the reason for this book.

To assemble the fragments of this story into a coherent whole, the authors have drawn heavily on their own memories, those of former Vietnam-era colleagues, and those of people who knew the four principal subjects of this story in places other than Indochina. We have benefited greatly from a body of writing by some of these former colleagues, providing details that we did not know and clarifying or firming up memories clouded by time.

Memories do play tricks, and there is no question that pitfalls are inherent in any narrative that depends heavily on personal recollections, especially those three decades old. But Vietnam truly was, for many people, *the* indelible experience and has remained whole, or nearly so, in their minds. Not only do former Saigon-based journalists remember with remarkable clarity events that occurred that long ago; shared memories of specific events coincide to an amazing degree. One might suppose that some of them had told their tales of that time and place more than a few times over the years. As for the reliability of those once-spoken words, direct quotes have been checked, wherever possible, with secondary or multiple sources and are as close to being accurate as we can make them.

So many people are entitled to special mention in this project that the term loses its meaning, yet there are several individuals without whom the book could not have been produced. Any such list must logically begin with Sergio Ortiz, who as a U.S. Marine Corps photographer in 1971 took the last known pictures of the four and was the last person known to have spoken with them at the helicopter pad before they departed on the fateful mission. Three other people had circular, interlocking roles that were crucial to relocating the crash site in Laos a quarter-century later—researcher William Forsyth, former Army helicopter commander James T. Newman, and journalist Michael Putzel.

Forsyth, a civilian investigator for the Hawaii-based Joint Task Force–Full Accounting (JTF-FA), the Pentagon agency that seeks Americans missing in action (MIA) on foreign battlefields, first heard of the Laos shootdown in 1993 while interviewing Newman on an un-related case. Newman had witnessed the incident on February 10, 1971, and the next day had flown Putzel, then an AP correspondent, near enough to the crash site to take photographs. It was from Forsyth's calls in 1994, seeking clues to the site location, that we learned the case was being investigated. It was Putzel's photograph, re-discovered twenty-five years after the fact, that enabled Forsyth to fi-nally pinpoint the location. And it was Jim Newman, again, who helped reconstruct details of the shootdown as far as they can be known.

We are especially indebted to Larry Burrows's son Russell and his wife, Bobbi, for details on the early years of the *Life* photographer whose name became synonymous with Vietnam; to Inger-Johanne Holmboe, Henri Huet's fiancée, who provided priceless letters, pic-tures, and recollections of that mysterious and complex man; to Ann Bathgate Walker, Kent Potter's last high-school sweetheart, who shared intimate, sometimes painful memories of a man she had loved in spite of herself; and to Kenro Shimamoto, who patiently answered questions through intermediaries in Japan about his younger brother Keisaburo.

Henri Huet's brothers, Paul and Yves, and sister, Jeanne Marie, recalled their childhood in Brittany and their prodigal's return to Indochina. Several friends of Kent Potter offered memories of Quaker school days in Philadelphia, most notably Tom Martin, who also described his timely reunion with Kent years later in Southeast Asia, Alice Maxfield, Robert Metz, David Thanhauser, and William Thode.

Janie Ellithorpe Trinkaus spoke about her late husband, Harold Ellithorpe, repeating his oft-told account of having been bumped from the fatal flight. Tsutomu "Tom" Kono's impeccable translation went well beyond literal Japanese to a deeper, more illuminating interpretation of writings by and about Keisaburo Shimamoto.

Officials of the two agencies concerned with MIAs kept us posted on search developments and facilitated our visit to Site 2062: Lieutenant Colonels Barbara Claypool, Roger King, and Franklin Childress; Major Joe Davis and Navy Journalist Second Class Jeff McDowell at JTF-FA; Colonel David Pagano and Johnie E. Webb Jr., the commander and deputy commander, respectively, and investigator Robert C. Maves, of the U.S. Army Central Identification Laboratory in Hawaii (CILHI); Lieutenant Colonel James Ransick and members of JTF Detachment 3 in Laos and, especially, the Site 2062 excavation team who accommodated our presence and needs: Army Captain (now Major) Jeffrey Price, the team leader; civilian anthropologist and site director Lisa Hoshower Leppo; Master Sergeant Ralf Hawkins and Tech Sergeant Aaron Carpenter, U.S. Air Force; Sergeant Carl Holden, U.S. Marine Corps; Staff Sergeant Michael Swam, Sergeant Bill Adams, Sergeant Don Anongdeth, and Specialist Michael Harsch, all U.S. Army.

Further credit belongs to freelance writer Brenda Smiley, the wife of coauthor Richard Pyle. On her first visit to Vietnam in 1995, Brenda talked her way into accompanying a JTF team into the field for an article in *Archaeology* magazine, establishing contacts that proved valuable for this book. Archaeologist-anthropologist Peter Miller offered expertise and guidance regarding the dedicated work of CILHI/JTF-FA teams in Indochina.

Dusadee Haymond of the U.S. embassy's public diplomacy office in Vientiane cut brilliantly through bureaucratic obstacles in Laos. Wendy J. Chamberlin, then U.S. ambassador to Laos (and later to Pakistan), explained today's U.S. diplomatic posture in Laos. Our government "minder," Mr. Soukhasavan Sanapay, was helpful and unobtrusive.

Retired Lieutenant General Hoang Xuan Lam and Colonel Tran Ngoc Chau recalled details of OPERATION LAM SON 719 (the U.S.-supported South Vietnamese invasion of Laos) and General Lam's abbreviated helicopter tour of the Laos battlefront. For several years we were thwarted in trying to track down any records or family contacts for any of the South Vietnamese helicopter crewmen who also died in the shootdown. Only in recent months did we finally locate informants familiar with the Vietnam Air Force's 213th Helicopter Squadron and learned the names of those lost. This is covered in the Afterword.

Information, advice, and/or encouragement came from many old Vietnam hands, notably Colonel Robert Burke, U.S. Army (ret.); Douglas Pike, an eminent authority on Vietnam's communist insurgency; Gerald Hickey, unquestionably the top scholar on Montagnard peoples of Indochina, and Jerome H. Doolittle. Robert Destatte, of the Department of Defense Prisoner of War and Missing Personnel Affairs Office, shared an amazing knowledge of North Vietnam's order of battle, including defenses arrayed on the Ho Chi Minh Trail in 1971.

William Hammond, an authority on Vietnam War press coverage, and Vietnam expert Dale Andrade, both of the U.S. Army Center of Military History, offered useful insights. Data on Kent Potter's Marine Corps reserve career came from USMC public affairs officers Lieutenant Colonel Scott Campbell, Captain Rob Winchester, and Captain Mike Newman. Doug Roesemann, former public affairs officer of 1st Brigade, 5th Infantry Division (Mechanized), dug out old maps to help reconstruct events at Camp Red Devil (Dong Ha), Khe Sanh, and along Route 9. Former scout pilot Bruce Osborne told how he spotted clues that led to Hamburger Hill. Richard Lennon recalled Henri Huet's visit to his Marine unit near the Demilitarized Zone (DMZ).

Helping to fill out the background of LAM SON 719, former pilots harkened back to their own ordeal of courage during the operation. Lieutenant Colonel Robert Clewell, U.S. Army (ret.), a/k/a Comanchero Six, was a fount of technical and historical knowledge, command wisdom, and human understanding.

In patiently drawing on his memory to help us reconstruct the VNAF shootdown, Jim Newman, a/k/a Condor Six, missed no opportunity to extol the fighting virtues of his beloved C Troop, 2nd Squadron, 17th Air Cavalry. Among former Condors who spoke in turn of Newman's courageous leadership and unstinting commitment to rescuing downed aviators were pilot/operations officer and unit historian Malcolm "Mac" Jones; Cobra platoon leader Charles Vehlow; Cobra pilots John Vasko, Mike Dempsey, and Jim Kane; Newman's crew chief, Charles Davis; crew chief Richard Frazee, aero rifle platoon commander Ed Kersey, pilot John Oldham, Newman's left-seater; pilots Cleveland "Slim" Pickens, Ross Eliason, Steve Karschner, Rick "the Mayor" Daly, and the late James Jones. Lieutenant Colonel Mike Sloniker (ret.) of the Vietnam Helicopter Pilots Association (VHPA) provided vital material on aircraft losses and casualties, as did VHPA member Bob Hamilton on other aeronautical questions. Former U.S. Ranger Randy White described heroic actions near the A Shau Valley.

The list of former and current news colleagues who encouraged and aided this project is long and their contributions immeasurable.

David Halberstam, who knows well the terrain, both in Vietnam and the publishing industry, gave this project a boost with his early and enthusiastic advocacy. Other ardent supporters from the outset were Peter Arnett and Bill and Rosemarie Tuohy. Likewise Tim Page, who was Horst's coeditor on the book *Requiem* and feels the seductive gravitational pull of Vietnam in ways that others may be pardoned not to understand.

Former and present AP staffers who provided help, ranging from wartime recollections and archival guidance to advice and encouragement: Eddie Adams, Vin Alabiso, Terry Anderson, Tad Bartimus, Ann Bertini, Sam Boyle, Harold Buell, Max Desfor, Linda Deutsch, George Esper, Les Glenister, Norman Goldstein, Denis Gray, Charles Hanley, Larry Heinzerling, Rikio Imajo, Susan James, Holger Jensen, Willis Johnson, Tom Jory, Jurate Kazickas, Rusty Kennedy, Guy Kopelowicz, Harry Koundakjian, Edith Lederer, David Longstreath, George McArthur, Hugh Mulligan, John Nance, Max Nash, Dang Van Phuoc, Robert Poos, Carl and Kim Dung Robinson, Mort Rosenblum, Rhonda

Shafner, Steve Stibbens, Jack Stokes, Kelly Smith Tunney, Neal Ulevich, Huynh Cong "Nick" Ut, Hugh Van Es, Edwin Q. White, Terry Wolkerstorfer, Ronen Zilberman, and Charles Zoeller.

UPI veterans whose memories of Vietnam were important, and in some cases essential, to the story: Leon Daniel, Joe Galloway, Nat and Helen Gibson, Dirck Halstead, Frank Johnston, David Lamb, Roger Norum, Bill Reilly, Bill Snead, Robert Sullivan, Kate Webb, and Nik Wheeler.

Other journalists, with past or current affiliations, who contributed: Steve Bell, ABC News; Kevin Buckley, *Newsweek*; David Burnett, *Time*; Ben Chapnick; Sal DiMarco, Jr.; Jed Duvall, Kurt Volkert, Jeff Williams, all CBS News; Marc Duvoisin, Philadelphia *Inquirer*; Dorothy Fall; Denby Fawcett; David Friend, *Vanity Fair*; Tony Hirashiki, ABC News; Chris Jensen, Cleveland *Plain Dealer*; Bob Jones, George Lewis, Arthur Lord, all NBC News; Catherine Leroy; Roger Mattingly; Don North, ABC News; Len Santorelli, Reuters; Co Rentmeester, John Saar, Dick Swanson, all *Life*; Wallace Terry, *Time*; and James Caccavo, *Newsweek*. Pham Xuan An spent part of an afternoon at his home in Ho Chi Minh City, recalling his double life as journalist and Viet Cong spy.

Our wives, Brenda Smiley and Ursula Faas, understood, supported, and shared our emotional and professional commitment to this long and, at times, exasperating project. Our agent, Tom Wallace, saw the book through eyes more experienced than ours, believed in it, and offered many excellent recommendations and suggestions.

We offer the work in memory, not just of the four whose lives and deaths it describes, but of all journalists who ever went in search of a story in Indochina.

A special thanks to all who have said, "I'm really glad you are doing this."

Richard Pyle
Horst Faas
New York, July 2002

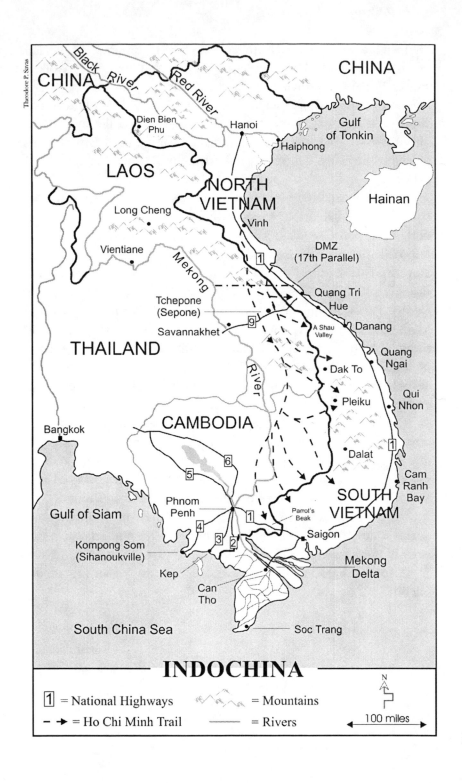

INDOCHINA

1 = National Highways   = Mountains

- ➤ = Ho Chi Minh Trail   = Rivers

100 miles

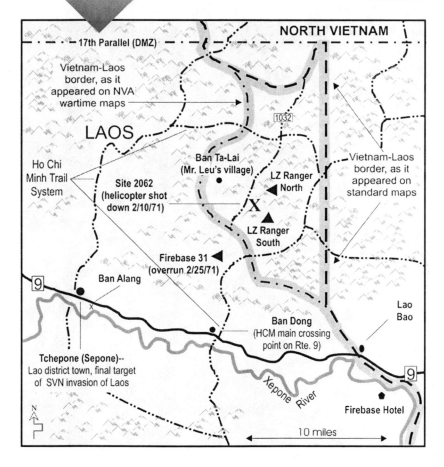

Lost over Laos

1 : The Flight

What it was really like in the helicopter's final moments, we of course can never know. From what is known of the people, it is reasonable to believe that some of those aboard the olive-green UH-1 Huey may have sensed impending disaster as it skimmed above the dark peaks and valleys of the Annamite Mountains of southern Laos, three other helicopters trailing behind.

Among the four civilian photographers riding in the cargo bay, Larry Burrows, a photographer for *Life* magazine, or Henri Huet, of the Associated Press, might have been first to feel a growing unease. Both men, in their early forties, had spent a decade covering combat in Indochina. Countless flights like this one had sharpened their instincts for danger, for knowing in the gut when things were not quite right.

Though half their age, Kent Potter of United Press International was a three-year veteran of covering the war and no less attuned to its special hazards. The same could be said of Keisaburo Shimamoto, a freelancer on assignment for *Newsweek*, who had been in and out of Vietnam since 1965.

Savvy born of experience might have caused any of the four to question why the flight from Firebase Hotel to Landing Zone (LZ) Ranger South, the second leg of this aerial tour of the battlefront, seemed to be taking so long. On the map, the distance between the two outposts was fourteen miles, a ten-minute flight in a Huey at maximum weight and speed. They should have been on the ground by now. The next logical thought would also have been the least comforting—that their two South Vietnamese pilots had missed LZ Ranger South entirely and were now lost over territory that was both unfamiliar and hostile.

Seated on the inside, facing each other, Burrows and Shimamoto felt—perhaps with some relief—the Huey's sudden tilt to the right, the beginning of a turn in that direction. It could be that the pilots had realized their mistake and were now circling back.

As the aircraft banked more sharply, Huet and Potter, riding in the open door on the right side, could look straight down, past their boots, to the steeply falling-away mountainsides and the gray-trunked hardwoods spiking upward from the jungle. Cameras at hand, eyes roving, they would have been watching for any sign of activity, any clue to the human presence, that they knew was down below.

They might also have noticed, off to the right in the middle distance, the raw slash of earth on a dark mountain, the intended destination that their pilots had overshot. Voices snatched instantly away by the rush of wind and engine clatter, they would have resorted to pantomiming the discovery with nods and thumbs-up gestures. "Over there, guys. LZ Ranger South ... everything's cool."

A last snapshot, had it been taken, would have captured the four photographers adjusting their gear, checking their Leicas and Nikon Fs, getting ready to go instantly to work on landing. Based on what they'd heard before leaving Firebase Hotel, Ranger South might be a hot LZ.

Sergeant Tu Vu, the young South Vietnamese Army photographer traveling with them, would be fiddling with his gear as well, and the other two passengers, Vietnamese Army staff colonels who had boarded at the last minute at Ham Nghi, would be sitting impassively, one clutching a briefcase, anticipating a quick return to solid ground.

The last snapshot might even have frozen the instant when someone looking down saw smoke under the dark trees and orange bolts of fire racing upward, curving toward them ...

2 : The Mission

Nearly three decades later, lifting off from the grassy field at Ban Alang base camp, our pilot, a New Zealander too young to remember the Vietnam War, circled the cluster of blue nylon tents we had just left and turned north, skimming above treeless brown hills dotted with old craters and crude forts whose revetments had collapsed over time into lumpy hillocks. The little red-and-white, French-built Squirrel helicopter flirted audaciously with each ridgeline as it rose to meet us before falling sharply away into yet another jungle-choked valley.

From Ban Alang to our destination was only seven minutes by air. On foot, someone had said, it could take three days of climbing and hacking through rainforest. How close, yet how far, was the nameless mountain where we were about to have a rendezvous with the past.

We were crammed five abreast on the narrow bench seat behind the pilot. On my left, my colleague Horst Faas was leaning out the open door, his hat brim flapping madly in the slipstream as he scanned the terrain below in search of targets for the 35mm cameras slung around his neck.

Up ahead, the serried peaks of the Annamite Range marched off into the smoky haze, a gray-green Chinese watercolor. It was the end of the dry season, and pocket-sized forest fires were burning in every direction, blackening hillsides to a smoldering checkerboard. I now knew what our escort officer, Lieutenant Colonel Roger King, had meant when he remarked, the day before, that "half of southern Laos is on fire."

Neither Horst nor I had ever seen these mountains so close at hand, yet they were as familiar as if we had been here many times. We had a true sense of the place. Thirty years before, as journalists for The Associated Press based in Saigon, we had flown frequently into wild country—a green sea of undulating elephant grass, or a sandbagged military outpost clinging to a narrow hogback ridge. But that had always been on the Vietnam side of the border.

These rugged mountains, the cordillera of Indochina running north to south through the panhandle of Laos, had been in those days the scene of history's most sustained aerial bombardment, as U.S. bombers hammered the Ho Chi Minh Trail around the clock, around the calendar. Our task had included reporting, as best we could, on this important part of the war, something not made easier by our inability to see it for ourselves. Southern Laos was off-limits, *terra incognita* to everyone but the warring parties. The only view of the Trail that outsiders might hope for was a fleeting glimpse from a commercial jetliner flying at 30,000 feet—an encapsulated world apart, from which, on a rare day when the haze lying over the jungle was not too thick, the eye might briefly discern the physical details of dark, mountainous outcroppings, a coiled stream revealing itself in a brief sun-flash, the vaguest trace here or there of a man-made track, perhaps even a plume of smoke that hinted at a war, distant and unseen.

Now, Horst and I found ourselves racing low over the mysterious mountains, accompanying a team of U.S. military search specialists to the very hillside where, it was believed, the helicopter carrying the four photographers and seven South Vietnamese soldiers had crashed and burned twenty-seven years and one month earlier.

Except for the old bomb craters, still unmistakable despite years of overgrowth, there was little to suggest the tempest that once ravaged this landscape. Over time, the jungle had blotted out most vestiges of the Trail, and except for a few dirt paths here and there, the tangled valleys and sun-scorched hillsides offered no clues to human habitation, old or new.

In recent years, and partly through our efforts, the site of the 1971 crash had been located, all but positively identified, and marked down on a list of sites to be excavated. After two bureaucratic delays, that effort was finally taking place. A nine-member team from the Joint Task Force–Full Accounting, a special Pentagon unit created in 1992 to trace the more than 2,000 Americans then still missing from the Vietnam War, hoped to verify the location beyond any doubt and to recover any human remains that might still be found after so many years. With luck, the team—made up of young U.S. military personnel and a civilian anthropologist—could resolve unanswered questions for loved ones of the four civilian photographers, just as they regularly did for the families of downed pilots and other military MIAs.

As the team had its mission, Horst and I had ours. It was a different one, and a dual quest. In the role of journalists, we hoped to determine the facts of what actually had occurred, beyond what was known from the eyewitness accounts. As friends and former comrades of the four photographers, we were making a pilgrimage of the heart, one that had been a long time coming.

That morning, at the government guesthouse in Sepone, I was awakened by a dream. It was one of those quick flashes that seem to occur just before the mind rising from sleep breaks the surface. In the dream, I was riding in the rear seat of a helicopter and saw the window below the pilots' feet suddenly disintegrate, shards of clear plastic floating away in slow motion.

Awake, I tried to mentally capture the dream before it dissolved. The light of a pale full moon filtered through a grimy window and the mosquito net draped over my bunk, casting odd shadows across the room, where Horst and Mr. Soukhasavan Sanapay, the official "minder" assigned to us by the Laos Foreign Ministry's information bureau, still slept. Outside, cowbells tinkled in the predawn, a reminder that this wooden house on stilts was part of a state agricultural test farm.

What did this dream mean? What does any dream mean? Not being given to belief in the occult, I could not see it, as some might, as a premonition of disaster, a warning against boarding the helicopter that in a few hours would take us on our first trip to the crash site. If anything, I figured, it could be just a venting of the subconscious, a way of releasing some of the long pent-up anticipation of this day, this place.

Lying awake, I retraced again the trail of events that had brought Horst and me back to Laos for the first time in a quarter of a century.

Both of us had last been here in March 1973, when Vientiane was the departure point for a group of journalists flying to Hanoi by chartered plane to cover the third and last release of U.S. prisoners of war— the final act in the United States' military withdrawal from Vietnam.

The Nixon White House was said to have issued an order that U.S. and foreign news media would have no access to the returning POWs until they were back in American hands. Whether the North Vietnamese were responding to the reported edict, or even knew of it, was unclear. But they gave our group of about thirty journalists what amounted to red-carpet treatment, a bus tour of Hanoi that included a stop at the prison compound known as the "Zoo," where we saw and talked to some of the last sixty-seven American prisoners in custody, then followed them in the bus caravan to the Gia Lam airport, where they were formally delivered back into friendly hands for the flight to Clark Air Force Base in the Philippines, the first leg on the long trip home.

That one-day trip to Hanoi had been a fitting capstone to my nearly five years in Indochina. A couple of months later, I left Saigon for good. It would be twenty-two years before I returned. In the meantime, I was to discover gradually, as many others did, what I had left behind in Southeast Asia. It was a large piece of myself.

From the day, almost from the moment, that the first word of the missing helicopter had reached us in a phone call to the AP Saigon bureau on February 10, 1971, I had taken a kind of proprietary interest in the event. At the basic level, this was predicated on having known three of the four photographers as friends. But it only began with that; those same friendships, after all, were shared by many people in Vietnam and elsewhere.

As chief of the Saigon bureau, an operation that involved some thirty news, photo, and technical people at any given time, I also felt a strong sense of responsibility. Not only had we lost one of our own; we had lost someone truly extraordinary.

Henri Huet, whom one colleague would sum up years later as "the kindest, bravest and most honorable man I ever knew,"[1] had occupied a unique place in his profession and in our immediate circle. His death was a shattering event. Yet there was no question of someone to blame, or what might have been done differently.

In his intrinsically dangerous profession, none knew better than Henri Huet how to calculate the risks, maximize the odds in his favor, to the extent that this *could* be done. And there was no way that a bureau chief, or anyone else, could have kept Henri from getting aboard that helicopter, any more than he would have chosen not to do so. For that to happen would have required the impossible—the certain foreknowledge that the aircraft was going to fall from the sky.

Within a day after the crash it was obvious that talk of survivors, of rescue, was meaningless. Given the location, any ground search of the area by friendly forces was clearly out of the question. There were reasons to believe that North Vietnamese soldiers might have visited the crash site, but nothing ever came of that, either.

From the jungle itself, there was only silence. We could not know that the war would continue for another four years, or that it would be more than two decades before anyone from the outside tried to find the hillside.

The world moved on, and most of us moved with it, to other lives, other stories, other wars. True, there were some among the old Vietnam hands who could not put the war's experience behind them—and never would. They were prisoners of an escape-proof past. Those of us who did not carry that burden could nod knowingly and say that we understood. We could imagine it happening to us and be glad that it had not.

Yet for anyone who had lived and worked as a journalist there in those years, Indochina was not easily erased, and there was no reason that it should be. The Vietnam War, we knew at the time and afterward, could well be the most important thing that ever happened in most of our lives. At least it would be always be there, a coal glowing, however faintly, in the banked fires of memory.

The lost helicopter of Laos hovered forever in that corner of my mind reserved for Vietnam. In its essence, the question was a journalist's question: What really *had* happened out there in the Annamites

---

[1] Letter from Robert Poos to the author.

that day, and why? Over time, the question reshaped itself into something larger and deeper. It became a mystery with a message—something from the past, not to be forgotten; something for the future, a story waiting to be finished.

Four photojournalists, reporting on a war, had gone to their deaths in a sudden, tumbling torrent of fire. It could be argued that such deaths as that served no valid purpose, that no photograph could possibly be worth that. Others would say it *was* worth it—that everybody dies, and what truly mattered was the record that these four had left, a marker far more enduring than any tombstone, a legacy that perpetuated mortality in ways that are denied to most people.

But those were not final answers; I looked for better ones.

None of the four—Larry Burrows, Henri Huet, Kent Potter, and Keisaburo Shimamoto—would have proclaimed any grand motive for what they did with their lives, yet all were men imbued with a purpose larger than themselves. In purest form, this was the reporter's creed—the telling of a story so that others might know it. In their case, it was to invite, even compel, the world to see Vietnam as they saw it, through a camera lens that illuminated, explained, told truths of what the war looked like and how it felt to be there.

It was therefore not right that they should be denied their own final truth, that the only monument to their commitment, their skill, and their courage should be a few bone shards and bits of metal, left out in the rain on a nameless, forgotten hillside.

That could be reconciled, I came to believe, only if someone were to go to that place, walk on that mountain, taste the thick jungle heat. Someone to go there, address any spirits that might exist, and say to them, "I am here. We are here. We have come to tell you that you are remembered, and well." And hope that an answer would come back in some form that we, the living, could understand.

Whatever the result of such a pilgrimage, it would be transcended by the very act of making it. Without that, at the very least, those four photographers—and, along with them, all the others who had died doing the same thing, even those of us who had done some of the same things and had *not* died—would be, forever, lost over Laos.

: :

Horst Faas and I, partners on this mission, had come to it by paths that began at the far ends of a world convulsed by World War II and gradually converged in the tropical latitudes of an Indochina at war with itself. Born in the same year, we had reached the age of awareness about the same time, but our boyhoods had been anything but mirror images.

Mine was spent in Detroit, which during the war had shelved its Motor City nickname in favor of another: the Arsenal of Democracy. At the nexus of the nation's manufacturing powerhouse, everything and everyone was in some way connected to the production of war materiel—tanks, trucks, jeeps, guns; everything that moved on wheels, and almost everything that caused the wheels to turn, flowed out of Detroit's converted automobile factories. It was claimed, with pride, that the last 1942 Dodge had been nudged off the end of the assembly line by the first tank.

Although geography made the chance of enemy attack on the American heartland remote, the city of Detroit took perverse pride in being the theoretical primary target. In a setting permeated by patriotic fervor to win the war on the assembly line, a boy's life was saving war bonds, scrap and paper drives, and Saturdays at the movies, where a dime provided transport to the jungles of *Bataan*, the desolation of *Sahara*, and the *Sands of Iwo Jima*.

Reality was ration cards, a sixth-grade teacher who also drove new army trucks from the factory to the railside loading dock, and the little white flags that seemed to hang in every window, with blue stars that sometimes turned to gold.

Horst's world was a world apart from mine. As a schoolboy living in the leafy Berlin suburb of Dahlem, he witnessed the first Allied air raids on the city, and "the fascinating spectacle of anti-aircraft action in the sky and the interruptions of school were not totally unwelcome." But things grew worse; after the family moved from Berlin to Kattowitz, in eastern Silesia, "the inevitable results were dramatically brought home to me each time the class had to stand at attention to listen to an announcement that the father or older brother of a classmate had died for Fuehrer and Fatherland."

As the end neared in early 1945, Horst's family spent six weeks in desperate flight from the advancing Russian forces, landing temporarily in—of all places—Berlin. By then, the air raids came three times a day, but "surprisingly, school continued to function until three weeks before the war ended." Amid the Soviet seizure and rape of Berlin, the family fled again, this time to northern Germany, remaining there for more than two years before finally escaping to Munich in the West, just before the Iron Curtain clanged down.

: :

As the red-and-white Squirrel droned above the Laotian peaks, Horst was thinking back—not to those precarious times in Germany, but to a humid dawn in June 1962 when he pulled himself and his bulky gear aboard a noisy, vibrating U.S. Army H-21 helicopter, loaded with South Vietnamese soldiers, near Soc Trang, deep in Vietnam's Mekong Delta.

It was his first-ever helicopter ride, the first of hundreds of such flights he would make over the next decade. Yet this one was indelibly fixed:

> Once loaded, the clumsy, banana-shaped helicopters swept upward in a narrow steep circle until the world at the tip of my lens became an endless lake of flooded field, criss-crossed by dikes and narrow straight roads. Being the last man aboard, I did as the last Vietnamese who climbed into the helicopter was doing. I sat in the open door, my feet dangling out. I soon lost my courage, closed my eyes and held on to the fixed machine gun beside me, its barrel pointing downward.
>
> The American gunner, crouching behind the gun and looking like a man from Mars in his flight helmet, seemed to understand. His right hand's index finger on the trigger, he used his left hand to grab my shirt and make me lean back, my eyes now staring at the ceiling of the helicopter.
>
> As the formation of twelve H-21s descended to the landing zone, all hell broke loose. Every helicopter gunner started firing, shell casings showering me, and I saw the bullets splashing into the water and the treeline beyond. My helicopter never landed, but hovered two or three feet above water and I realized there was no way back. The soldiers behind me pushed forward. I let go, jumped into the water holding my two cameras high over my head. The water was surprisingly cool at that early hour, the gooey mud lukewarm and rather pleasant.

The soldiers ran forward firing, a steady crackling sound, with intermittent thumping of exploding grenades, added to the machine guns of the helicopters that ended only when they were out of sight. I found it all frightening, confusing, exciting—and exhilarating. Since there was no place to hide, I remembered that I had come here to take pictures, and within seconds I had some excellent photographs of troops attacking from helicopters and racing across the open paddies toward the bank of a canal. Scenes that would become standard fare of mine and other photographers' war coverage.

Minutes later it was all over. As the soldiers reached the treeline and some small huts, they had ceased fire and nobody was shooting at us. Reaching the firm ground of the canal bank, I saw my first victims of the war, a few old people, a hideously wounded young woman holding up her child. An American captain and his radio operator tried to organize help for them.

: :

Cresting yet another ridge, we suddenly found ourselves above the crash site. On a barren mountain ridge we could see a parked helicopter, a twin to ours. There was also a blue tent, like those back at Ban Alang. People were standing on the ridge, looking up at us, shielding their eyes from the bright morning sun.

Our pilot circled out away from the hillside and hovered, giving Horst a chance to make some unobstructed aerial shots of the scene. Although the location of the crash site still was officially tentative, my eyes told my heart that this was it. No question. The steep slope, the clearing surrounded by thick vegetation—they looked almost exactly as I had imagined it a hundred times. The only surprise was a trace of an old roadway that emerged from the trees, curled the length of the open ridge, and disappeared into the foliage at the other end.

A newly carved foot trail led down to the area being excavated, already marked off with tape in the crosshatch pattern of an archaeological dig. The digging, in fact, had begun the previous day. Officially, it was known already as Site 2062, the number having been assigned in more or less chronological order to the list of MIA cases in Indochina.

There had been some 2,200 Americans still unaccounted for in

1992, when diplomatic agreements with the three communist governments—Vietnam, Laos, and Cambodia—opened the way to full-scale exploration of the wartime crash sites and the cumbersomely named Joint Task Force–Full Accounting was signed into existence by then–Defense Secretary Richard Cheney.[2]

Since the JTF's inception, its Hawaii-based search teams had located, explored, and excavated scores of crash sites in the three countries of Indochina. The overall results did not seem particularly impressive—in six years, only about 100 sets of remains recovered in Indochina had been identified as American. Yet the searchers, as we would soon discover, approached the task with an unflagging energy and enthusiasm, like prospectors forever driven by the hope of gold nuggets in the next pan of pebbles.

Whatever the team found at Site 2062 would follow the usual procedure: It would be shipped back to the U.S. Army's Central Identification Laboratory–Hawaii, where teams of forensic experts would employ a variety of scientific techniques toward identification. CILHI was itself a legacy of Vietnam, a spin-off of the wartime U.S. Army mortuary at Saigon, which had received and processed the American dead for return to the United States.[3]

But that part of the story lay well ahead. The first order of business now was to establish unequivocally that this place was where the South Vietnamese helicopter had gone down on February 10, 1971, and then to find whatever physical fragments of the eleven people it had carried might still rest amid the soil and stones.

Our New Zealander eased the Squirrel to a gentle landing next to its parked twin. Horst and I unbuckled our safety belts and scrambled out the left-side door. We felt a rush of excitement and a hundred other emotions as we stepped, for the first time in our lives, onto the rocky, hard-packed remnant of the Ho Chi Minh Trail.

---

[2] "Joint" refers to forces of different services combined for a common mission. MIA search teams are drawn from the U.S. Army, U.S. Air Force, and U.S. Marine Corps. The host country provides official assistance and recruits local villagers to help with the work.

[3] Some MIA remains have been identified through a single tooth—Vietnam was the first war in which the U.S. government had dental records for every participant—and in recent years through DNA matches with family members. But some 900 sets of remains are stored at the CILHI lab in Hawaii. Officials conceded that most will never be identified and, ultimately, may be interred in a common grave.

3 : The Mountain

For nearly three decades the Huey lay in scorched and twisted fragments on the slope, sun-blistered in the dry seasons, washed by driving monsoon rains, slowly buried by time. For four more years after it fell, the *bo doi*, the ant-army of North Vietnam, continued marching past—soldiers, supplies, and munitions moving to the battlefields in the south.

In a relentless campaign to stop the ant-army, U.S. Air Force and Marine Corps F-4 Phantom fighter-bombers flying from Danang and Thailand, and A-6 Intruders and A-4 Skyhawks catapulted from U.S. Navy carriers in the South China Sea, shrieked over the mountainside, unleashing steel canisters that burst in midair, spewing hundreds of baseball-sized bomblets into the forests, where they waited in silent ambush for an errant human step.

When the shooting ended in 1975, the People's Army of Vietnam simply vanished, victors in the twentieth century's longest and third-bloodiest war. With them went the antiaircraft guns—perhaps some of the same ones that had tracked our colleagues' helicopter and shot it out of the sky.

As the mountains fell silent and the tropical forest began to reclaim what was rightfully its own, the human inhabitants, members of the Bru tribe of Montagnard, who had fled the indentured servitude of the *bo doi* and the howling of the bombers, drifted back to resume their lives as slash-and-burn farmers. Hardy, sinewy people with coffee-colored skin, they had found the scattered wreckage of the helicopter. Some, believing strongly that spirits were present, kept their distance from the hillside. Others, more practical, scavenged the largest pieces of metal for use in rebuilding huts or to sell at the scrap market that had sprung up in one village for that purpose.

Beyond the mountains, the communist victory had been a complete one. All three Indochina states were now controlled by leaders schooled in Soviet or Chinese socialism yet beholden to neither of those giants. The three countries had different languages and different cultures and took different paths to their utopian goals.

Vietnam, divided in two by the Geneva Accords of 1954, was reunited twenty-one years later in a shotgun marriage of politics. Hanoi, a quaint little city that had scarcely changed in the two decades since the French were driven out, was now the capital of all Vietnam. Saigon, the onetime Paris of the Orient, had been renamed Ho Chi Minh City, a move that might eradicate its political past but not entirely its strumpet character. The new communist order, dominated by northerners, could only suppress but not abolish the historical distinctions, grounded in regional and ethnic origin, that had long defined Vietnam not so much as two countries but as three—Tonkin in the north, Annam in the center, and Cochin China in the south.

However, the former Republic of Vietnam (i.e., South Vietnam) had ceased to exist, and thousands of military people and civilians with former connections to the fallen regime or its American patrons were sent to so-called reeducation camps. Many emerged after months or years, only to find themselves condemned permanently to lives of struggle and privation for having been on the wrong side. Over time, hundreds of thousands of southerners, including many ethnic Chinese, would flee, risking their lives as "boat people" to escape the new repression, often dying in their quest for safety on distant shores.

In Cambodia, the Khmer Rouge finally emerged from the jungle shadows and set about proving to a terrified people that the worst was still ahead. Supported and encouraged by the North Vietnamese, these onetime jungle outlaws had grown into a guerrilla army, controlled by paranoid leaders and suffused with xenophobia and an almost feral bloodthirst. The graceful capital of Phnom Penh and other cities knew no mercy as the Khmer Rouge's angry, black-clad peasant soldiers, many of them barely teenagers, force-marched virtually the entire population of some 8 million people into the countryside, where they would be enslaved for years in a nightmarish scheme to reinvent agrarian society, literally from the ground up. Before the outlandish experiment ended, nearly 2 million Cambodians would be murdered or die of disease and starvation in what became known as the Killing Fields.

Compared to those other states, the immediate transition to a new order in Laos was relatively quiet, swift, and smooth, a far cry from the street fighting and coup attempts that had marked previous changes of government in Vientiane, the dusty little capital city on the Mekong. A truce that ended fighting among Laotian political-military factions in 1973 now became the basis for a peace agreement, under which the communist Pathet Lao, formerly just a faction of the governing coalition, took full control. After a decade as the command center for the so-called Secret War in northern Laos, the United States embassy closed its doors—but only for one day. It then reopened, the new face of innocence, just another nondescript diplomatic outpost in a small third world capital.

The war in Laos and its cast of amazing characters faded into history. Legendary spies retired. Cowboy-booted Air America pilots cashed their last tax-free $1,000-a-week paychecks. General Vang Pao, the gold-bedecked warlord who had led the CIA-supported army of Hmong tribesmen from Long Cheng, his Shangri-la–like mountain stronghold, saw the futility of continuing the fight. Along with his wives and relatives he was taken by his American sponsors to Montana to begin a life of exile in the high country. A number of die-hard followers stayed behind. From time to time, bombs exploding randomly in public places in Vientiane served as reminders that vanquished and vanished were not the same.

Across northern Laos and along its frontier with Vietnam, the detritus of war lay scattered on mountainsides and in jungle ravines. In the southern panhandle, where the Ho Chi Minh Trail, not political or territorial gain, had been the main focus of the fighting, the hulks of tanks and trucks, rusting relics of unfinished journeys, were embraced by the jungle growth. Here and there on the hillsides, shreds of titanium with U.S. aircraft markings and serial numbers glinted dully in the sun.

Winners and losers counted casualties. Along with hundreds of thousands of civilians killed in the fifteen years of war, more than half a million *bo doi* were dead or missing, many buried in mass graves that might never be found. Though just as dead, nearly 300,000 killed or missing in the service of South Vietnam were ignored in the totals. As military cemeteries in the north contained symbolic markers over empty graves, some in the south were obliterated, as if their occupants had never existed.

At the war's end in 1975, the U.S. score sheet for Indochina showed 58,000 dead, 591 prisoners repatriated from communist control, and 2,583 missing in action or—in the Pentagon's official phrasing—"unaccounted for, body not recovered." More than 1,600 of these were in Vietnam. Another 800 were in Laos and Cambodia, with a handful in southern China. Although the majority were fliers, the MIAs included members of all service branches, even the U.S. Coast Guard, and, originally, 101 civilians.

Eventually, the U.S. Department of Defense, over the complaints of MIA family and activist groups any such action would be premature or was politically motivated, would write off more than 600 cases—almost all of them aviators lost over water, the rest in vaporizing explosions or unknown circumstances. After a year-long review, the Pentagon's POW-MIA Office said there was "virtually no possibility" of finding those remains, "regardless of any future effort" by anyone.[1]

The civilian list was more than halved by the swift repatriation of forty-seven people from communist custody when hostilities ended.

[1] The 591 POWs were released in several stages during "Operation Homecoming" in early 1973, as part of the Paris Accords. The main group of 560, mostly fliers, were returned to U.S. hands at Hanoi's Gia Lam airport on February 12, March 5, and March 28. Of those, 94 had been captured in South Vietnam and 9 in Laos. Twenty-seven other POWs were freed at the South Vietnamese district town of Loc Ninh, north of Saigon, on February 12, 1 in China on March 12 and 2 more in China on March 15. The war's last repatriated American was Robert White, released at Long Toan, South Vietnam, on April 1. At different times earlier in the war, 118 prisoners had been freed, or managed to escape—76 Americans (64 military, 12 civilians) and 42 of other nationalities.

The longest-held were two people taken prisoner in China in November 1952; the briefest, a person captured in South Vietnam on April 30, 1975, the very day of Hanoi's final victory. Three others escaped custody, two were rescued, and ten sets of remains were subsequently recovered and identified. The remaining thirty-eight represented a spectrum of war-zone civilians. Eight were pilots for Air America, the so-called CIA airline that operated mainly in Laos. Eight others were government contract workers; four were journalists; four were missionaries, two of them women. There were two members of the Merchant Marine; a salesman, a hunter, a tourist, and nine U.S. citizens of "unknown vocation."

The four missing American journalists on the list included two freelance photographers who had vanished in Cambodia in April 1970, another who disappeared there in 1972, and a *Newsweek* stringer last seen alive on a Vietnam road in 1972. There was a fifth, though not on the original list. The shootdown of the helicopter in Laos had received wide attention in the world's press at the time, but later, as Pentagon statisticians compiled the roster of Americans missing and presumed dead in Indochina, the name of Kent Potter, a civilian whose death in the crash of a South Vietnamese helicopter in Laos had no obvious U.S. connection, simply slipped through the cracks.

The American MIA search mechanism had gone through several incarnations during the war. As early as September 1966, a year after the first U.S. combat troops arrived, a unit called the Joint Personnel Resolution Center (JPRC) was set up as part of MACV's Studies and Observations Group, or SOG—a secretive Saigon-based operation whose innocuous name offered no hint to the clandestine reconnaissance and raiding missions that it carried out in Cambodia, Laos, and North Vietnam. Six years later, in January 1973, JPRC was absorbed into the Joint Casualty Resolution Center (JCRC), a new, stand-alone entity created under the same Paris Peace Accords that mandated the U.S. withdrawal from Vietnam and the repatriation of prisoners of war.

Whereas the main purpose of the JPRC had been the recovery of Americans thought to be held prisoner in the jungle, the new mission included searching for human remains. But this was hampered from the outset by the fact that the two Vietnams were still in a shooting war, and most of the MIAs were in communist-held territory where Americans were at risk. It soon became evident, in fact, that JCRC's searchers were not safe anywhere. In December 1973, nine months after the Paris Accords went into effect, an unarmed JCRC team was ambushed as it landed by helicopter 12 miles southwest of Saigon. The leader, Captain Richard Rees, and a Vietnamese crew member were killed, and four Americans and three Vietnamese wounded.

Despite the various obstacles, JCRC operators in South Vietnam did manage to recover forty-five sets of remains, later identified as American, in the first two years after the Paris agreement. Twenty-three other bodies were voluntarily returned by the North Vietnamese. Elsewhere in Indochina, JCRC found itself blocked at almost every turn. Its attempts to set up liaison offices in Hanoi, Phnom Penh, and Vientiane were refused. In Cambodia, continuing strife between the government and the Khmer Rouge ruled out any field search operations. Peace reigned in Laos, but nothing happened on the MIA search front. The "casualty resolution" section of the Laos agreement was so vaguely worded that it offered no legal basis for setting up a procedure to seek out the missing in action. Out of frustration, the Joint Casualty Resolution Center eventually moved its headquarters from Saigon— first to Thailand, then to Hawaii.

With the fall of Saigon in April 1975, the ensuing Khmer Rouge seizure of Cambodia and the communist takeover in Vientiane, all American MIA field search activity in Indochina effectively ended. The JCRC still existed, but was now relegated to operating on the fringes—interviewing refugees for information about sightings of live Westerners, location of crash sites, and other clues to the fate of missing Americans, as well as keeping up contacts with Vietnamese officials in the hope that they might gradually become more responsive on the POW-MIA question.[2]

---

[2] Defense officials have never ruled out the possibility of Americans alive and held against their will in Indochina, and this remains the first priority of POW-MIA policy. Of 1,906 "firsthand live sightings" between the war's end in 1975 and late 1999, 48 were "unresolved"—39 "Americans reported in a captive environment" and 9 in a "noncaptive environment," that is, working or living with families. Of the rest, 1,300 were matched to people previously accounted for—returned prisoners, missionaries, civilians jailed on criminal charges; 45 were correlated to pre-1975 sightings of civilians unaccounted for, and 513 proved false.

Moves toward normalizing U.S. diplomatic ties with Indochina were stymied in the late 1970s by several obstacles—"boat people" fleeing repression, Vietnam's invasion of Cambodia, and Washington's new coziness with China, by then hostile toward Hanoi. But the politically and emotionally freighted POW-MIA issue remained central. Veterans' and MIA family groups opposed lifting of economic sanctions against Vietnam until all Americans were "accounted for." In 1984, Vietnam made its first voluntary repatriation of bone fragments; after that it was almost routine for U.S. visitors to Vietnam to depart with remains doled out mainly, or so it seemed, for political effect. These rituals fed suspicion—ultimately admitted by its officials—that the People's Republic had a store of bones waiting to be released at opportune moments.[3]

After the initial spate of news reports and speculation, the story of the February 1971 helicopter crash in Laos faded from the public mind. The seven South Vietnamese soldiers and the four news photographers were presumed to be dead. As far as is known, no one from the outside ever visited the site, and—as was the case with many military aircraft crashes in the mountains—the exact location was not known. The twin obstacles of politics and geography stood in the way of any inquiry or search. If the Laotian government ever received an outside proposal, whether official or private, to look for the site, it did not act on it.

The diplomatic impasse gradually dissolved after the first Bush administration relaxed the embargo, allowing U.S. companies to trade and invest in Vietnam, and Hanoi agreed to allow full MIA searches. In early 1992, Defense Secretary Dick Cheney signed an order creating the Joint Task Force-Full Accounting as successor to JCRC, empowered to conduct search and recovery operations in Indochina.[4]

At last, the United States would be able to explore vast areas that had been long sealed off but were sure to contain remnants of missing aircraft and, possibly, information as to the fate of their crews.

Initially, it was widely assumed that most records of the defeated South Vietnamese military establishment had been destroyed, obliterated along with the government it had served. Indeed, some were. But

---

[3] A civilian anthropologist working for the JTF-FA recalls that during his first visit to Hanoi he passed a certain nondescript building near Gia Lam airport and a companion, an American who had been there for some time, remarked, "That's where they kept the bodies."

[4] The Clinton administration ended the embargo and normalized ties in 1994.

the great bulk of military documents left behind in Saigon were carefully gathered up, collated, and indexed by the North Vietnamese victors, who, being communists, were also bureaucrats to the core. That this compendium of history exists is uncontested, yet even decades after the war it remains stored away in files in Hanoi, inaccessible not only to outside scholars and researchers, but even to other government agencies of the Democratic Republic.[5]

Whatever records might or might not exist in Hanoi concerning the Laos helicopter crash, the incident did have at least one other toehold on history—a single scrap of paper that had somehow survived and found its way into United States military archives. It was a list of the Vietnam Air Force combat losses for 1970 and early 1971. Among the entries, it showed:

10.2.71 12.30 XD677.477 UH1H 68-15715 4 (crew) 7 (passengers)
10.2.71 12.30 XD565.520 UH1H 65-15528 4 (crew)

The date, the time, the aircraft data, and the number of people they carried were accurate. The six-digit grid coordinates, if correct, narrowed down to a few dozen square meters in the XRay Delta quadrant on the map of Laos. Yet another source, a United States record of all aircraft losses in Southeast Asia, known as SEAloss, put the location at XD563.523. While any one of these grid coordinates might have been precise enough for future exploration, investigators would find years later that none of them were accurate enough to pinpoint the crash site of the first helicopter.

There was, however, another important bit of evidence: a grainy, black-and-white photograph, which was taken the day after the crash from another helicopter, hovering at a discreet distance yet close enough for the camera to capture details of the crash site. It showed a barren mountain ridge pocked with bomb craters and what appeared to be a primitive road curling along its top, above a steep slope with a dark smear—a shadowy ravine—running down one side.

As time passed, the photo itself was all but forgotten, tucked away among its owner's papers in an attic in Washington, D.C.

---

[5] A leading American expert on Hanoi's military, Robert Destatte, quotes two former members of the People's Army as saying the collection and indexing of captured military archives began "immediately after" the fall of Saigon.

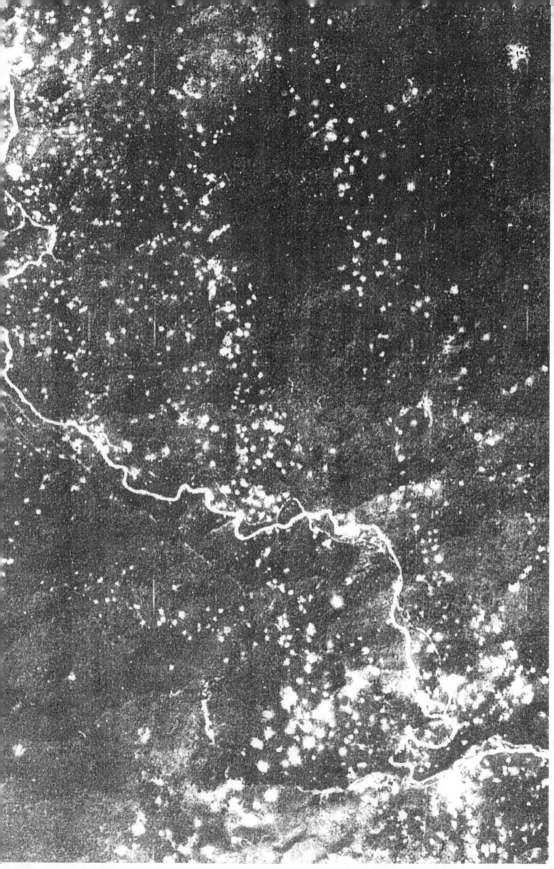

PREVIOUS PAGE: Old French Route 1032, part of Ho Chi Minh Trail, from 70,000 feet. This May 1971 photo by SR-71 spy plane was matched to another picture to locate crash site. White spots are bomb craters.

THIS PAGE: JTF-FA search team helicopter on ridge above crash site. Note steps cut in hillside path leading down to excavation area (bottom of photo).

FACING PAGE, TOP: Sgt. Michael Swam (left) directs Lao workers at Site 2062. BOTTOM: Tech Sgt. Aaron Carpenter examines old film.

ABOVE: Last photo of the
four photographers before
their fatal flight; (left to
right), Shimamoto, Huet,
Burrows, Potter.
RIGHT: Awaiting invasion,
Henri Huet (left) and Kent
Potter shared rations at
border.

TOP: Huet, Burrows at border. BOTTOM, LEFT: Keisaburo Shimamoto. BOTTOM, RIGHT: ARVN photographer Sgt. Tu Vu.

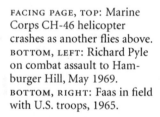

FACING PAGE, TOP: Marine Corps CH-46 helicopter crashes as another flies above.
BOTTOM, LEFT: Richard Pyle on combat assault to Hamburger Hill, May 1969.
BOTTOM, RIGHT: Faas in field with U.S. troops, 1965.

ABOVE: Flaming CH-46, caught by Faas's lens.
LEFT, TOP: The only live VC Faas ever saw face to face.
LEFT, BOTTOM: Medics work to save Faas, wounded in groin by shrapnel, at Bu Dop in 1967. Medic said years later, "I thought you were a goner."

ABOVE: Faas and Pyle at Site 2062 during March 1998 excavation. LEFT: Recovered camera parts proved Site 2062 was right place. Leica body (upper left in photo) is believed to be Burrows'. No other items were traceable to specific owners.

4 : Larry Burrows

Within the news fraternity working in Vietnam, no one commanded more respect than Larry Burrows. Tall, gaunt, and nearsighted, with a toothy smile and tousled hair, the London-born photographer of *Life* magazine at age forty-four was not the perfect model of a dashing combat correspondent. His thick glasses made it hard to meet his gaze; one acquaintance said Larry always seemed to be focusing "somewhere beyond the point he was looking at." Yet poor eyesight did not prevent him from visualizing a scene, framing a composition, that others could not see.

Burrows did not like being known as a war photographer, as if that were the only meaningful aspect of his calling. He was proudest of his photo essays on classical works of art and cultural subjects, and he did not hesitate to tell people that he actually preferred the hush of a museum to the excitement of combat. The fact remained, however, that in the 1960s the name Larry Burrows was most closely identified with pictures of armed conflict in Indochina.

Born Henry Frank Leslie Burrows on May 29, 1926, an only child whose father was a British Railway employee, he grew up in the section of north London called Finsbury Park, a working-class neighborhood best known as the home of the Arsenal football club. His parents were very private people who stuck to a quiet but firm family routine. Going to the movies on Saturday evenings was an unswerving ritual.

Known then as Harry, the diminutive of Henry, Burrows had an unremarkable early boyhood. He was thirteen in 1939 when Adolf Hitler's blitzkrieg across Poland launched the war that would soon engulf the globe. Whether or not there was a connection, it was about this time that the boy became interested in photography as a hobby. His paternal grandmother bought him his first camera.

Young Burrows's enthusiasm for his newfound craft was not fully shared by his parents. His father wanted him to pursue a career that would be dependable and steady, not involving a lot of risk. He could scarcely have imagined the perils that his son would one day face willingly. In later years, Larry himself spoke of the profound effect that life during the London Blitz of 1940 had in developing his journalistic senses. It motivated him, he once said, to "show the interested people and shock the uninterested" into recognizing the horrors of war.

Around 1942, the teenager became acquainted with some of the American servicemen who then were thronging wartime London. He took snapshots of them at a dance hall and in other off-duty pursuits. He remembered years later how he was drawn to the visitors, most of whom were just a few years older than he. The Yanks were clearly better off than their British cousins, but they were different in other ways as well. Some of them befriended the gawky, stuttering London lad with the camera. "He clearly was fascinated by things American, and it would be fair to say he was quite taken with the young Americans he met," his son, Russell, says today.

Burrows's keen interest in photography earned him his first job as a tea boy at the London-based Keystone photo agency. Eventually, he was given a chance to learn darkroom and laboratory work and, at age sixteen, moved into *Life* magazine's London bureau as a darkroom apprentice. The job still included fetching cups of tea for others, but those now included many of the most famous professionals of the day, among them Robert Capa, David "Chim" Seymour, George Rodger, and John Morris, who, along with Henri Cartier-Bresson, would later found the Magnum photo agency.

It was around this time that the young Harry Burrows became Larry Burrows, a name given to him by American friends—whether soldiers or staffers at *Life* is not certain—to distinguish him from another Harry. The new name stuck, and most people who met Burrows later in life probably assumed that his first name was Lawrence.

Nearing the age for wartime military conscription, he tried to enlist in the Royal Merchant Marine, but to his surprise and dismay, he was rejected. The ostensible reason given by examiners was poor eyesight, but Larry himself would always insist there had to be some other reason. After all, he explained, he had passed the vision test by getting prior access to the eye chart and memorizing it.

Turned down by the military, young Burrows was conscripted into national service as a civilian, but his assignment left much to be desired; he was put to work in a coal mine. This proved a terrible ordeal for the already high-strung youth. After sixteen months, his nerves were so frazzled by the claustrophobic labor that his former bosses at *Life* petitioned the government to have him excused.

The idea that a person with poor eyesight could serve the cause as effectively in a photo darkroom as in a coal mine evidently made sense to someone in Britain's wartime bureaucracy. The request was approved, and Larry, escaping the colliery, was soon at work again in the magazine's photo lab, handling the film brought back by its stable of top war photographers and listening to their stories.

On June 6, 1944, as the Allies invaded France, launching the long-awaited final drive across Europe to destroy Nazi Germany, Robert Capa, *Life*'s premier combat photographer, went ashore with the troops. His pictures from the Normandy beachhead were certain to be among the most dramatic and important of the war. A day later, the urgent package of film landed on a desk in the London bureau and was rushed to the darkroom. But most of Capa's priceless photos would never be published. As if some demonic saboteur was afoot in the lab, a technician erred in the developing process—"overcooking" the film, it was called later—and ruined all but 11 of the more than 150 frames.

While everyone who mattered agreed that he had nothing to do with it, the Burrows name became linked with the Capa film incident merely by virtue of his having been there. Larry spent the rest of his life denying it, but it must have strained his good nature to have to deal with it. He often said he knew the real culprit—yet he did not name him. He also liked to point out that Capa himself had been very forgiving about the whole thing.

However, the idea that it had been the great Burrows who ruined the great Capa's D-Day film was too delicious to just fade away, and no number of denials could dispel it. The cruelest resurrection of the story came in 1994. In a story marking the fiftieth anniversary of the Normandy invasion, *Time* magazine, *Life*'s sister publication, recalled the episode in a publisher's note, saying that the young Larry Burrows, of all people, had committed the mistake.

Surrounded by some of the best in the business, Burrows learned his craft swiftly and well. He began photographing works of art for *Life*, which taught him about composition and lighting and other techniques that would help him develop a special aptitude for studio and museum photography. Having worked in the laboratory—considered by many photographers an onerous chore—he understood, in taking a picture, the photographer's adage that half the creative process takes place in the darkroom.

Burrows's first work on record in *Life* archives includes photos of a foreign ministers conference in London in 1945. He also was offered a chance to join the fledgling Magnum agency, but he declined. His thinking, according to son Russell, was that it was better for someone getting started to stick with a magazine that set standards for others, rather than take a chance on a new agency with uncertain prospects. But he could not know that in two decades his work would be compared with that of Capa.

Burrows was still only twenty when, in January 1947, he met Vicky Dickins, who had recently joined the magazine's business side and was working for its travel service. It was a case of instant romance, and they were married in July of that year.

Vicky's family were British expatriates—her father had been a harbormaster in Shanghai before the war, and except for a brother who was back in England, the family were taken prisoner by the Japanese on December 8, 1941. They spent three years in the Lung Hwa prison camp, later made famous by the book and film *Empire of the Sun*. Her parents remained in China after the war and sent a gift of money to the newlyweds. The timing was fortuitous. Larry used it to buy a used Speed Graphic 4x5 camera that he had been "drooling over," according to Russell. It was a camera he could use in studio portraiture and studies of objets d'art in museums that would become a Burrows specialty.

Using ever more sophisticated equipment, Larry made the rounds of London's centers of culture, photographing paintings, sculpture, and historical artifacts. Young Russell sometimes accompanied his father on what he recalls as "interminable museum trips." Larry's favorite was the Victoria and Albert, where he often worked by special permission after midnight, when the underground connecting South Kensington and Picadilly was quiet, with no vibrations to disturb his time exposures that might last up to two hours.

From his London base in the late 1950s and early 1960s, Burrows also roved widely, mixing photo essays on famous sites and works of art with pictures of strife in Iraq, Iran, Cyprus, Lebanon, and the Congo. His camera captured Queen Elizabeth II; the Queen Mother; an aging, irascible Winston Churchill; and other notables of the mid–twentieth century.

On these assignments he became a man of meticulous preparation and attention to detail. If it was a parade or other preplanned public event, he would reconnoiter the route or location ahead of time, taking note of vantage points from which he could get the most effective shots. Although more than six feet tall, Burrows sometimes climbed on the shoulders of his driver or a reporter colleague to get the all-important "elevation" on a crowd shot. This in turn led to another innovation: the inclusion of a small aluminum ladder in his traveling gear, a trick he may have picked up during a visit to Japan, where the swarming newsphoto corps often resembled a gaggle of housepainters.

Like many professional photographers with studio experience, Burrows traveled with a great deal of equipment, even to war zones. Son Russell says that getting Larry's metal Halliburton cases packed and ready for a major assignment was "a family affair" in which everybody had a part. He designed his own cases, with special lint-free padding for cameras and lenses. He preferred hotel rooms with two beds—one to sleep in and the other to lay out his cameras and lenses.

In Saigon, Burrows generally reserved Room 103 at the Caravelle. It was a corner room overlooking the street, where he could observe any unusual event occurring in Lam Son Square, the city's busiest intersection. Steve Stibbens, a Marine Corps photographer assigned to the military paper *Pacific Stars and Stripes* who became a Burrows protégé, recalls Larry "laying out his aluminum cases, about ten of them, in a certain order, ready for action." The cases contained a variety of lenses, cameras, and gadgets, which Burrows handled almost lovingly, "like a kid with a bunch of new toys," Stibbens says. "He was especially proud of a matchbook-sized camera in a cigarette package that he said would serve him one day to get that secret photo in a forbidden situation."

Don Moser, a former Saigon bureau chief for *Life*, wrote of Burrows: "He carried four cameras even in combat (usually two Leicas and two Nikons, the favored tools of war photographers of the 1960s) and owned every piece of equipment ever made and some which he'd concocted himself." That was true; while covering the independence of the Congo in July 1960, Burrows had been caught in street rioting, and his gear was smashed. According to Russell, Larry finished the assignment with a camera he'd cobbled together from undamaged parts.

By the early 1960s, Larry's reputation was so firmly established that *Life* considered transferring him from London to the United States to cover the heady excitement of the Kennedy White House. He was already in Washington when his editors offered him an even more appealing alternative: assignment anywhere in the world that the magazine had a bureau. Burrows opted for Asia and moved the family to a residence and operating base in Hong Kong.

There, with Larry on call for breaking news assignments anywhere in a vast region stretching from New Zealand to India, Vicky's experience in the *Life* magazine travel office paid new dividends. Along with Russell, she worked the phones skillfully to book space on crowded airplanes. And in those days of relaxed or even nonexistent airline security, she could find out the names of passengers and negotiate directly with them to give up their seats.

Operating from his Hong Kong base, Burrows was likely to show up anywhere, and when least expected. Jeff Williams, then with AP, remembers traveling with a Gurkha unit in Malaysia in 1965—the

Gurkhas were tracking Indonesian infiltrators involved in President Sukarno's *"Ganjang Malaysia"* ("crush Malaysia") campaign—and was "dragging along at the rear, when Larry Burrows, in a clean photographer suit, with a towel around his neck, appeared from nowhere." Recalls Williams, "he was grinning, and said I better move to the front. 'Stay at the front if you want to see the action,' he said, and away he went."

The staccato sounds of warfare emanating anew from Indochina were just beginning to draw the world's attention, and Burrows was among the first photojournalists to discover this place of drama, intrigue, and colorful people in one of the world's most photogenic settings. Over the next decade he would return again and again to Indochina, and his best-known work would be achieved there. "This strange war fascinates me," he once wrote. By 1963, Burrows had won the first of two Robert Capa Awards, given by the Overseas Press Club in New York for "superlative photography requiring exceptional courage and enterprise."

In a profession that did not lack for rampant egos and self-anointed geniuses, Burrows seemed uncommonly secure. Once, visiting the AP's Saigon bureau, he saw photos just brought in from the field by AP photographer Henri Huet and was so impressed that he urged his own editors at *Life* to use them, which they did.

He was the natural leader of the photojournalists' circle in Southeast Asia, and given his age, his professional reputation, and his affable nature, he could hardly have avoided becoming a father figure to the younger photographers. He liked to quote *Henry V*—"we happy few, we band of brothers," and former colleagues say Larry could be kinder toward novices than seasoned pros like himself. According to Steve Stibbens, one night, after they had covered a Vietnamese student draft protest together, Burrows told him, "I watched you. I like the way you work." Says Stibbens, "That was enough encouragement to last me a month, but that's the way he was, eager to share his ideas with a new kid on the block."

Actually, Burrows's generosity toward others was more selective—especially when they happened to be other *Life* magazine photographers. These rivals entered the Burrows domain, particularly Vietnam, at their peril. "He was extremely protective of his territory.

No one else was really welcome there," says Co Rentmeester, a Dutch-born photographer who was assigned as *Life*'s second staffer in Asia in those years.

Dick Swanson, who arrived in Saigon in early 1967 as a freelancer and soon became a local addition to the magazine staff, paid the price when he volunteered to take an assignment in Pakistan for Burrows, who was away from Saigon at the time. On Burrows's return, recalls Swanson, "Larry took me to dinner and made very clear to me the pecking order of the Saigon bureau." Although he called it a "dressing-down," Swanson says he and Burrows did the assignment together and became good friends.

Like many Westerners who first arrived in Indochina in the early 1960s, Burrows regarded South Vietnam's cause as a righteous one, yet he seldom offered this personal view in public. In one rare commentary, in a 1969 *Life* photo essay, he described himself as still "rather a hawk" but skeptical that Saigon's forces could "fight and survive on their own" once the Americans left. "The prospects seem to me doubtful," he wrote.

Although he generally steered clear of the politics and polemics that spun out of "concerned" photojournalism, Burrows was of that breed of photographers who were acutely conscious of the human misery they portrayed. Among the stories that affected him most deeply were two depicting the plight of Vietnamese children caught in the war.

First it was a twelve-year-old girl named Nguyen Thi Tron, who had lost a leg to a U.S. helicopter attack. Burrows befriended Tron and her family and photographed her progress in learning to walk on an artificial leg. Don Moser wrote that Larry worried about Tron becoming overly dependent on him and tried to conceal his feelings—"not always successfully"—by acting like a "cheerful uncle."

Later came Nguyen Lau, a ten-year-old boy who suffered paralyzing wounds and was sent to the United States for corrective surgery. Burrows set out to chronicle what was to be Lau's happy return to his native village, only to find the boy treated as an outcast—unable to speak his own language and ridiculed by other children. *Life* reporter John Saar said Larry was so aggrieved over Lau's situation that he mulled over the idea of adopting him.

But the story that best defined Larry Burrows—for his editors at *Life*, his working colleagues, and many an aspiring young photographer—was "Yankee Papa 13," a 1965 photo essay that dealt up close with courage, commitment, and futility in war.

Burrows had returned again and again to the same Marine Corps helicopter unit, shooting more than a hundred rolls of film as the pilots flew various combat missions, including the ferrying of Vietnamese troops into battle. Then came the mission that would make the story: A helicopter had gone down, and the one Burrows was riding raced to the rescue. Bullets zinging past his head, Larry photographed the desperate efforts of his aircraft's crew chief, James Farley, to rescue the mortally wounded copilot of the downed ship. The resulting photo spread included the cover and several pages of *Life*, ending with a shot of the exhausted chief Farley slumped on a foot locker, privately grieving over the flier's death and his own inability to save him.

"Yankee Papa 13" won Burrows his second Capa Award. Among other things, it underscored his capacity to get inside his subject matter, to bore in on the most sensitive aspects without seeming to intrude or violate a confidence. Larry acknowledged having "moments of doubt" about "capitalizing on other men's grief," but he did not let this turn him or his lens away from the essential photographic moment. "I concluded that what I was doing would penetrate the hearts of those at home who are simply too indifferent, and I felt I was free to act on that condition," he said.

Burrows's penchant for combat troubled *Life*'s editors after a time; they wanted him to ease back on dangerous assignments. Burrows admitted in candid moments that he, too, worried sometimes about pushing his luck. But he also knew there would be no pictures without risk.

And like others, he struggled to explain what drove him. If people were looking for cosmic answers, they weren't there. "I am no more courageous than anyone else," he said in one interview. "I just feel that photography is important and I will do what is required to show what is happening. I have a sense of the ultimate—death. And I must say, 'to hell with that.'"

In late January 1971, Burrows was in Calcutta, shooting a story on poverty. The local situation "had him quite worried," Russell recalls. "A bomb exploded on the steps of a police station, and he didn't know who the good guys were. He knew his way around in Vietnam, but Calcutta was very unsettling by comparison." Given that, one can almost imagine Larry hearing with relief of the impending South Vietnamese invasion of Laos. Indochina was familiar ground, his home turf—and this was clearly a major story, perhaps Cambodia all over again. Horst, who was also on assignment in Calcutta at the time, remembers Burrows rushing to collect his gear and catch a flight out.

I was walking across the park in front of city hall when I happened briefly to encounter Burrows, coming from the direction of the JUSPAO office in the Rex Hotel. He told me he had just returned from India, and was on his way to the AP photo bureau. "I hear there's a big operation up north," he said. I filled him in quickly on the basics—that the South Vietnamese were preparing for a major offensive, a cross-border attack into Laos, with American air support but no ground forces. I do not recall what he said in response. When I returned to the bureau a short time later, Larry was still there, talking to photo editor James Bourdier and some others in the photo office. After a while, he emerged, and with a wave good-bye, was out the door, on his way north to Quang Tri.

There, in the fog and rain at Camp Red Devil, the base of the U.S. Army's 1st Battalion, 5th Mechanized Infantry, Burrows found a press camp already teeming with journalists from Saigon and beyond, among them his old friend Henri Huet.

For the first time ever—or at least in the memory of press corps veterans—U.S. and South Vietnamese military officials were refusing to allow civilian journalists into the battle zone. But the ban did not discourage them from pushing as close to the action as possible. On February 6, a group of journalists, including Burrows, Huet, John Saar, and several others, hitched a ride in a South Vietnamese military convoy heading west from Quang Tri to the border, where the forces were marshaling for the attack, then just two days away.

As dark descended, the armored column halted and bivouacked about a mile east of the border, deploying its tanks and armored tracks in a semicircle in a forest. Jeff Williams, by then with CBS, remembers Burrows arriving in a jeep with a Vietnamese driver. Recognizing Williams and his cameraman, Norman Lloyd, Larry flashed a toothy grin, reached into his pack, and came forth with a can of beer, which he handed to Williams. "It was still cool, such a treat—as he knew it would be," says Williams. He and Lloyd found a comfortable spot to share their unexpected gift, sitting with their backs to the bank of a dry river bed, a few dozen yards from where the encamped Vietnamese soldiers were preparing and eating their evening rations.

Williams and Lloyd had shared no more than a few sips of the precious beer before a U.S. Navy A-6 Intruder jet, suddenly and without warning, screeched low overhead, dropping cluster bombs, which exploded in fiery strings among the parked tanks and armored personnel carriers. Everybody scrambled for safety, huddling in the nearest ditch or behind whatever cover they could find. Williams and Lloyd rushed back to find "dead and wounded lying everywhere, people shouting, radios crackling, the air full of dust and smoke," says Williams.[1] Six ARVN soldiers were killed and fifty-one wounded in the few seconds of the mistaken attack.

Roger Mattingly, a freelance photographer with the convoy group, had first heard of Larry Burrows in 1965 when his high school teacher, who had sold some of his own work to *Life*, "came into class waving a copy of the magazine containing the 'Yankee Papa 13' story, saying it was the best thing he had ever seen and would change the course of the war." Mattingly wasn't sure what that meant, but bought his own copy of the issue, and "I knew that was photojournalism at its best."

Now, eating rations with the armored column at the side of Route 9, Mattingly was surprised to see Larry Burrows, whom he had never met. While he was "working up the nerve to introduce myself," the jet raced overhead and the area exploded in chaos. For a few moments, time was paralyzed, until it became clear that the attack was over. "I guess Burrows, with his experience, figured it out first and came out of the ditch and started shooting. I followed him and watched him working," Mattingly recalls. But the first priority was to get wounded Vietnamese soldiers away from the burning armored vehicles that were

---

[1] The TV crew used camera lights to help illuminate the scene so medics could work on the wounded. Lloyd's hastily shot film was put into a CBS shipping bag and given to an American medevac helicopter crew but never made it to Quang Tri—"probably pitched into the jungle," says Williams.

starting to cook off. "The light was failing and Burrows knew it," says Mattingly. "But when I asked him to help with a wounded man, there was no hesitation on his part. He grabbed the other end of the trooper, and we hustled him back to the aid station. Then he started shooting again. The man knew his priorities."

The next morning, as a light rain softened the grimy scene of dead bodies and blackened wrecks, Mattingly shot a picture of Burrows, his craggy face enveloped by sadness and fatigue. "Watching him work was the most revealing experience I had while in Vietnam," Mattingly would later write. "If a cardinal is a prince of the church, Larry Burrows was a prince of photojournalism."

5 : The Trail

Our journey to the crash site, on a steep hillside in what Horst referred to one day as "the remotest place on Earth," had its genesis in the earlier journeys of many others—the thousands of North Vietnamese soldiers who had trod these mountains on the 300-plus-mile march from their homeland to southern battlefields.

Hardly had the French been defeated at Dien Bien Phu in 1954 and the country divided by international convention before Hanoi's communist leaders turned to their next task—a takeover of the newly independent, noncommunist Republic of Vietnam, by whatever means necessary, and at whatever cost. The key would be patience, sustained effort—and the Ho Chi Minh Trail.

According to one account, the Trail officially came into existence through a military order issued in Hanoi on May 19, 1955, which by design or coincidence happened to be the birthday of its wispy-bearded namesake. Although North Vietnamese documents do exist that call it *Duong Ho Chi Minh*—literally, Ho Chi Minh Trail—it was more commonly referred to as Truong Son Strategic Supply Route— *Truong Son*, or Long Mountains, being the range that it crossed from

North Vietnam to Laos. By any name, it would become a stupendous achievement of strategic planning, engineering, logistics management, camouflage, and road maintenance. For sheer sustained accomplishment, the Trail might rank in military annals alongside Alexander's third-century-B.C. trek to India. The ability of the People's Army to move heavy equipment, even tanks, down the mountainous roadways during the 1972 and 1973 offensives was somehow evocative of Hannibal steering his elephants across the Alps.

In the first five years, the military conduit was contained wholly within Vietnam, snaking across the DMZ and down the eastern side of the Truong Son into the A Shau Valley west of Hue. But persistent attacks by Saigon's forces, disrupting the supply flow and inflicting severe manpower losses, eventually forced Hanoi's strategic planners to look for an alternative route. The map clearly showed but one choice, and in 1960, they decided to shift the entire operation to the west, out of Vietnam and into Laos. While the weather patterns on the other side of the mountains were the opposite of Vietnam's, and frequently harsher, there was little danger from attack. Politically, the intrusion represented a de facto violation of Laos's neutrality, but the Vientiane government was powerless to do anything about it.

Over the next fourteen years, this ever-changing network of roads and pathways paralleling the sharp spine of Indochina fed war materiel by the hundreds of tons and troops by the tens of thousands southward, first to support the native Viet Cong insurgency, and later to enable Hanoi's near-total control of the war against Saigon and its American patrons. More than 1 million *bo doi* traveled the Trail during the Vietnam War, and for many of those it was a one-way trip. To avoid the issue of Laotian neutrality, Hanoi simply denied to the world that any such activity was going on there and even produced maps on which the Vietnam-Laos border angled several kilometers to the west of where standard maps—including those used by allied forces—showed it to be. The sensitive neutrality issue at first kept the United States from officially admitting that it was bombing the Ho Chi Minh Trail in Laos, and it never openly acknowledged the reconnaissance teams that regularly crossed the border to gather intelligence on the Trail.

The main north-south artery of the Ho Chi Minh Trail followed an old French secondary road, but contrary to the image, it was far more than a single highway coursing down through the Annamites. It was an intricate ganglion of old roads, new roads, pathways, river fords, and makeshift bridges that ran some 300 miles from the 1,300-foot Mu Gia Pass on the Vietnam-Laos border to the forests of eastern Cambodia. All along the route, feeder trails spun off to the east, leading into South Vietnam. The Trail complex was thirty miles across at its widest point in the Laos panhandle, and estimates of the actual road mileage varied wildly. In 1971, according to American analysts in Saigon, the Trail included more than 1,500 miles of seasonal roads, some capable of heavy truck traffic, and nearly a dozen waterways to supplement the jungle paths. After the war, North Vietnamese officials would claim that the Trail's total mileage was more than twice the American estimate.[1]

Initially, the North Vietnamese tried to build corduroy roads of fallen logs, but abandoned that idea—perhaps to save wear and tear on the trucks or their drivers' kidneys—and also had to contend with rockslides, flash floods, and malaria, in addition to the ever-present threat of the American B-52s and fighter-bombers. A special 25,000-member unit of the People's Army known as Transportation Group 559 had overall responsibility for operating and maintaining the Trail's logistical infrastructure that included underground storage areas and troop quarters, hospitals, and concealed fuel dumps. The regular units were augmented by a force of 20,000 youthful "volunteers" who helped to maintain the roadways, repairing bomb damage, filling in washouts, and building detours.

Moving mainly at night in relays that took one to two days each, the trucks jounced and crawled along the primitive routes between supply transfer points or military way stations, called *binh tham*, where drivers rested and vehicle maintenance was performed. Covering the same stretches of roadway over and over, drivers became so fa-

---

[1] While the Ho Chi Minh Trail in Laos was much more secure against U.S. and South Vietnamese attack, the monsoons on the western side could paralyze backcountry traffic for weeks, and Hanoi never quit trying to reopen the original routes on the Vietnam side. This effort was reflected in the NVA's determination to control the A Shau Valley, from which one key road led east toward Hue and another, known to Americans as the "yellow brick road," ran south to connect with Route 14 in the Central Highlands. Once the American forces withdrew this became easier, and by 1972 the North Vietnamese were using bulldozers near the A Shau to help lay a fuel pipeline from the DMZ to Kontum, in the highlands.

miliar with the twists and turns that they could negotiate them without headlights. Some trucks traveling in the daytime had windshields removed to avoid reflections that could betray them to cruising reconnaissance aircraft. The way stations also maintained control over subordinate communications posts that were spaced a day's foot-march apart. Bicycles were used to haul cargo over makeshift bamboo bridges and through riverbeds that the truck convoys could not negotiate.

By 1969, the Trail had become a battleground unto itself, bombed virtually around the clock by the Americans and defended by hundreds of Soviet- and Chinese-supplied antiaircraft weapons, ranging from .51-caliber machine guns to long-barreled 100mm guns able to hit targets at 10,000 feet. The *phao phong khong*, or antiaircraft artillery battalions, also were part of Transportation Group 559. When the traffic flow hit its peak that year, the United States Navy and Air Force were flying more than 500 sorties a day against the Trail. Along with the rain of high explosives and the antipersonnel cluster bombs—"area denial weapons" in Pentagonese—came a variety of sensors that could detect sound, vibration, infrared heat signature, or the scent of vehicles and soldiers on the move.

Some ideas worked and some didn't. The North Vietnamese learned to spot the sensors camouflaged as plants and move them to locations where bombs would fall harmlessly. The "people-sniffers" supposedly could be fooled by animal urine. At one point, it has been reported, the Americans came up with a scheme to cover steep sections of the Trail with laundry detergent, on the theory that the first rains would turn roads into slick, sudsy deathtraps, sending truck convoys plunging into the nearest ravine.

Anecdotal accounts suggest, in fact, that no idea was too outlandish for at least a preliminary look, and some fell into a category that journalists like to call "too good to check." In 1970, over bottles of warm Tiger beer on an overnight train in Thailand, a retired U.S. Army colonel, who claimed to have been part of the brainstorming team on Trail-related dirty tricks, described a few ideas that he said had been tested and rejected as impractical. The "world's largest lawn mower," according to the colonel, was a giant blade slung under a heavy-lift helicopter to chop the tops off trees—reducing "triple-canopy" jungle to double-canopy, and so forth. Did it work? "Hell, no," snorted the colonel, who then went on to describe his personal favorite, which he called the "world's longest razor blade." This, he explained, was an extremely long piece of sharp spring steel, wound tightly into an innocent-looking coffee can, which was then placed inside a room or hut. When a timing mechanism blew the lid off, the spring would explode from the can like a Slinky toy run amok, filling the confined space in seconds and slicing to pieces anything inside. The colonel was vague about whether this diabolical device was ever put to actual use.

In the coverage of the Vietnam War, day-to-day news from Laos and Cambodia rarely made headlines; neither did the Ho Chi Minh Trail. Officials at the U.S. embassy in Vientiane were willing to talk on background—not for attribution—about the conflict in upcountry Laos, but questions about the *other* one in the southern panhandle were turned aside. That, they said, was part of the Vietnam War, and for that the U.S. Military Assistance Command–Vietnam (MACV) in Saigon was the place to ask for details. But even if Laos's neutral status required MACV to decline comment on any U.S. activity in the country, there were officials in Saigon who could, and would, provide a reasonably clear picture, based on intelligence estimates, of North Vietnamese troop and supply movements along the Trail and the allied countermeasures being used against them. As these military sources spoke about Laos only on background, or deep background, we were in effect telling readers we considered them trustworthy.

And while MACV's daily communiqués seldom if ever included specifics on Laos beyond the bare bones—no mention of actual target locations or bomb damage assessments—it was often possible to figure out from the volume of air strikes whether activity was intensifying over the Trail, indicating possible change in the overall battlefield situation. It may not have been far removed from the reading of tea leaves, but U.S. spokesmen generally did not dispute reports that were reasonably accurate.

If Cambodia ever had any prospect of staying out of the war next door, it was negated by the very existence of the Ho Chi Minh Trail, which terminated in its eastern provinces. From there, a last spiderweb of feeder trails funneled North Vietnamese troops and supplies across the border into the South Vietnamese Third Military Region, which included a number of large rubber plantations, the clear jungles of

"War Zones C and D," and Saigon itself, sixty miles to the southeast. To meet this threat to the capital region, the Americans set up temporary bases astride the "infiltration routes," with the express purpose of drawing the enemy into battle. Hanoi's commanders accommodated them by launching battalion-sized nighttime attacks that never more than dented any of those bases, but frequently resulted in heavy losses to their own forces. Or so the U.S. command claimed; press trips to the bases after battles rarely revealed khaki-clad *bo doi* corpses or "blood trails" equal to the reported "body count." One explanation for this was that the combination of artillery, small arms, and air strikes was so devastating as to pulverize the attackers beyond a precise reckoning.[2]

In Phnom Penh, Cambodia's head of state, Prince Norodom Sihanouk, lived in a state of high-dudgeon denial. The fervent nationalist, known among diplomats and journalists as "Snooky" and almost always described in news reports as "mercurial," had decided early in the game that Cambodia's best chance of survival was to declare itself neutral. In reality, it was a gambit that offered no more protection for Cambodia than it had for Laos.

Despite what was absurdly obvious to anyone who cared, Sihanouk publicly insisted that there was neither a Ho Chi Minh Trail nor a foreign army in eastern Cambodia and charged that such contentions by the United States were part of a scheme to justify an impending U.S. invasion. Privately, while forced to concede that he was powerless to expel the Vietnamese, Sihanouk appeased them by furnishing rice and even allowed them to use the southern Cambodian port of Kompong Som as a secondary supply conduit. The truck route from the port, also called Sihanoukville, became known as the Sihanouk Trail.

By 1965, the quixotic Sihanouk's relations with Washington had become strained to the breaking point. He severed diplomatic ties and charged, in an endless string of complaints to the United Nations, that armed reconnaissance flights by U.S. aircraft along the border were "acts of aggression" that violated Cambodian territory. This, in turn, resonated with domestic critics of the deepening U.S. involvement in Vietnam. In late July 1966, "Americans Want to Know," a private dele-

---

[2] General Creighton Abrams, the U.S. forces commander, told the author in 1970 that the border firebases were intended to lure the North Vietnamese into meat-grinder assaults.

gation of seven U.S. civil rights leaders, writers, and self-described "pacifist militants," arrived in Phnom Penh on what they called a "fact-finding mission."

Prior to leaving home, the group, which included Floyd McKissick, director of the Congress of Racial Equality, author-activist Kay Boyle, radical lawyer William Kunstler, and American Friends Service Committee spokesman Russell Johnson, had denounced U.S. policies toward Cambodia, saying that the Johnson administration's claim that Hanoi and its acolytes were using Cambodian "sanctuaries" to attack South Vietnam was actually a pretext to prepare the American public for a major expansion of the war.

On arrival, the peace delegation split into two groups, one touring the Cambodia-Vietnam border area, the other visiting Kompong Som. After a few days, the activists returned to Phnom Penh, declaring that they had been right: There was no evidence to support Washington's "fables" concerning supply trails or foreign troops. "Members of the American mission were able to ascertain the complete tranquility of the regions, where no trace of the presence of Viet Cong was noted," the official Cambodian radio station announced. They also met with Sihanouk to discuss his complaints about border violations and, according to one report, "could find no indication of wrongdoing on the part of the Cambodian government."[3]

Thirteen months later, Prince Sihanouk indulged his penchant for showmanship by playing host to former U.S. First Lady Jacqueline Kennedy, who had expressed interest in touring Cambodia's most famous archaeological site, the twelfth-century Khmer Dynasty ruins at Angkor Wat. Many foreign journalists were invited to Phnom Penh to cover the visit of Kennedy and her escort of the moment, Britain's Lord Harlech.[4] At some point amid the social whirl, the subject of the purported jungle sanctuaries was raised by visiting reporters. Si-

---

[3] The radio report was quoted in the *New York Times*, August 4, 1966. Other references in Kay Boyle papers, University of Delaware Library. In a 1988 biography of Boyle, Sandra Spanier wrote that the group "traveled the Ho Chi Minh Trail and the Sihanouk Trail day and night, without finding any evidence of such military action." While in effect confirming the trails' existence, the writer did not explain what purpose they had, if not military.

[4] Larry Burrows's photo coverage of the Kennedy visit made the cover and six inside pages of *Life*.

hanouk, perhaps emboldened by his peace group–propaganda triumph of the previous year, openly suggested that members of the media might visit the eastern border region to see for themselves that no foreign soldiers were there.

The prince's offer became a prime topic of conversation among visiting journalists at Hotel Le Royal, but only two, Horst Faas and George McArthur of AP, decided to take up the challenge. As it happened, Faas had just come from covering a secretive U.S. military operation in War Zone C, on the Vietnam side of the border. Officers had shown him field maps that indicated, among other things, the suspected location of communist camps on the Cambodian side. From this, Horst had sketched out his own rough map showing where a jungle camp was believed to exist.

Dressed in ordinary civilian clothes—McArthur was wearing street shoes—the AP pair hired a taxi and drove down Highway 1 toward the Vietnam border. McArthur recalls that they stopped at a district police post, where an officer agreed to escort them—only to make his excuses when he learned where the two journalists were heading. From his sketched map, Faas was able to identify a bend in the road where they should stop. Leaving the taxi beside the highway and walking about 200 yards into the forest, they came upon a crude road made of felled trees, which led to a clearing in the woods. There they found huts, a makeshift jungle pharmacy, and other evidence of recent use by Viet Cong troops. The camp was exactly where it had been marked on the American maps. Fortunately, it also was, for the moment, deserted. Looking back, both men reflect with amazement at the foolhardiness of their foray. Any Viet Cong, North Vietnamese, or Khmer Rouge would have regarded the sudden appearance of two Westerners in civilian clothes with great suspicion; the map probably would have sealed their fate as spies. It was, Horst says, "the stupidest thing I ever did."

By late 1969, the presence of large Vietnamese forces was eroding security in the Cambodian countryside—and public confidence in Phnom Penh. Sihanouk moved to shore things up by restoring diplomatic ties with the United States and appointing a "national government of salvation" to stabilize the domestic and military situation. But it came too late. In March 1970, with Sihanouk away on a world tour, civil protests flared in Phnom Penh. The targets of this less than spontaneous uprising included the embassies of North Vietnam and the National Liberation Front, both of which were sacked. On March 18, as Sihanouk was departing Moscow for Beijing on the next to last leg of his tour, the unrest boiled over into a coup d'état that ousted him from power. General Lon Nol, an obscure officer that Sihanouk had chosen to lead the salvation government, became the new head of state. He lost no time in declaring a new Cambodian alliance with the South Vietnamese and the Americans.

With few foreigners based in Phnom Penh, the wire services were dependent for day-to-day coverage on a resident press corps that consisted mainly of two Cambodians, who lived together and divided stringer chores—one filing to AP and Agence France Presse, the other to UPI and Reuters. As the March 18 coup developed, all links to the outside—telephone circuits, the international telex at the post office, and the airport—were shut down, silencing not only the stringers but also the only Western reporter who happened to be in Phnom Penh. Three days earlier, Jeff Williams, the AP's Hong Kong–based roving correspondent for Southeast Asia, had slipped into the country as a tourist. Now, Williams faced what he has called "a journalist's nightmare—big story, no competition, but no way to get it out."

By the time Williams managed to file a heavily censored report the next day, AP had already broken the story—from Saigon. A visiting Asian press group was paying a scheduled courtesy call that day on South Vietnamese President Nguyen Van Thieu, who stunned his guests by suddenly announcing that Sihanouk had been deposed. Peter Arnett, who was present as the New Zealand delegate to the press group, quickly found a telephone in the palace and called the AP bureau with the first confirmed word of an upheaval. Peter's voice was calm, but edged with excitement, as he dictated the report that would dramatically change the war situation in Indochina.

The impact went well beyond Sihanouk's becoming a man without a country. In moves aimed at driving the Vietnamese out of his country, Lon Nol shut down the supply port of Sihanoukville and sent his inexperienced army on the attack, only to have the North Vietnamese and Viet Cong retaliate with force that soon imperiled Phnom

Penh itself. Within days, South Vietnamese troops also were operating on the Cambodian side of the border, ostensibly with Lon Nol's approval, and it was only a matter of weeks before the Americans followed. In late April, the U.S. invasion that had so fixated Sihanouk finally happened—though not, as he had feared, to take over Cambodia. Using the less incendiary term "incursion," President Richard Nixon announced that American forces were crossing the border to find and destroy the main NVA-VC headquarters, the Central Office for South Vietnam, or COSVN—in effect, the southern anchor of the Ho Chi Minh Trail.

The two-month allied campaign that followed consisted of thirteen field operations. Only two actually involved American forces, which were restricted by congressional edict to a thirty-kilometer (eighteen-mile) swath inside Cambodia. While critics in the United States assailed Nixon for spreading the war to neutral Cambodia, in Saigon the invasion was seen as a logical response to a preexisting military situation. The Kent State debacle in early May deepened the controversy but did not noticeably affect the combat operations or speed an American pullout.

The invaders claimed afterward to have captured enough small arms and heavy weapons to outfit scores of North Vietnamese infantry battalions—possibly co-opting any immediate plans by Hanoi for an offensive against Lon Nol's forces, and giving Saigon an unaccustomed military advantage. But that was overshadowed by the Americans' failure to find the elusive COSVN, with its purported multilayered underground complex of barracks, hospitals, and storage bunkers. The U.S. withdrawal from Cambodia on June 30 left the field to the South Vietnamese and the Cambodians, now allies of convenience against the communists.

Meanwhile, the new Indochina front was drawing news correspondents from Saigon, Europe, and elsewhere. They found Cambodia at first glance a sort of quaint fantasyland, where the government's soldiers rode to war on commandeered Pepsi-Cola trucks and put Buddha medals in their mouths to protect them from enemy bullets. The chief military spokesman, Major Am Rong, had studied at Louisiana State University and lamented to one reporter that during his time there "we never beat Ole Miss." Among reporters, his name became an unhappy metaphor for the new government's military bumbling.[5]

Quiet on the surface, Phnom Penh pulsated with a steamy undercurrent of sex, drugs, and corruption. At the Hotel Le Royal, the de facto headquarters for foreign journalists, the pungent aroma of marijuana—Cambodian Red, or Khmer Rouge, it was inevitably dubbed—drifted through the screened bungalows and around the swimming pool. The more adventurous visited Madame Chum's, or Chantal's, a local opium den that some began referring to as the Foreign Correspondents Club of Phnom Penh. There was much amusement among the media when two visiting staff aides to the Senate Foreign Relations Committee went to dinner with some American reporters and discovered, too late, that their food had been laced with marijuana. The joke was short-lived when the outraged pair reported the prank to the committee.

Beyond the city limits, Cambodia was a different world, where the reward for reckless behavior could easily be death. Beginning in April 1970, less than a month after the coup, journalists began disappearing on trips into the countryside. Over a few weeks, nearly a dozen were captured by Viet Cong or other irregular forces. Some were held for a few days and then released, chastened by their good fortune. More drove out Route 1 toward the Vietnam border, or down other highways radiating out from the city, and vanished. Between April 5 and April 16, the border area known, for its map configuration, as the Parrot's Beak became a trap from which ten journalists from half a dozen countries did not return.

Among these were the Americans Sean Flynn, the son of actor Errol Flynn, who was on photo assignment for *Time*, and Dana Stone, a freelance cameraman for CBS News. While other journalists climbed aboard old armored cars for a government-sponsored press junket, Flynn and Stone roared ahead on motorcycles. The tour caught up with them near Chipou, where an empty car sat crosswise in the road. It belonged to French photojournalist Claude Arpin and Guy Han-

---

[5] The amateurishness extended to attempts by the new regime to censor outgoing news reports. AP's Hugh Mulligan remembers one story being held up because, the censor explained, "you misspell guerrilla. Two r's in guerrilla."

noteaux, a reporter for the French magazine *L'Express,* who had driven out earlier in search of Gilles Caron, another Frenchman, who had not returned from a trip the day before.

As the journalists' tour group waited by a roadside food stand for what might happen next, Flynn and Stone wheeled their bikes around the car—and into oblivion. Akira Kusaka, a correspondent for Japan's Fuji Television, and his cameraman, Yujiro Takagi, also ventured ahead—and they, too, vanished. It wasn't clear whether the two Japanese had misunderstood the situation or had taken a chance that as Asian noncombatants they could make friendly contact with the Viet Cong, as several Japanese reporters in Vietnam had done. In the space of two days, seven foreign journalists had disappeared. Two days later, the list increased to nine with the disappearance of Georg Gensluckner, an Austrian freelancer, and Dieter Bellendorf, a short, one-eyed German cameraman for NBC who claimed to have served in the French Foreign Legion and was famous in Saigon for keeping his gold bars and money in a cage with his pet cobra. Later, intelligence reports filtered out of eastern Cambodia telling of groups of Caucasians or Westerners being seen in Viet Cong or Khmer Rouge custody, but none of the missing journalists were ever found alive.

As Steve Bell, an American correspondent for ABC-TV who went from Saigon to Phnom Penh in 1970, recalls it, "Journalists ran the roads in mostly air-conditioned limos left over from the tourist era— in the early days, lovely cars and idyllic countryside. Every few days someone didn't come back in the evening." Bell and his crew were among those who were captured by Viet Cong but got away; he credits cameraman Terry Khoo with saving their lives by insisting that the tall, blond son of Iowa was an Australian and refusing to accept the guerrillas' offer to keep him and let Khoo and others go free.

In late May, TV crews for American networks CBS and NBC were not so lucky. Six CBS men in two vehicles drove down Highway 3 toward the town of Takeo. Ignoring warnings at a Cambodian army roadblock, they blundered into a Viet Cong ambush. CBS correspondent George Syvertsen, producer Gerald Miller, cameraman Ramnik Lekhi, and their driver-interpreter, Sam Leng, were killed when their jeep was hit by a B-40 rocket grenade. Cameraman To-

moharu Iishi and soundman Kojiro Sakai had waited a short distance behind but were captured, along with three NBC men—correspondent Welles Hangen, cameraman Roger Colne, and soundman
Yoshiniko Waku—who had pursued their network rivals down the
same road. All were executed a day later. The only survivor, a Cambodian driver for NBC, reported that Hangen also brushed off warnings at the roadblock. "If CBS goes, we go," were his last known
words. Taken together, it was the war's bloodiest single incident involving journalists.[6]

In meetings around the hotel swimming pool, the journalists in
Phnom Penh formed a committee to protect themselves, setting out
guidelines for running the roads and how to behave if captured, reg-
istering all members of the press corps, and indoctrinating new ar-
rivals on the perils of Cambodian coverage. The safety rules recommended that reporters "look civilian rather than military"—the
reverse of the combat-area dress code in Vietnam—watch village activity along the roads to make sure peasants were going about their
affairs normally, and always get back to the city by three o'clock in
the afternoon. Traveling in groups was essential, even though it
might lead to a false sense of security.

Just after sundown on another day, Steve Bell encountered a worried UPI reporter, Kate Webb, in the hotel driveway. Webb—who
would later survive her own ordeal of capture in Cambodia—reported
that two of her colleagues, Pulitzer Prize–winning photographer Kyoichi Sawada and recently arrived reporter Frank Frosch, were hours
overdue on a trip down Highway 2. The next day, a UPI stringer found
their car, riddled with bullets, and the bodies of Sawada and Frosch.
They evidently had been marched off into a field and summarily executed. Sawada's body was cremated in a Buddhist ceremony at a Phnom
Penh pagoda, where Bell remembers being "the only non-Asian family

---

[6] The bodies of Syvertsen, Miller, Lekhi, and driver Leng were retrieved within days, those of
Sakai and the NBC crew in a JTF-FA search in 1992. Iishi's remains were never found. "It
took twenty-two years, but if something happened to me, I would want someone to look
for me," said Arthur Lord, a former NBC colleague and friend of Hangen, who played a key
role in arranging the JTF-FA search. An excellent account of the TV crew murders, and of
the Cambodian media experience in general, is *A Cambodian Odyssey,* by then–CBS (and
former AP) correspondent Jeff Williams and CBS cameraman Kurt Volkert. It was published in 2001 by Writers' Showcase, an imprint of iUniverse.com, Inc., Lincoln, Nebraska.

member." In the Japanese custom, a priest brought the ashes in a small steel container, and mourners used chopsticks to lift out bits of fire-whitened bone and deposit them in two memorial boxes—"one to Sawada's wife, the other to his girlfriend."

By the end of 1970, twenty-five foreign journalists were dead or unaccounted for in Cambodia. The strangest case involved the last one, a mysterious young Dutchman named Johannes Duynisveld, who had passed through Saigon on his way to Phnom Penh, saying he planned to work there as a freelance journalist. One day in September, he left the capital and disappeared, as so many others had.

Nothing was heard of Duynisveld until late December, when the Dutch military attache in Saigon was notified that the body of a Dutchman was in the morgue at the Bien Hoa military base. According to military officials, a group of Viet Cong guerrillas had walked into an ambush by South Vietnamese Rangers in the Parrot's Beak and during a firefight, some Rangers saw a blond foreigner carrying a weapon, who cried out as he was hit by bullets. In a post-action sweep, the Rangers recovered the body, along with a battered pocket diary.

By the description, the diplomat at first feared the dead man was AP photographer Hugh Van Es, a countryman whom he knew to be in Cambodia at the time. But the diary identified its owner as Johannes Duynisveld. It fell to Van Es, on his return to Saigon a few days later, to translate the Dutch-language entries. Some were in a code which, Van Es recalls, "I could never break." From the rest of it, however, he learned that Duynisveld had been secretly hired in Phnom Penh by Louise Smyser Stone, to try to find Dana and bring him back. Louise Stone had stayed on at the hotel Le Royal after Dana and Sean Flynn disappeared, insisting that Dana was alive and would turn up any day.

According to the diary, Duynisveld had managed to link up with a Viet Cong unit and had traveled with it for several weeks. His intermittent entries told of constant movement, occasional contact with other forces, and the threat of bombing by South Vietnamese aircraft. The last entry was a couple of days before the ambush.

Nothing in the diary suggested he had found any clues to the fate of Dana Stone, but Louise was extremely distraught that it had come into our hands. She insisted that it belonged to her and begged us not to write about it, saying the revelation that someone had been searching for her husband could panic his captors into killing him and cause trouble for her with Cambodian officials.

Although that was debatable, it created an awkward situation. After some discussion, we compromised—in Louise's favor. I wrote a story about the diary that said Duynisveld had been looking for Stone and Flynn, but I did not reveal that she had hired him. We gave her the diary. Going to the wire just before Christmas, the story attracted little attention. Duynisveld was buried in Saigon. His possessions were sent to his family in Leiden, Holland.[7]

---

[7] Louise Stone died in her native Kentucky in 2001 after a long, debilitating illness. She never gave up hope that Dana would return.

6 : Henri Huet

If Larry Burrows had a peer as combat photographer, it was friendly, handsome Henri Huet. "Henri goes to war the way other people go to the office," Horst liked to say. Admirers, describing him to newcomers to the war zone, would remark that "Henri has spent more time pinned down in rice paddies than most photographers have spent in Vietnam."

Such hyperbole contained more than a grain of truth; probably no journalist covering the war had spent more days and nights in the field, sitting, walking, or flying with the troops, sharing their miseries, and bringing them a fresh breath of the world they'd left somewhere.

Huet was a complex, almost mystifying figure, gregarious yet private, a talented painter, a charmer of women, a terror at chess, a hail-fellow-well-met who lived quietly and did not drink or smoke. Fortunately for the law, someone once said, he had become a combat photographer instead of a confidence man.

In the fields of combat, he was utterly self-sufficient and at ease yet was not afraid to say that he was afraid. "I hate zee ay-lee-cop-tair," he would sometimes remark, after returning to the Saigon bureau with pictures and meticulous notes on what he had witnessed.

In a war where many professional soldiers regarded journalists with attitudes ranging from wary mistrust to outright contempt, the seemingly guileless Frenchman was welcome everywhere, using his glacier-melting grin to break down the most media-hostile field commanders. Edwin Q. White, an AP reporter and Saigon bureau chief who was particularly close to Huet, wrote that it was common for other journalists to be greeted in the field by an officer saying, "Where's Henri? Tell him to come and see us."

Henri's way with the camera—his impeccable composition and sure timing—was widely recognized among his press colleagues, particularly by other photographers. "Henri doesn't miss," declared Larry Burrows, who could easily have viewed Huet as a rival but instead embraced him as a friend and companion. Of course, it helped Henri's standing with the turf-conscious Burrows that he did not work for *Life* magazine.

The more general accolades for Huet's work were curiously long in coming, and some never did. Six different AP staffers would earn a Pulitzer Prize for Vietnam-related work, yet the man who made covering the war in his native land his life's purpose was not among them.

Even Horst, who was Henri's immediate boss in Saigon for five years, concedes that he came to fully appreciate his talent only years later, as the cocreator of a book and museum exhibit on Vietnam War photographers. "I always knew from handling his film on a daily basis that Henri was a great photographer, but I didn't realize how great until I saw the body of his work in its entirety," says Faas. "He might have been the best of all."

Henri Gilles Huet was born the second of four children of a French father and a Vietnamese mother, on a plantation owned by her family in Dalat, a farming area of Vietnam's Central Highlands. Gilles Pierre Louis Raoul Huet was a civil engineer who first went to Indochina to survey a route for a Dalat branch of the Saigon-Hanoi railroad, and stayed on to build roads and bridges for the French colonial government.

While some family details are obscure, the parents were never married and did not live together. *Le pere* (father) Huet, as eldest son

Paul still calls him, was away from the Dalat plantation much of the time, managing highway projects, and the four children, raised by their maternal grandparents, rarely saw their mother, who managed a separate business, a transportation company. The old man was "very secretive about our mother and we never knew her name," only as "maman," Paul recalls. She was originally from "high society in Hue," and as small children, the Huet brood were taken to visit maternal relatives in Saigon. "We did not know who they were," he says. "I was very young, and I remember seeing an old man seated on a throne, with fingernails reaching to the floor."

Despite the parents' frequent absences, the children lived well on the farm that covered nearly 1,000 acres, with a hundred acres devoted to coffee and the rest given over to fruit orchards with exotic fruits such as Japanese plums, citrus groves, and grazing land for sheep and dairy cattle, with a montagnard workforce of Moi tribesmen producing enough crops to feed the local villages and export to lowland markets.

The main villa had its own large vegetable garden, a formal garden overlooking a pond, and a nearby bamboo grove "swarming with cobras," Paul remembers. The plantation also served as a lodge for visiting hunters—Dalat not only was the farming capital of Vietnam, but teemed with other wildlife, including elephants, tigers, and barking deer.

Gilles Huet had begun his family late in life. He was 46 when Paul was born in 1924; then came Henri in 1927, Yves in 1929, and a daughter, Jeanne Marie, in 1930. So proud of his progeny that he gave all three boys the middle name Gilles, the father decided in 1933 to send them to France for proper schooling. After their mother died of a fever in 1937, he sent Jeanne Marie as well to live with a cousin in the Huet family's spacious home in Roz-sur-Couesnon, a small town 25 miles east of the historic port city of Saint-Malo, and near Mont Saint-Michel, the coastal landmark castle where Brittany and Normandy meet.

Getting the children out of Vietnam ultimately proved to have been a wise decision. When the Japanese Imperial Army invaded Indochina, the elder Huet hid his hunting rifles, but was thrown in prison after they were discovered. He would spend most of World War II in detention, and would never fully regain his health.

Living with their father's relatives in Roz-sur-Couesnon, Henri and his siblings grew up French, seeing their father only during his home leaves every three years or so. While the *metisse*, or mixed French-Vietnamese, tend to be exceptionally handsome people, they were not readily accepted in French society. Henri as a child was relegated to what he described, years later, as a kind of secondary status in his adopted family. He was forced to work long, arduous hours on a farm in Rennes, near his home, and his dark, Eurasian features made him the target of schoolmates' racial slurs. He compensated for this by excelling at soccer and in art classes, where he found a more welcoming atmosphere, and won numerous prizes and praise from his teachers.

Although France was under Nazi occupation from 1940, the effect this had on Henri's early teenage years is unclear. He was seventeen when the Allies invaded France in June 1944 to sweep the German occupiers back from the coast. In that same year, Henri began four years of study at the prestigious *lycée* and *Ecole des Beaux Arts* in Rennes. In late July, the U.S. 4th Armored Division, leading the Allies' breakout from Saint-Lo in Normandy, drove across the neck of the Brittany peninsula, capturing a series of river crossings and smashing German resistance. Saint-Malo, 25 miles from Roz-sur-Couesnon, had formed part of Hitler's "Atlantic Wall" and was 80 percent destroyed.

The advancing Americans seized Rennes in the first week of August. One can only speculate whether Henri Huet and his schoolmates were among the welcoming citizenry as Sherman tanks of the 37th Armored Battalion, the division spearhead, rumbled through the town, with cigar-chewing Lieutenant Colonel Creighton Abrams standing, as always, in the turret of the command tank.[1]

By his own account, Henri had been planning on an art career. But as World War II ended, something interceded, something that would draw him back to Indochina. Brother Paul had enlisted in the French Army in 1945 and spent the next three years in Indochina as

[1] Abrams went on to fame as General George S. Patton's "favorite tank commander," leading the armored spearhead that broke the German siege at Bastogne in December 1944, relieving the surrounded troopers of the 101st Airborne Division and symbolically ending the Battle of the Bulge. While Henri Huet often photographed Abrams as commander of U.S. forces in Vietnam, it seems doubtful that he ever knew the craggy-faced general was the same officer who had liberated him a quarter of a century earlier.

CLOCKWISE FROM UPPER LEFT: Young Larry Burrows in London studio; Faas and Burrows in Saigon, 1967; fatigued Burrows with Leicas on February 7, 1971, morning after mistaken air strike.

TOP: "If your pictures aren't good enough...." Burrows (in background) gets close up on touring Queen Elizabeth II in Fiji, 1963.
BOTTOM: Larry and young friend on Thailand location for film, "The Ugly American."

ABOVE: Burrows shields face during helicopter medevac at Mimot, Cambodia, 1970; and (left) walks in stream with troops.
BELOW: Always striving for the unusual shot, Larry fixes camera to H-21 "Flying Banana" helicopter, 1996.

A masterpiece of engineering, the Ho Chi Minh Trail was Hanoi's road to battle for men and materiel. Maintenance crews worked constantly, filling bomb craters, clearing landslides.

CLOCKWISE FROM UPPER
LEFT: Monsoon rains
restricted truck traffic for
weeks at a time, forcing
North Vietnamese to rely
on simpler means of transport (above). More than a
million troops traveled the
network that meandered
through some of world's
most rugged jungle terrain
(left). For many, the journey was one way.

ABOVE: Huet children at Dalat, 1932, with father, Gilles, and Vietnamese wife. Children, from left to right, are Jeanne Marie, Yves, Paul and Henri.

RIGHT: Even native son Henri Huet was not immune from Vietnam's oppressive heat.

CLOCKWISE FROM LEFT: Henri and Inger-Johanne in Bangkok, 1970; Inger-Johanne Holmboe with Henri's ex-wife Sonia, son Joelle, daughter Sandrine in New Caledonia, 1970; Gilles Huet, 1954; Henri with daughter Sandrine in Saigon.

RIGHT: Gen. Westmoreland congratulates Henri on 1967 Capa Award in New York; others are AP board chairman Paul Miller (center), AP general manager Wes Gallagher.

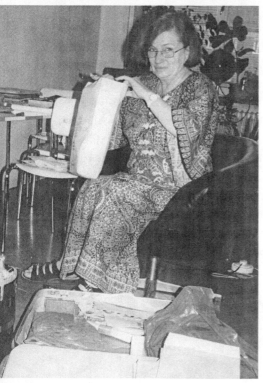

CLOCKWISE FROM TOP LEFT: Journalists
sometimes had to help out; as when
Henri held a blood transfusion bottle.
Henri at Con Thien (above), moments
after being wounded by artillery shrapnel; a Marine a few feet away was killed.
Inger-Johanne (left) preserved Henri's
papers after his death.

an electrician. A year after he returned, it was Henri's turn. In 1949, at age twenty-two, he was drafted into the military. Offered a choice of occupational specialties, he made a life-determining decision. "I didn't want to be anything like a radio operator, so I said photographer," he recalled in a 1967 interview.

He was sent to a military photography school at Rochefort, where he earned a certificate in aerial photography from the Marine Nationale, the French navy. He also volunteered for Indochina duty and a year later was back in Vietnam, reconnecting with his father, by then retired at the farm in Dalat. The elder Huet, who was never the same after his prison camp ordeal, would hang on in Indochina until expelled by the communists in May 1958; he then returned to France and died the following March of cancer, aged eighty-eight.

In his last years before expulsion, the elder Huet had acquired a new female companion, La Co, who helped him manage the plantation. Before leaving for France, the old man gave Henri full authority to deal with the estate as he saw fit. Henri encountered "all sorts of legal problems and fights with La Co," Paul Huet recalls.

Peace had been short-lived in Asia. In 1950 the Korean peninsula was engulfed in war, and French Indochina was on the cusp of revolution, led by a communist named Nguyen Ai Quoc, alias Ho Chi Minh. As the anticolonial war spread across the country, Henri saw it mostly from above, shooting aerial reconnaissance photos from pontoon-equipped seaplanes for officers to use in planning field operations.

Stationed at Cat Lai, a naval compound ten miles outside of Saigon, he ran the photo laboratory and occasionally went into the field with troops—perhaps sixteen times in all, he recalled later. On the first such operation, the commanding officer insisted that Henri carry a weapon. He refused. "I was only there to take pictures," he said in a 1967 interview. "Carrying a gun was not my business." The officer finally forced him to hook some hand grenades to his belt, but Henri claimed to have lost them in the first couple of hours, and "nobody ever asked me to carry a weapon again."

In 1952, Henri took his discharge from the military, but rather than return to France he stayed on in Saigon for the next decade, putting the photographic skills learned in the Navy to work as a civilian.

At first he worked in a Saigon photo studio, then as a contract photographer for the U.S. embassy's economic mission. His duties there included recording on film the activities of the Asia experts, diplomats, and politicians—among them Vice Presidents Richard Nixon and Lyndon Johnson—who came in a steady stream to take their soundings of the new Republic of Vietnam, a pro-Western democracy spun out of the Geneva Accords.

Henri also got married—to Sonia Piotrowski, a Russian-Vietnamese who worked in a Saigon restaurant owned by her parents. A son, Joelle, was born in 1959 and a daughter, Sandrine, in 1960, but the marriage was not to last.

By that time, fresh mutterings of political thunder could be heard in the languid Paris of the Orient. Triumphant in the north, the Viet Minh were now fomenting unrest in the south; and in the countryside, a new communist-led insurgency, soon to become known as the Viet Cong, was taking shape. Within two years it had become a fever. Politicized Buddhist monks took to the streets, sometimes burning themselves to death in grisly protests against the repressive policies of President Ngo Dinh Diem and his regime, dominated by the country's Catholic minority.

When matters finally boiled over in November 1963, Henri was in the streets with his cameras. Amid the turmoil of a coup d'état in which Diem was overthrown and murdered along with his police-chief brother, Ngo Dinh Nhu, he took photos that were splashed across six pages in *Paris-Match* magazine. Henri Huet had become a news photographer.

His success as a freelancer covering the continuing turbulence in Vietnam led to a full-time job, in early 1965, with UPI's Saigon bureau. In almost no time Henri won the agency's $100 best-photo-of-the-month award and probably would have won it many more times had he stayed longer. But a newfound friend, AP photographer Eddie Adams, persuaded him to jump to the rival news service. Money was the lure that overcame loyalty. "At UPI, Henri was making sixty-five dollars a week and didn't want to leave," Adams recalls. "He said, 'They gave me a job as a photographer.' I told him we'd pay him two hundred a week."

As Henri Huet was carving out a reputation as one of the world's best photographers, he also was generating a personal legend. Though not by design, it was encouraged by such anecdotes as the occasion when he returned from the field bleeding from a wound yet dropped off his film at the UPI bureau before going to the hospital.

After he joined AP, the mystique grew, helped along by the fact that Henri Huet was not much given to talking about himself. Other than the basic facts—that he was born in Dalat of mixed parentage, was a French citizen, and had a former wife and two children in New Caledonia— even close friends and colleagues knew relatively little about him.

All of which served to build the mythology. There was, for example, a story that Henri, who was slight in stature, had once carried a wounded American officer for three days through the jungle. If this was true, why was such an astonishing feat not widely known?

A few former colleagues also remember hearing that Huet had been captured by the Viet Minh in the fall of Dien Bien Phu in May 1954 and had spent months in a prison camp before being released. One claims that he was told this by Henri himself. But most former friends say they never heard this story, and no military records or other evidence appear to support it.

In May 1954, Henri had been out of the French navy for two years and, as far as is known, was living and working in Saigon. To have fought and survived at Dien Bien Phu was a special badge of honor among French war veterans, a distinction that perhaps even humble Henri Huet could not have resisted making known. On the other hand, says Eddie Adams, "Henri was so damn modest that he could have won the Medal of Honor and never bothered to tell anybody about it."

Within the Saigon press corps, Huet was widely regarded as the quintessential combat-wise photographer, courageous yet cautious, and always the professional—helping others but asking nothing. Reporters loved to travel with him in the field, although at least one, former UPI reporter Joe Galloway, learned early in the game that this could be an unnerving experience.

One day after arriving in Vietnam, Galloway—still in civilian clothes and a total stranger to everything Vietnamese—found himself literally shanghaied by Huet from the Danang airport to cover a story at a base that had been attacked by the Viet Cong. They helped retrieve the bodies of two dead U.S. advisers, then spent the night with weapons in hand, helping to guard the advisory team's compound in

Quang Ngai against an expected guerrilla raid. It was an introduction to Vietnam that Galloway would never forget.

Henri's colleagues wondered how someone so friendly, even jovial, could also be so private and tinged with melancholy. He lived alone in a Saigon apartment and often, upon returning from the field, would vanish for days, then reappear, ready for more action.

His aversion to alcohol apparently stemmed from childhood, when relatives put calvados-soaked cloths over his face to induce sleep. At holiday parties and departing-staffer dinners, he ordered "orange squash." Adams recalls that Henri had a special preference for Fanta, a bottled orange soda. "I didn't even know what it was," says Adams.

Having learned chess at an early age, Henri was good enough to beat all comers, military and civilian. During assignments in I Corps, he found time to display his boyhood soccer skills at the Danang Press Center, and on one occasion he teamed up with Steve Stibbens to rig a makeshift mast and sails on a derelict rowboat, in which they cruised up and down the Danang River.

Huet spoke French, some Vietnamese, and a very Gallic form of English, but he communicated in no medium more effectively than his pictures. Along with their extraordinary reach into the soul of a soldier, they revealed a native son's sensitivity to the plight of people trying to live normally amid fear, death, and destruction. He romanced Vietnam's landscape with his lens, capturing the beauty in its moods, mist, and menace, sometimes revealing the introspective artist behind the shield of sunny optimism.

Other photographers found Henri Huet, like Larry Burrows, a kindly mentor. "He was my boss at UPI and he taught me the dark-room," says British photographer Tim Page, four times wounded and himself a Vietnam press corps legend. Dana Stone, the red-haired former Vermont lumberjack who arrived in Vietnam as a tourist, spent some time hanging out with military units, and eventually found work as a photo freelancer, credited Henri with teaching him how to work and survive in combat. Stone said that when he first went into the field, he was so raw that he didn't even know how to rewind the Nikon F camera that UPI had given him. "Henri showed me how to do it, didn't laugh at me or anything," he said.

In January 1966 came the incident that would define Henri Huet as a combat photographer in the way that "Yankee Papa 13" had defined Larry Burrows. And in the peculiar way their destinies seemed to be intertwined, Burrows himself would have a hand in it.

Huet and an AP reporter, Robert Poos, were with troops of the U.S. 1st Cavalry Division at An Thi, on South Vietnam's central Bong Son Plain, when they were ambushed by a mixed force of North Vietnamese and Viet Cong regulars. For some twenty-four hours, the unit truly was in that classic Vietnam mode—"pinned down in a rice paddy"—during which the two AP men pitched in to handle ammunition and assist with the wounded.

In the eruption of gunfire that followed the first shot from a communist soldier's AK-47, Poos and Huet split up to join different platoons. It was a way to maximize their news and photo coverage—and reduce the odds of both being killed or wounded. Poos found the 3rd Platoon by sprinting across a field and plunging headlong into a muddy ditch. From there, he could see Henri at a distance, "ignoring the bullets cracking around him while rapidly snapping photos."

Early in the battle, Henri fulfilled his own myth by helping to rescue a wounded man. When a trooper was hit by enemy fire and fell between Henri and another soldier, "they hardly broke stride but grabbed the wounded guy on either side and dragged him to the trench line," said Poos. "The thing everyone noticed about Henri was his absolute fearlessness, or, perhaps, indifference to fear, is a better way to put it."

Fortunately for the newsmen, these troopers of the 2nd Battalion, 7th Cavalry Regiment, were seasoned and well-led, many of them veterans of the battle at Ia Drang two months earlier. They did not panic, even when it became clear that an enemy force had slipped behind them, blocking their route of withdrawal.

As the situation worsened, Huet and Poos stayed together most of the time, huddling with GIs in the sandy trench, reasonably well protected from enemy fire. "We could tell by the sound—'sing-whang-whop'—that bullets were very close, at waist level. But Henri stood and knelt on the lip of the trench snapping shots of a medic working on the wounded. I was flat on my back, and I couldn't believe he wasn't getting hit. A couple of guys yelled, 'Henri, get down!' but he did so only when he'd used up a roll of film and had to reload."

The men in the trench narrowly escaped death when three rounds from a U.S. howitzer fell short, smashing into the parapet just yards away. "Henri said, 'I don't think we are going to make it out of this, Bob,'" Poos recalls. "That was the last thing I wanted to hear because he, more than anyone I knew, had the experience to assess such situations accurately and dispassionately."

With the onset of darkness came heavy rain, and the two journalists volunteered to help guard the makeshift hospital, a section of trench where the medic, Thomas Cole, was tending the wounded. Only Poos had a sidearm. "Even in this situation, where we figured we could be overrun and wiped out in the next twenty-four hours, Henri was consistent about not using a weapon. He was the only person I know who could have done that with no one thinking less of him. Everyone just figured it was some sort of personal ethics issue with Henri and accepted it."

Lieutenant Colonel Robert McDade would later call Huet "the bravest man I ever saw," and Colonel Harold Moore, commander of the 1st Cav's 3rd Brigade, said he would have decorated him on the spot if he had the power to do so. As cavalry reinforcements arrived, Huet and Poos managed to get aboard helicopters taking out the GI dead wrapped in ponchos. While Poos phoned his story from the nearest base at Lai Khe, Huet headed straight for Saigon with his film.

Normally, the Saigon bureau would transmit a few of its best photos of the day to New York by radio, then ship all film and negatives by airfreight to New York and Tokyo. On this day, recalls John Nance, who was the photo editor on duty, "Henri came in with so many good pictures that the desk was overwhelmed." Nance sent the New York office a quick rundown of Huet's pictures, but editors there, trying to cope with a busy news day elsewhere in the world, messaged Saigon to transmit only his "two best."

As Nance remembers, "We argued by telex that Henri's pictures were truly exceptional, and when New York saw the first couple of shots, they took a stack, each one terrific." The key sequence of photos showed Cole, his grimy face partly obscured by a battle dressing, giving water in a C-ration can to another wounded GI. Huet, still in his own dirty uniform, was calmly reading out caption material from his notebook when Larry Burrows entered the AP photo office. He had just returned from an operation in the Central Highlands, and some-one had told him about the An Thi fighting. "I hear Henri got some great stuff," he said. Nance spread the freshly developed black-and-white photos across the desk. Larry scanned them, then pointed to the shot of the wounded medic. "That's a *Life* cover," he said.

Burrows then promised Nance and Huet that he would urge his editors to use the AP photos in the magazine. He did, and they did—putting Henri's medic on the cover and filling six pages inside with other pictures of the battle of An Thi.

The year 1967 was a momentous one for Huet. In April, he flew to New York to receive the Overseas Press Club's Robert Capa Award for the An Thi pictures. People who knew Henri Huet only as the slight, smiling figure in combat fatigues caked with Vietnam's *terre rouge* were startled to see the sophisticated, slicked-back version in dark suit and tie.

A few months later, Henri and Dana Stone were together covering U.S. Marines under siege at Con Thien, a hill outpost just below the DMZ. The North Vietnamese were bombarding the Marines con-stantly with mortars and artillery, and Henri, who theretofore had suf-fered only a minor scratch or two in combat, was caught in the open as an artillery round suddenly slammed into the muddy hill.

Two Marines—one of them standing five feet from Henri—were killed, as most others managed to dive into trenches and bunkers. Hearing the call for medical assistance—"Corpsman up!"—Stone climbed from his hole and raced to find Henri lying in a shallow trench, with shrapnel in one arm and his right leg, which was broken. The Marine who was killed apparently had shielded Henri from the full blast.

Huet was evacuated, first to an aid station, then to Danang and Saigon, and finally to New York, where within days he was undergoing surgery on his mangled leg. There, he had another close call—in its way as dangerous as any he had encountered in Vietnam. During the operation, a fumble-fingered doctor accidentally shut down the oxy-gen supply; Henri, unable to move or cry out, nearly died before the mistake was discovered.

Recovery from the wounds lasted months, and when doctors fi-nally released him, Henri took time off to play tourist. He visited

Philadelphia, then traveled to Montreal, Cuba, and Mexico. His companion on the trip to Acapulco was a young Belgian photographer's model, whom he had met during his convalescence. Although they apparently went so far as to discuss marriage, friends do not recall Henri mentioning this after returning to Saigon. Nothing is known of the Belgian girl except her first name, Cecile.

Henri did not get back to Saigon in time to cover the 1968 Tet Offensive and the siege of Khe Sanh, but he was soon in the field on other stories. The war was shifting—the U.S. forces peaked at more than 549,000 in early 1969 and then began a slow, piecemeal withdrawal, but the fighting continued at intensive levels, and Henri was running the same risks that he always had to get pictures.

By June of that year, AP executives in New York became so concerned about Huet's continuing exposure to danger that they pressured him into leaving Vietnam for a safer assignment. In what seemed at the time a reasonable solution, AP's Tokyo photo editor, Max Desfor, offered Henri a spot on his staff.

Henri accepted the transfer reluctantly. A going-away party at fellow AP photographer Rick Merron's Saigon apartment served only to emphasize the camaraderie that he would miss, along with the excitement, and, above all, the photos that only the Vietnam War could generate.

No change, at least within the hemisphere, could have been more drastic, or more profound, in its impact on Huet. Although the large Tokyo bureau was one of AP's most prestigious and a huge money-earner for the news agency, the tightfisted bureau chief did not lavish funds on coverage of Japan itself.

In a country of picturesque landscapes and unique culture, awash in colorful festivals, Henri could hardly get out of Tokyo—and the assignments in the capital were dull and repetitious. There was little in the way of hard news, and almost never was there an exclusive. Every valid news event in Japan that merited photo coverage was overwhelmed by hordes of Japanese photographers.

Tony Hirashiki, a TV cameraman who had worked in Vietnam for ABC News, encountered his friend Henri one day on a street in the Ginza. "I was very happy to see Henri in Tokyo, and I asked him where he was going," recalls Hirashiki. "He was embarrassed. He told me he was on his way to cover a Rotary International meeting."

Henri blamed his immediate boss, Desfor, for keeping him tied down in bureau routine, especially the darkroom, which he detested. That was not entirely fair; Desfor, an old pro who had won a Pulitzer Prize for photography in the Korean War, was as beholden to the bureau chief's penny-pinching dictates as was the rest of the Tokyo staff. And in retrospect, Desfor himself concedes that the assignment had been to no one's advantage: "Henri's work in Tokyo was professional, but mechanical. You could see he wasn't happy. His heart and soul were still in Vietnam."

Henri's first act on arriving in the AP office in the Ginza each morning was to grab the "Asia Incoming" clipboard off the news desk and devour the overnight reports from Saigon. After a time, Desfor noticed that Henri had stopped carrying his Leica. In Vietnam, where the unexpected was always to be expected, that was unthinkable; he would never have left his apartment, even to go to breakfast, without a camera on his shoulder. Desfor thought Henri was losing his edge. "I guess the peace was beginning to settle in on him," he says.

On December 31, 1969—New Year's Eve—Henri met Inger-Johanne Holmboe, a Swedish journalist and art expert in Tokyo. Their meeting was occasioned by a postcard from the Belgian model Cecile. From Paris, Cecile had written to *Cher Henri* to say that she could not come to Tokyo to get married, as they had planned. *"Je suis tres desolée,"* she began ("I am very sorry . . ."). In a rare breakdown of the Japanese postal service's vaunted efficiency, the postcard had landed in the mailbox of Inger-Johanne's apartment in the city's Bunkyo-Ku ward.

Up to that point, Inger-Johanne says, Henri had been just a next-door neighbor, if a somewhat annoying one, whose halfhearted attempts to strike up a conversation she, a recent divorcée, had gently rebuffed. The postcard would change all that.

"I knocked on his door and said, 'Listen, Mister, please tell the postman not to put your mail in my mailbox.'" As Henri stood in the doorway, offering Japanese-style obsequies for having inconvenienced her, Inger-Johanne could see past him into the apartment, where an unfinished portrait of a woman rested on a painter's easel. When the art connoisseur expressed interest in the painting, Henri invited her in. The portrait, Inger-Johanne believes, was of Cecile.

Henri, it turned out, had sent Cecile money to come to Tokyo to get married, but she confessed in the postcard that she had spent it on other things and could not make the trip or, for that matter, get married at all. Though saddened by the unexpected news, Henri managed to shrug it off. It being December 31, two solitary people toasted the new year with champagne and began a friendship that would quickly grow into something deeper and more passionate.

Inger-Johanne had studied Asian art and culture as an exchange student at the University of Pennsylvania in the early 1960s. Now she was living in Japan, writing freelance articles on those subjects. Soon, she and Henri began talking about a partnership, traveling around Asia and producing stories and pictures on art, culture, and tourism.

They also fell in love, and it began to appear as if Henri Huet might at last put Indochina and the war behind him. In fact, with Inger-Johanne's encouragement—and unknown to AP—he was sending out discreet job feelers to other news and photo agencies and major magazines.

In one letter to Larry Burrows in Hong Kong, he asked about a rumor that *Life* was looking for a new contract photographer in Southeast Asia. On April 9, Burrows wrote back that the information was "way off beam." The magazine, he said, was actually cutting back on its Asian operation, and editors' interest in Indochina seemed to be flagging. "World Wide *Life* is very much on a close budget and there have been very few requests for stories, even from us hired hands!" Burrows said. "As a matter of fact I now hold a Cambodian visa and N.Y. are not interested in coverage unless all hell breaks loose, who knows when that might happen."

Henri's new career as the shooting half of a travel-and-culture reporting team was not to be, either.

In March 1970, the overthrow of Prince Sihanouk's regime in Phnom Penh plunged Cambodia fully into the war. Henri told AP he wanted to go back to Indochina and strongly hinted that if the company refused he would quit and return on his own. But before all that came to an awkward showdown, the problem resolved itself. In early April, as the Cambodia story burgeoned beyond the level of sideshow, the AP Saigon bureau put out a call to New York for reinforcements—reporters and photographers with Vietnam experience.

On the photo side, Henri was candidate number one. In New York, AP photo chief Hal Buell messaged Tokyo: "Would like to send Huet [to Vietnam] for approximately one month, beginning soon's can." Max Desfor could not and would not stand in the way. Within two days, Henri Huet flew home—to Indochina and the war.

One of his first assignments upon returning was to southern Cambodia, with this author, to cover operations of South Vietnamese troops trying to move westward along the coast toward Sihanoukville, the Gulf of Thailand port that for years had served as a second supply conduit for communist forces in Vietnam. In the Mekong Delta town of Ha Tien, we took refuge from a violent monsoon in a hotel that was all but empty—no beds, no water, no people. Spectacular webs of lightning crazed the sky, accompanied by unbroken rolls of thunder that lasted through the night. Henri was in an ebullient mood; the weather gods were putting on a *son et lumiére* show to welcome him back.

The next morning, after a ferry ride across the river to Cambodia, we found a South Vietnamese helicopter unit and wangled a ride to Kep, a coastal resort town that marked the ARVN forces' farthest advance. We arrived to find that the communist troops had pulled out overnight, leaving a town wrecked and virtually deserted by its civilian population. On borrowed bicycles we headed west along the coastal blacktop.

A few kilometers beyond Kep, South Vietnamese troops manning a roadblock warned us to go no farther; the area beyond was controlled by the enemy. Considering the way journalists were vanishing on Cambodian highways, it was advice worth taking, and we did.

Henri slipped back into the Saigon routine as if he'd never left, making several forays into Cambodia with the Vietnamese and the Americans. When asked about Tokyo, he offered little more than a Gallic shrug. He never returned there. Instead, he wrote to the New York office and asked that his reassignment to Saigon be made permanent, to which AP management eventually agreed.

In July, he used some vacation time to travel to Hong Kong, Thailand, Malaysia, and Indonesia with Inger-Johanne. In Jakarta, they paid a visit to Joe Galloway, the UPI correspondent who several years earlier had been dragooned by Henri into covering combat on his second day in Vietnam as a new reporter. Galloway greeted his old friend warmly: "You're still alive?"

Then, in December, Henri and Inger-Johanne made another, long-awaited trip to New Caledonia. Henri had written to his children and was eager to see them; ideally, he wanted legal custody, but there seemed no practical way to achieve that.

In Noumea, they found Henri's former wife, Sonia, and the children living with a sea captain, and financially distressed despite Henri's own monthly support. After five days with Joelle and Sandrine, Henri came away deeply troubled by their situation. He told Inger-Johanne that if anything happened to him he wanted her to try to get custody and care for the children. She promised this, and he wrote a note giving her power of attorney, as his fiancée, to handle affairs "in case of an accident during my assignment with AP in Vietnam." He specified that his life insurance should be used for his children's welfare and education, adding that he doubted Sonia's ability "to administer correctly large sums of money."

Back in Saigon, the year 1971 began with wide speculation about plans by U.S. and South Vietnamese leaders for another cross-border invasion, this time into Laos. Henri soon joined the flow of journalists heading north to cover the buildup and wait for a chance to join the push into Laos if and when it occurred.

There was, however, a problem: His Vietnamese residence visa was about to expire. This would require him to leave the country again, just long enough to renew it. This bit of bureaucratic red tape was a recurring annoyance for foreign residents in South Vietnam, but it could not be ignored. The government enforced the rule rigidly, particularly in the case of journalists, and problems with the foreign ministry were something that members of the Saigon press corps tried hard to avoid.

Henri knew all this yet insisted on staying at the northern front, even though his continued presence there was not absolutely necessary. AP had at least three other staff photographers and three reporters in the area, any one of whom would be available to cover the action in Laos if and when the opportunity arose.

Among them was Huynh Cong "Nick" Ut, who from age sixteen had worked his way up to become a photographer under the tutelage of Faas and Huet. Starting out, he had worked as an AP photo darkroom assistant after his older brother, Huynh Thanh My, was killed while shooting the war for AP in 1965. It was Henri who first used the nickname "Nic," meaning "last brother," which naturally transformed into "Nick."

Ut recalls that he had put his own name at the top of a press sign-up list for Laos, but when the time came, he deferred to his mentor's seniority: "Henri said he wanted to go to Laos for a day, so I said okay." After so long, the Saigon visa office would just have to wait some more. No press helicopter was going into Laos without Henri Huet.

Over the next couple of days, the photographers hung out at the border, taking photos of the military activity, and each other, as the columns of South Vietnamese vehicles and flights of U.S. helicopters streamed into Laos.

On February 9, word was passed at the U.S. Army press tent at Khe Sanh, where many of the journalists had dropped their gear: If the weather improved, General Hoang Xuan Lam would make a flying inspection tour of the Laos front the next day and had room for a handful of journalists. From Khe Sanh, Huet relayed a message via colleagues to the AP photo desk in Saigon: He would stay "one more day" to be on the first trip into the battle zone.

Huet, Burrows, and the others spent that night at Khe Sanh, sharing the ten or so cots in the press tent with a handful of military photographers. The latter were assigned to record the war for the U.S. Army and the Marine Corps, and some entertained ambitions toward a career in news after leaving the military. They were frankly awed by the idea of bunking with these famous, combat-seasoned professionals. "To us it was like being lodged with the gods," says Christopher Jensen, then the leader of an Army photo team.

Jensen, who had met Larry Burrows once before, at the press camp in Danang, remembers being "amazed" by two things about the *Life* photographer: "First, he carried pajamas, and second, even though we were just Army photographers, he treated us with civility, as if we were colleagues, a graciousness that stunned us." The soldiers, who had military sleeping bags, reciprocated by loaning poncho liners to the four civilians as protection against the wet February chill. "The next morning was pretty routine," Jensen recalls, "with all of us sitting on our cots, sharing our shivers and griping about the cold, in search of a little warmth and caffeine from canteen cups of coffee."

People were rummaging through the Army-supplied C-rations, looking for suitable breakfast fare and something to pack along for later. In Vietnam, C-rats were always within easy reach wherever the

U.S. military was present, and they spawned their own grunt-gourmet superstitions. The canned peaches, the fruit cocktail, and the pound cake were considered special treats—as were the canned apricots, until a story circulated among troops that they were bad luck, that people tended to get killed after eating them.

Chris Jensen remembers Henri Huet as the "liveliest" member of the group in the Khe Sanh press tent that morning. "He saw himself as the winner of the C-ration breakfast sweepstakes when he found his box contained a can of pound cake. He said, 'This is going to be my lucky day.'"

7 : Bao Chi

The Saigon press corps was an ever-changing cast of characters from many countries, drawn to the flame of the most important story of the decade. The journalists carrying the required South Vietnamese and U.S. press credentials ranged between 200 and 400 at a given time, depending on the changing intensity of battlefield activity. The largest contingent of *bao chi*—Vietnamese for journalist—was, of course, American, followed by British, Japanese, French, Australian, and lesser numbers of Germans, Italians, Koreans, Scandinavians, Indians, South Africans, Dutch, and Canadians. Dozens of local Vietnamese—reporters, photographers, technicians, drivers, "fixers," and office workers—also worked for the foreign agencies, newspapers, and TV networks.

It was an eclectic mix in other ways as well. There were old Asia hands with a historical, above-the-battle perspective, cynical Korean War retreads who scoffed quietly at the ambitious young Ivy Leaguers now peppering their sacrosanct profession. There were even a few World War II–vintage correspondents, one of whom had a habit of calling the Vietnam GIs "doughboys"—a term actually dating from World War I.

In the cutthroat world of network television, a Vietnam tour was de rigueur for everyone, whether an anchor-star of the evening news or a newcomer eager for a shot at the big time. Some stayed for long periods; for others the war was just a quick turn, known as "getting your ticket punched." Most of the familiar faces on American TV news programs of the last quarter-century once were seen doing "stand-up-pers" against a backdrop of Vietnamese countryside or Saigon's traffic-clogged avenues.

Obtaining credentials to work as a journalist in Vietnam was not difficult, and it carried no obligation to cover combat. Overall, no more than a third of the members of the Saigon press corps actually went into the field.[1] To qualify for press cards from the Saigon government and the Joint U.S. Public Affairs Office (JUSPAO), one needed only a valid visa and a letter—two letters in the case of freelancers—attesting to employment as a journalist in Vietnam and responsibility for personal finances. Although reporting agendas varied widely, the *Washington Post* and *God's News Behind the News* were technically equals in the eyes of JUSPAO.

Given these less-than-rigid standards, the Saigon press corps attracted not only serious journalists but also a steady trickle of adventurers, thrill-seekers, and other people of doubtful background and questionable purpose. Behind the wry jokes about "spooks" (i.e., intelligence operatives) lurking in our midst was the recognition that in fact there probably were some people using journalistic cover for espionage. Journalists had access to all manner of officials and some knowledge of military plans; almost any kernel of tactical information had potential intelligence value. Thus, a certain amount of discretion was observed. But few in the media were deluded into thinking military security could be maintained in the hothouse of rumor and intrigue that was Saigon.

Only after the fall of Saigon in April 1975 did the truth emerge. The communist takeover was still in its early hours when one of AP's

---

[1] Figures cited by William Hammond, senior historian, U.S. Army Center of Military History, in a 2000 study for the Joan Shorenstein Center for the Press and Public Policy, Harvard University. In 1968–1969, the average age of members of the Saigon press corps was thirty-five. By 1971, this had dropped to thirty-three as younger people arrived and some of the older hands, having established themselves professionally or perhaps simply having had enough of Vietnam, went on to other things.

longtime Vietnamese photo stringers walked into the bureau to reveal that he had been a Viet Cong undercover agent all along. Soon after, *Time* magazine's chief Vietnamese reporter, Pham Xuan An, dropped the even more stunning bombshell that he also was a spy—in fact, a senior commander in the National Liberation Front.

An, a native southerner who had attended college in the United States and worked previously for Reuters, was the acknowledged dean of the South Vietnamese press corps and, for several years, the voice of Radio Catinat, as Saigon's political rumor mill was long known. Every day, from his regular table at the Givral coffee shop on the corner of Tu Do Street, formerly Rue Catinat, An dispensed tidbits of Saigon's convoluted politics and presidential-palace machinations to a rapt audience of disciples—the Vietnamese reporters who worked for the foreign press and networks. These reporters then returned to their offices with the latest inside information from their "sources." It was no mystery where the information was coming from, and a standing press corps joke was that anyone with An's connections must be CIA. If any of his Vietnamese admirers suspected that An was a communist agent, they surely didn't advertise it, but no one in the foreign press ever imagined that the courtly, smiling *Time* reporter was living a dangerous double life and that during his periodic absences from the city he was slipping back into the jungle to teach tactics and confer with his communist superiors.[2]

Even without such pulp-fiction intrigues for inspiration, Vietnam promised journalistic adventure in an exotic setting—and a career opportunity too good to pass up. The obvious risks of covering a war were trumped by having a share in the biggest story of the time. There also was, in some minds—mine, at least—a sense of obligation to one-

---

[2] In postwar years, former press colleagues have not criticized An for his subterfuge, but Hanoi's leaders made clear they didn't fully trust a spy with friends in the West. In 1990, his government promoted An in retirement to one-star general; seven years later it refused to let him travel to the United States for a war symposium. In an interview in Ho Chi Minh City in April 2000, An told this author that he had believed in the communist cause as representing Vietnamese aspirations for independence, that he never dealt in "disinformation," and more than once he had saved *Time* from publishing information he knew was not true. "Most important were things that I knew, that I never told to anyone," he said. Of his one-star promotion, he said: "I told them that because I had experience with the French army, the Viet Minh, the U.S. Army, the South Vietnamese Army, and the Viet Cong, they should make me a five-star general. I don't think they understood my sense of humor."

self. If there was a Vietnam, you had to be there. To paraphrase a popular slogan of the antiwar movement, if they gave a war and *you didn't come*, would you not regret it forever? This idea was never better summarized than one night in the Saigon bureau in early 1969. Viet Cong guerrillas were shelling the city. As the sharp crack of another 122mm rocket echoed in the street outside, AP reporter Edwin Q. White calmly cranked a new sheet of paper into his typewriter, put the world on hold while he relit his pipe, and said, "If you are a journalist at this time in the twentieth century, and you are not in Vietnam, just what the fuck *are* you doing?"

By the timing of birth, my father had been too young for World War I and too old for World War II. During the second war, he was a dedicated home-front warrior, active in Detroit's Red Cross emergency preparations and fulfilling the defense-related responsibilities, such as they were, of an urban high-school principal. While he never spoke openly of it, I believed that my father regretted not having shared more fully in what was the consummate life-realizing experience of his American generation: the triumph of the democracies over fascism. It wasn't something he would have said without being asked, and I never did. Yet my brother Daniel and I both recognized that this was a private burden for him. And even if military service was not essential to every youth's passage to manhood, I knew from his example that there was no way that I could go through life having missed the opportunity, as he had.

This was not entirely by choice. The Korean War was over, but the Cold War dominated the day's news, and every able young male in the United States still faced an obligation to serve two years of military duty. At age twenty, trying to recover in summer school from a failed college sophomore year, I decided to meet this duty head-on. One day I cut classes, went down to the draft board office, and volunteered for the U.S. Army. Although I couldn't know it at the time, the headlines that summer foreshadowed events that would eventually change my life. They told of the communist siege of Dien Bien Phu, a French military stronghold in Indochina, also called Vietnam—a place of strange names that I, like most Americans, knew almost nothing about.

Years later I would realize that volunteering for the draft had been the first life-changing, no-turning-back decision I had ever made on my own. At the time, it filled me with a sense of achievement, and I rehearsed how to coolly drop the news at the dinner table that night. "Guess what I did today?" I said when the moment arrived. "What?" asked my mother. "I volunteered for the draft," I said, with what I hoped was casual aplomb. "I'm going in the army." My mother was aghast; her youngest son was going off to get killed. But my father sat, looking bemused. "Well," he said finally, "good for you. I think you made a smart move." He shook my hand. He understood what I had done and why I had done it. This little drama repeated itself years later when I told my parents, by then retired in southern Ohio, that I had again volunteered—but this time to go off to an actual war. That I would be going as a journalist, rather than a soldier, was little consolation to my mother. As before, my father understood. No one could know better than he that once the question came up there was but one answer.

No journalist could arrive in Saigon for the first time without some apprehension about the dangers and his own ability to measure up. The Pan-Am approach into Tan Son Nhut airport—a steep maneuver designed to minimize exposure to sniper fire—did nothing to calm the initial nerves; neither did the sight of sandbagged revetments, F-4 Phantoms in camouflage taking off laden with bombs, or the mad jostling by tiny women to get to the head of the immigration line. The first blast of Saigon's Turkish-bath humidity and the ride through streets teeming with traffic, past buildings ringed with necklaces of concertina wire, created a further sense of plunging into the abyss.

Once there, these newcomers were generally accorded the benefit of the doubt on the theory that they wouldn't have been sent to Vietnam if they couldn't handle the task. Yet they would remain novices—what the grunts called FNGs, or "fucking new guys"—until tested as to their fitness. And, indeed, Vietnam had its own way of sorting out the unsuited. Some would-be war correspondents arrived full of bravado, only to discover, after a few weeks—or, in some cases, a few days—that they would rather be somewhere else. One TV reporter with a large reputation back in the States got off the plane, holed up in the Caravelle Hotel for forty-eight hours, and went back to the airport. Others came, ostensibly for short tours, and stayed on for months or even years, hopelessly beguiled by the strange allure of war in the tropics. Such people "tended to get over-involved, identified with a time that is now obsolete," Tim Page has since written. "The war days had been the ultimate in experience, laden with a magic, a glamorous edge that none who went through it can truly deny."[3] Wally Terry, one of the first black reporters to cover the war, found Saigon a place where everyone was a brother. "I covered the civil rights movement from Selma and Birmingham to Watts and Harlem, and I have never felt the kind of connection to my fellow journalists on those stories as I did with the ones I worked with in Vietnam," he has said.

By 1968, Saigon had become a wartime capital in which it still was possible to live a modified version of normal life, and many journalists had spouses or companions with them. Although my wife, Toby, had spent several years as an airline flight attendant, this was her first venture abroad. She quickly found friends—among them Jolynne D'Ornano, the wife of our landlord—and wrote a story about living in Saigon for the hometown paper, the *Detroit News*, which duly published it in its Sunday magazine. Our first apartment was above a dress shop a block from the office; later we moved into the AP's building, inheriting a Chinese maid and a cat from the previous occupant, AP bureau chief George McArthur.

For journalists, Vietnam was a war of transition. It was the last one covered with the old-fashioned tools—typewriters, dial-up phones, radio teletype circuits, photo darkrooms; the first one in which television was a presence and news was relayed globally by satellite, although CNN broadcasting live from the scene was still two decades away. The TV networks spent staggering sums of money on war coverage, airshipping film—not yet videotape—to Hong Kong and Tokyo for transmission; the world's first living-room war was at least eighteen hours old by the time it reached television screens in the States. The term "word-processing" was not yet coined. Computers first turned up in newsrooms around 1973, two years before the communist tanks crashed through the gates of Independence Palace.

Vietnam also was the last war—and along with the U.S. space program, the last major running story—in which the Associated Press, a

---

[3] Tim Page, *Derailed in Uncle Ho's Victory Garden* (London: Scribner UK, 1999), p. 13.

nonprofit news cooperative owned by member-subscribers in the United States, went head-to-head with its Scripps-Howard–owned rival, United Press International. AP and UPI (and, to a lesser extent, Britain-based Reuters and Agence France Presse) were at the nexus of Saigon's journalistic subculture. Among them, the two U.S.-based agencies were dominant; Vietnam was, after all, an American version of a Southeast Asian war, in which the British and the French were now been-there, done-that bystanders to someone's else misadventure.

Always skating on the financial brink, UPI in later years would fall victim to a string of mismanagement disasters, a shell of its former robust self, somehow staying afloat despite constant retrenching and revolving-door ownership. In Saigon days, UPI was still very much in the game, making the most of comparatively limited resources in a valiant effort to match the wealthier AP's coverage of the war. One almost had to be a wire-service veteran to truly appreciate the relationship. AP's bureau overlooking Saigon city hall and UPI's at 19 Ngo Duc Ke Street were several blocks apart, and the two staffs moved in separate social orbits. Other than rubbing shoulders at the daily U.S. Command briefings known as the Five O'clock Follies, AP and UPI reporters might go weeks in Saigon without crossing paths. In the field, it was a different matter. There, they often traveled together, sharing C-rations, camera film, and, in certain situations, information.[4]

Both agencies were proud, tightly knit groups, brimming with brio, exulting over scoops and favorable "play reports" from the home office. One wall of the AP bureau held a bulletin board covered with messages of praise for the staff's pace-setting coverage of the Viet Cong sapper attack on the U.S. embassy during the 1968 Tet Offensive. That story in fact had been one of AP's greatest moments; Kate Webb of UPI told an AP friend that it had been, comparatively speaking, one of UPI's worst days. The staffs consisted mainly of handpicked volunteers from domestic or foreign bureaus, supplemented by news and

---

[4] The wire services had their own internal language, based on "cablese," the abbreviated form that was a holdover from days when telegraph messages were charged by the word. In UPI's lexicon, AP was "ROX," possibly referring to AP headquarters at New York's Rockefeller Plaza. UPI also used "grandma," alluding to AP's purported stuffiness. AP called UPI "osn" (opposition), or "brand X." Reuters reflected an outsider's view—calling AP "primary," UPI "secondary."

photo stringers recruited locally from Saigon's ever-changing pool of freelancers. The rigors of the job, whether in the field or spending long hours at desks, winnowed out those who could not perform. "Not a bank clerk in the bunch," former UPI photo chief Bill Snead said when asked to describe the people he worked with in Saigon. The same was true at AP, where the mission—to be first with the story and quick to follow it up—was likened to assaulting a beach and then moving inland. Not for nothing was AP sometimes called "the Marine Corps of journalism."

Within the head-to-head competition, there were commonly perceived differences, for AP had long had a reputation as the more cautious, and more reliable, of the two agencies. Although there was no shortage of talent, guts, and resourcefulness at UPI, there was a definite tendency to overreach. We regularly took calls from other news organizations saying they were unable to confirm something that our competitors had reported, asking what we knew about it. Sometimes we had an answer, sometimes not. One example, recalled by a veteran TV network journalist, was a UPI story claiming that "three battalions of Viet Cong" had "surrounded" Saigon—a fairly scary prospect for anyone who didn't know how utterly implausible that was. After a UPI reporter got into print with a story telling how the "Black Angel of Death" had hovered over the scene of a recent clash, AP staffers who had been on the scene were mock-admonished for having missed the manifestation and were urged to be extra vigilant lest the Black Angel pay a return visit.

Both agencies rotated staff reporters, photographers, and stringers in the field and, with their own twenty-four-hour communications circuits to the world outside, could stay abreast of breaking events in real time. This was important for the many newspapers and broadcast outlets around the globe that were depending on them for quick, detailed reports from the war zone. It also made the wire-service bureaus important points of contact for both resident and visiting correspondents. Each agency developed its own circle of allies, swapping information and comparing notes, while protecting sources and contacts as best they could. Most reporters who made the rounds of both agencies were reasonably discreet, but the warning flags went up for those who seemed too eager in purveying press-corps gossip. One newspaper reporter who kept a mailbox in the AP bureau was barred from the premises after he was caught in the off-limits area of the newsroom, thumbing through a clipboard full of confidential messages.

By mid-1968, the war was in its sixth, seventh, or eighth year, depending on how one measured it, and the Saigon press corps had undergone at least three major evolutions of personnel. Most of the original cadre of young correspondents who had attracted attention for their tough reporting in the early 1960s, before most people knew where Vietnam was, had long since gone on to other things. Not so at AP, where the staff experience in the war zone was unmatched by any other news organization. Horst Faas, Peter Arnett, and Edwin Q. White had been covering Vietnam since 1962, a year before the coup that overthrew and killed President Ngo Dinh Diem; several others had come in the big influx around the same time that the first U.S. combat forces arrived in 1965. The combined experience revealed itself daily in the staff's depth of knowledge and understanding, of Vietnam the country, and of Vietnam the war. Newer staff members could learn a lot just by sitting in the bureau and remaining silent.

Being handpicked in New York to join this elite group did not guarantee a warm reception in Saigon, and it was a relief to be made welcome by these people whose names I knew so well but had never met. The first day in Saigon featured a staff lunch at the nearby Royale Hotel, a gracefully shabby holdover from the colonial era, which had been a regular AP hangout since the early days when Faas lived there. In a dining room graced with white tablecloths, the walls filled with the framed insignia of French colonial-era air squadrons, the wrinkled Corsican owner, Monsieur Jean Ottavi, smiled enigmatically through an opium haze as his waiters served up passable French fare with imported "Algerian red" wine over ice.

Among others I met on that first day were the bureau chief, George McArthur; George Esper, who regularly bylined AP's daily war roundups, pursuing sources with a tenacity I had never seen; and a genial French-Vietnamese photographer, Henri Huet, who had recently returned to Vietnam after recuperating from wounds in a New York hospital. McArthur, who had been Faas's companion in the reckless Cambodian adventure a year earlier, was central casting's version of a foreign correspondent—a fast, fluid writer, veteran of Korean War coverage, hard-drinking bachelor and *bon vivant* who once lived on a houseboat on the Nile and had recorded a string of romantic escapades from Paris to the Philippines. Like most of the old Asia hands in the press corps, McArthur sympathized with the American purpose in Vietnam—though not necessarily with the way it was being conducted—and in inveterate AP style kept a wall between facts and feelings. When Ho Chi Minh died in 1969, it was McArthur who wrote insightfully of Ho as a national hero, "the only Vietnamese who became a world-renowned figure in his own lifetime," whose passing was being mourned in every part of the country, north *and* south.

The bureau was a gathering spot for other journalists, and in the first days I met several press corps icons. McArthur's close friend Keyes Beech was a *Chicago Daily News* warhorse whose book, *Tokyo and Points East,* a collection of Korean War dispatches, had enthralled me years earlier as a young GI in Japan. Robert Shaplen, the gravel-voiced Asia correspondent for *The New Yorker,* served as a kindly, gurulike friend to young reporters, in the way that Larry Burrows was to young photographers. Robert S. Elegant, or "Arrogant," as he was sometimes called, affected a monocle and an imperious charm. His *Los Angeles Times* colleague Jack Foisie, iron-tough and prematurely bald, had earned his journalistic spurs in World War II, covering the Italian campaign for *Stars and Stripes,* getting drunk with Ernie Pyle, and at some point adopting "ya-hoo!" as a permanent substitute for "hello." Don "Skinny" Wise of the London *Daily Mirror* and Ian Brodie of the *Express* were inseparable friends who traveled together on assignments, witnessing the same events and interviewing the same people yet managing to turn out remarkably different versions of the same story for their Fleet Street arch-rival employers.

Listening to these war-wise veterans reinforced my concern about having arrived too late in Vietnam. John Wheeler, an AP reporter who had written brilliantly of the siege of Khe Sanh and spiked his conversation with vague allusions to doomsday—a legacy, I decided, of earlier service in the Strategic Air Command—assured me that I was anything *but* late. "This war's going to go on for a long time, and it's going to get even more dangerous for us—for the press," he said. Years later, I realized how prescient Wheeler had been. No one could know in 1968 that the war would continue for seven more years or that deaths of journalists would more than double during that time. I also began to absorb the lessons of the Saigon bureau, among them that the value of U.S. "diplomatic sources" generally was in inverse proportion to their rank; that except for soldiers in the field, truly useful news sources in Vietnam were almost always anonymous in print and were kept that way even in casual conversation. Carl Robinson, a conscientious objector who had quit his job with the U.S. aid agency in disgust over its policies and joined AP as a photo editor, became my close friend and guide on matters Vietnamese. Married to a Mekong Delta native, Carl spoke the language, cared passionately about the people, and agitated constantly to improve our reporting on Vietnamese politics—the weakest link in almost every foreign news organization's coverage. I also found that, for all its potential for clashing egos, the AP Saigon bureau managed to remain free of the internecine conflicts that plagued other news organizations, particularly the TV networks. Ultimately, many of us would come to realize that the camaraderie of that group was the strongest and most enduring in a lifetime of shared experiences and adventures as journalists.

My first story in Vietnam was a feature on U.S. soldiers who were using geese as an early-warning system at Saigon's Y-bridge, in case the Viet Cong attacked it again as they had during the "Second Tet" flare-up of fighting three months earlier. The inspiration had come from ancient Rome—where the squawking of the sacred geese of the capitol had aroused defenders in time to repulse the invading Gauls in 390 B.C. Lacking a library, we had to scramble to find that information in a place like Saigon, but photo editor Max Nash somehow located a reference book.

Then came an introduction to the helicopter, the mode of transport that would become so familiar over the next five years. Though nowhere as intense as Horst's first helicopter experience had been, the invitation to accompany two military officers observing an Arc Light mission—a B-52 raid—offered a first taste of war, up close and violent beyond imagination. After a twenty-minute flight northeast from Tan Son Nhut, the Army UH-1 Huey went into an orbiting pattern at 2,000 feet. The open doors afforded a view of flat, shimmering land, mountains in the distance, and, closer at hand, a brown river that goose-necked through thick mangrove and jungle. My earphones screened out the wind rush and dulled the engine noise, and a voice inside was clear, laconic: "One minute…." "Thirty seconds…." As an officer nudged me and pointed to a bend in the river, a mile or more away, a garden of huge brown flowers, each with a fiery red center, bloomed suddenly across the placid landscape. Though strapped in, I grabbed the edge of my seat as concentric shock waves visibly roiled outward from the target, rocking the helicopter like a canoe caught in the wake of a speedboat. Three bombers, unseen at 35,000 feet, had unlimbered ninety tons of high explosives on a box-shaped target area a half-mile long and a quarter-mile wide, where military intelligence had earlier deduced the presence of a hidden enemy base camp. As the smoke drifted off, our pilot flew low over the target, now a moonscape offering no hint that anything was alive—or ever had been. I would witness many more Arc Lights, but none, perhaps, to match the cataclysmic grandeur of the first.

The Associated Press bureau was in the Eden Building, a six-story colonial-era warren of offices and apartments, filling half a block in downtown Saigon. Some stores and restaurants opened on the street, while inside was a cool, dark arcade of boutiques offering refuge from the city's oppressive heat and sudden downpours. The location was ideal—close to the Continental Palace, the Caravelle and Rex Hotels, and many of the city's remarkable collection of Corsican-run French restaurants. The MACV briefing room was just across Lam Son Square, beyond the huge, hideous concrete sculpture of two soldiers, known to the foreign community as the "buggery statue."[5]

Two rickety elevators and several stairwells led to the fourth floor—actually the fifth, by the French system—where AP and NBC occupied the two halves of what had once been a German embassy consular office. In the AP's large, tile-floored main room, an L-shaped wooden counter separated the reception area from the cluster of news desks with telephones and typewriters and a radio booth for monitoring broadcasts. Clipboards for visitors, updated with Vietnam copy and stories from the incoming World Wire, were atop the counter. The

---

[5] No one could decide whether the statue of one soldier behind the other depicted a U.S. adviser pushing his ARVN counterpart into battle, the ARVN hiding behind the adviser, or two ARVN soldiers attacking the National Assembly.

bureau chief's office and teletype room opened off one end of the room; at the other end was the photo department and darkroom. Staff photos and maps covered the walls, and battlefield souvenirs and a plaster bust of the late President Diem provided a kitschy décor. A generator ran emergency lights during power failures, which were frequent during the rainstorms that deluged Saigon with clockwork precision every afternoon during the monsoon.

As next-door neighbors, AP and NBC shared a primitive bathroom, a balky, cramped elevator known as the "flying coffin," and a symbiotic relationship in covering the story. If an NBC camera crew happened on a minor skirmish at a bridge in the Mekong Delta, the information might make a paragraph or two in the AP's daily roundup, piquing the interest of NBC editors in New York and giving the Saigon crew a selling point for its film of black pajama–clad bodies lying in the road. In this circuitous way, another vignette of Vietnam, another shard of the war, might rate a couple of minutes on the next night's Huntley-Brinkley report.[6]

McArthur had his ways of putting new staffers to the test. When he sharply criticized one of the first stories I wrote, I told Toby I feared my career as a war correspondent might be over before it began. When I got the courage to tell him this, he all but apologized, saying he "hadn't meant it that way," and sent me on my first assignment "up north," which meant to Danang. The mode of transport to this second city of South Vietnam, the former colonial port of Tourane, was the U.S. Air Force C-130, an efficient, all-purpose cargo aircraft whose four turbo-prop engines shrieked and roared in deafening determination to deliver the goods. Passengers sat on canvas sling seats with no windows and no amenities except what they brought. From Wheeler I learned to bury myself in three hours' worth of the cheap paperbacks he called "C-130 literature."

---

[6] The NBC bureau also boasted an array of colorful characters that sometimes seemed more like a sitcom cast than a news bureau. They ranged from the legendarily brave Vietnamese cameraman, Vo Huynh, to a junior staff assistant who wore a steel helmet with his pajamas in case of nighttime rocket attack. And, of course, there was Dieter Bellendorf, the German cameraman with the pet cobra. Bitten once as he reached into the cage for his wallet, Bellendorf saved his own life by slashing his finger to bleed out the poison—then disposed of the cobra, he explained, by "feeding it to my python."

The Danang Press Center, a MACV facility run by the U.S. Marines, was a motel-like compound, allegedly once a French brothel, on the banks of the Danang River. Major news organizations kept permanent quarters there for staffers covering the war in South Vietnam's five northernmost provinces just below the DMZ, known collectively as Military Region I, or Eye Corps.[7] At least half the battlefield action in Vietnam was taking place in this area at any given time, and AP, like other agencies, kept reporters and photographers there on a full-time basis. The press camp had its own restaurant, bar, and outdoor movies on the patio, which often played to a backdrop of rocket attacks on the nearby Danang Air Base and the Marine helicopter base at Marble Mountain. Over time it acquired its own legends, such as the Marine officer who put a pistol bullet through a slot machine that wouldn't pay off, as well as the visiting radio reporter who never left the compound, but recorded the sounds of bridge guards shooting at suspicious floating objects in the river for the "combat actuality" he sent back to Long Island.

A Marine at the press center's operations shack pointed me to the AP "hootch," which I found to be a dormitorylike setup, with four bunk beds, a bathroom, and a shelf full of helmets, flak jackets, and web gear. Two men were there, both in dusty military fatigues, when I walked in. I introduced myself to the stocky, red-haired fellow in thick glasses, who turned out to be freelance photographer Dana Stone, then working for AP.

"How long you been in country?" he asked, noticing the new black-market fatigues and boots that fairly screamed my FNG status. "About a week," I admitted. Dana simply nodded. No comment, no sign of being judged, no hint of the lofty disdain that the answer had evoked from some other people I had encountered. Dana Stone knew that everybody was once a new guy. Everybody had to learn how to rewind the camera.

Dana introduced me to the skinny Vietnamese who watched us from a lower bunk. Like Stone, he had just come in from the field. "This is Dang Van Phuoc," said Stone. "Call him Phuoc. He's a photographer. The best." Phuoc stood up, grasped my hand in the Vietnamese

---

[7] South Vietnam was divided into four administrative parts, called Military Regions, or Corps, from north to south. The Roman numeral "I" became "Eye Corps" in daily usage. MR II, or "Two Corps," included the Central Highlands; MR III, or "Three Corps," the Saigon region; MR IV, or "Four Corps," the Mekong Delta.

manner, and peppered me with questions in machine gun–rapid broken English: "You come Saigon? When you come? Today? You stay Danang? Maybe tomorrow we go field. Go Rangers." Phuoc saw my hesitation. "No problem," he said, grinning. "We go Rangers. You stay me, be okay. No problem." Stone chuckled. "No problem. You stay him, you get fuckin' killed. Phuoc likes to walk the point."

Phuoc laughed in delight. I was yet to learn what others knew, that this engaging child-man, with his impish humor and the energy of a herd of horses, had great instincts as a photographer and was 100 pounds of raw courage. Perhaps no Vietnamese earned the admiration of American and other foreign colleagues that was bestowed on DVP, as we sometimes called him. By the time we met, he had been wounded four times and, during the second Tet fighting in Saigon a few months earlier, had carried a wounded American, possibly twice his weight, to safety on his back.

Marine Corps officers at the Danang press camp respected Phuoc to the point of reverence, telling stories around the bar about his exploits. A favorite was how he had persuaded two North Vietnamese soldiers and a wounded sixteen-year-old female Viet Cong hiding in a bunker to surrender, saving their lives.

Some of the Marines also knew Phuoc's personal history—that when Phuoc was twelve years old some Viet Cong cadre had come into the Central Coast village where the family lived, pulled Phuoc's father, a local official, out into the street, and killed him in front of the boy and his mother. Phuoc knew who the killers were and nursed the idea of revenge ever after, carrying a pistol along with his camera gear. But the opportunity to exact justice for his father's death never materialized.

On a hot day in February 1969, Phuoc was walking—if not on the point, close to it—with an ARVN Ranger patrol through open fields south of the Danang Air Base when a Viet Cong grenade, thrown from a hidden bunker, exploded in his face, taking out his right eye. Miraculously, Phuoc survived the devastating wound, and after months of surgery and rehabilitation in Tokyo, he returned to Vietnam and to work, sighting his Nikon F with his other eye. While persistent headaches muted the blithe spirit, Phuoc's mischievous cackle at one of his own practical jokes could still be heard. Doctors at the U.S. Army hospital in Bien Hoa administered a follow-up brain scan, pronounced Phuoc normal, and gave him the results—a long piece of graph paper filled with squiggles. George McArthur remembers Phuoc showing it around the AP and NBC bureaus, "challenging anyone to produce equal evidence of normalcy."

A few days after my introduction to Danang and the irrepressible Phuoc, I was in the field, hearing shots fired in anger for the first time in my life. Leonard Santorelli, a Reuters reporter who also had recently arrived in Vietnam, and I were accompanying Marines on a cordon-and-search operation in an area south of Danang that the Americans had dubbed Dodge City. The concept was simple: The Marines encircled a target area of several square miles, then moved systematically toward the center, squeezing the enemy in a shrinking net. It was classic Vietnam, in the sense that local and main-force Viet Cong units operated in the area, mingling with a peasant population whose underground bunkers might conceal a family seeking safety—or a squad of armed guerrillas. The day was unbelievably hot. Machine-gun fire stuttered ahead and off to our right. The Marines, laden with heavy rucksacks and weapons, kept slipping on the narrow paddy dikes and falling, cursing, into the water.

We found what passed for shade near a deserted thatched hut and drank from canteens. The water was lukewarm, all but useless against thirst. "Why are you here?" I asked Santorelli. "Because you are," he replied. There was elemental truth in that droll British wit. Dodge City, Vietnam, was not a place that many people would want to be under any circumstances, and the individual decisions of two novice war correspondents to go there were predicated in large part on the reassuring presence of each other, doing something together that neither of us, at that point, would have wanted to do alone. Companionship was more than someone to talk to; it was a confidence-multiplier, and sharing the story—even with a direct competitor—seemed a reasonable trade-off for having a witness to the risking of one's neck.

AP's Saigon staff drew strength and confidence from knowing it had a strong advocate at the corporate helm in New York. The general manager, Wes Gallagher, had been a highly respected World War II correspondent whose distinctions included having been rescued from under an overturned jeep in North Africa by a young Army lieutenant colonel named William Westmoreland. Within AP, Gallagher's reputation as a martinet stemmed less from any actions he took than the brusque manner and fearsome, beetle-browed glower with which he terrorized everyone at Fifty Rock (a reference to the AP office housed in Rockefeller Plaza). Gallagher hung AP's prestige on its Vietnam coverage, impressed U.S. newspaper editors and publishers with its quality, and rejected demands from no less than President Lyndon Johnson that AP transfer "that Australian"—meaning the pesky, New Zealand–born Peter Arnett—to a different assignment.

During his first visit to Saigon in 1964, Gallagher was appalled by the primitive conditions of the AP bureau on Rue Pasteur, where the bathroom doubled as a photo darkroom; even a visiting VIP from the home office had to wait for Horst to finish developing the latest batch of film before using the facilities. In typically decisive style, and despite the objections of then–bureau chief Malcolm Browne, Gallagher ordered a search for bigger quarters. When Horst's wife, Ursula, reported that the German consular office was moving, the AP grabbed the space and offered half to NBC.

Gallagher's surehanded grip in New York settled or prevented internal disputes that inevitably arose from covering such a highly charged story. But even for him, this was not always possible. On May 6, 1970, Arnett returned to Saigon from the Cambodian front with a story about U.S. armored troops charging into the bomb-shattered rubber plantation town of Snuol, tearing down the Cambodian flag and looting the ruined shops of brandy, soft drinks, and electronic gear. Editors at AP's Foreign Desk in New York, who at that point were seeing everything related to Vietnam in the context of the shooting deaths of four protesting students at Ohio's Kent State University two days earlier, excised the looting references from Arnett's copy and sent a message to Saigon:

> We are in the midst of a highly charged situation in Unistates regarding Southeast Asia and must guard our copy to see that it is down the middle and subdues emotion.... We don't think it's especially news that such things take place in war and in the present context this can be inflammatory.... Let's play it cool.

In their quest to subdue emotion, the Foreign Desk editors forgot that two other New York desks—the World Desk, which filed to AP subscribers overseas, and the Broadcast Desk, serving hundreds of

Stateside radio and TV stations, also received the Saigon incoming wire, and both of these, blithely unaware of any concern, sent out Arnett's original story unchanged, even as U.S. newspapers were receiving the Foreign Desk's sanitized version. The Foreign Desk also somehow failed to consider that Arnett might not have been the only reporter at Snuol—and in fact, he wasn't. Leon Daniel, a top UPI staffer, was there, too, and his story included the colorful antics of the GIs. It was only a matter of time until newspaper editors began calling AP to ask whether UPI's version was true and, if so, why AP didn't have the same information.

Horst, who was in the bureau when New York's let's-play-it-cool admonition arrived, predicted that if the situation was not rectified quickly the proud and volatile Arnett would resign. And indeed, when informed by telephone of what was going on, Peter stormed into the bureau and fired off a private message to Gallagher, saying he had been "personally and professionally insulted" by New York's editing decision and would not compromise his reporting to meet some perceived need in New York that had nothing to do with battlefield reality.

Peter did not threaten to quit as Horst had feared, but the implications of the unprecedented situation were not lost on the staff. No one questioned New York's right to edit copy, but to make changes for political reasons was flat-out unacceptable. Worse was the idea that editors there did not trust the Saigon correspondents to report a story— incredibly, one that had involved personal risk. In a show of solidarity, the staff informed the Saigon bureau chief, David Mason, that if Peter quit we all would go. Even as we committed to it, such a move seemed unimaginable. There was a twinge of fear—perhaps what the *Bounty* mutineers must have felt. We knew that if a staff revolt became real, then it would be far bigger news than what had happened to Arnett. But we knew we were right. Mason, whose perpetually worried expression belied a sure diplomatic instinct, immediately sent his own cable to Gallagher, backing Arnett and declaring, without mentioning the staff ultimatum, that a crisis of confidence existed in the bureau.

The two messages were enough. New York led the Snuol story to reinstate Arnett's original reporting. To nail the whole affair down, Peter leaked the story to Kevin Buckley, *Newsweek*'s Saigon bureau chief. In the magazine's account, Gallagher took full responsibility for what he called an "error in judgment," even though, as far as we knew, the decision had been made on the Foreign Desk. It was, in the end, the kind of response we had expected.

The Five O'clock Follies—a pejorative coined by early Saigon press-corps cynics and so apt that it was adopted by U.S. military officers as well—referred to MACV's daily news briefing for correspondents, held every afternoon in a seedy building on Lam Son Square. For the Saigon-based news media, the Follies were the social and informational highlight of the day, an opportunity to mingle, compare notes, and hear what the U.S. embassy, MACV, and the South Vietnamese military had to say about the course of events. Spokesmen from each agency and service branch were customarily present to deliver oral battle reports, hand out press releases, and answer questions. When the war was in one of its periodic battlefield lulls, the Follies might last only a few minutes; at other times, they could turn into a protracted shouting match over almost anything—from MACV's refusal to divulge information to which reporters felt they were entitled, to hair-splitting arguments over semantics.

Such exchanges, with the press ganging up on the spokesmen, may have reinforced a perception among some officials that the media was conspiring to embarrass or discredit the U.S. military, a view, however ridiculous, that has endured for decades among some former officials. Media-savvy officers knew the opposite was true—that reporters had no group agenda, and if they did, the competitive demands of a story of such transcendent importance would prevent any collusion or attempt at unified action. One former commander of the MACV public affairs office recalls the military's view of the press corps as one of "grudging respect," acknowledging that its members also "were volunteers, courageous and intelligent," though inclined to exaggerate the failures and misdeeds of U.S. and South Vietnamese forces while ignoring those of the North Vietnamese and Viet Cong. "The general feeling was that the press was a necessary evil, and had to be tolerated, but no one got up in the morning saying 'God, I am so happy the press is over here reporting the war,'" the officer said. "Lots of people wished for an Ernie Pyle, but saw no one like that."

Considering that terrorist bombs were not unknown in the city, Follies security was amazingly lax. Except for a couple of "white mice"—South Vietnamese cops were never called anything else—loitering on the sidewalk, there was nothing—no metal detectors, bag searches, or other safeguards—to prevent anyone from slipping into the ground-floor briefing and wreaking destruction with a well-placed grenade. The fact that such an incident never occurred was perhaps a sign that Hanoi's strategists believed, as did disaffected U.S. and South Vietnamese officials, that press coverage of the war was helping the communist cause.

As early as 1964, U.S. officials had recognized that the American effort in Vietnam was suffering serious credibility problems, stemming partly from U.S. officials' inability to explain a war of attrition that, with few decisive events, seemed to be going nowhere. Citing a State Department directive, Assistant Secretary of Defense Arthur Sylvester declared that a less-than-honest information policy would create "suspicion and distrust," eroding public and congressional support for the war effort. "Credibility is the key to the successful discharge of the [U.S.] mission's responsibility to provide a full and accurate understanding of the U.S. involvement in Vietnam," it said. "As a priority matter of great importance, the [U.S.] mission should refrain from any information activity which would tend to mislead the media, or which would otherwise be damaging to mission credibility." It was an interesting policy statement from an official who also became known for having defined a concept known as "managing the news."

Sylvester's cautionary dictum could not have been more right, but it could not protect the Follies from scorn and ridicule. In one report assessing American policy in Vietnam, *Time* magazine quoted an AP story calling the briefings "the longest running tragi-comedy in South East Asia's theater of the absurd." In practice, MACV's spokesmen were capable of dissembling, withholding information or allowing it to be misinterpreted. "Sometimes ... for security reasons they misled reporters—which backfired when the truth emerged elsewhere, often within hours," says the former senior officer. "Of course some reporters made ludicrous charges—that if you don't give them information, you're lying. Actually that's called withholding information and frequently it's a good idea, depending on the situation."

There was, however, a certain amount of media posturing on the Follies. Some of the most vocal critics were among that 70 percent of accredited journalists who stayed close to Saigon and depended heavily on them—particularly the reporter for a New York daily, who not only used the JUSPAO office as his "bureau," but shamelessly accepted spoonfed tidbits of information to support his editors' demand for some sort of "exclusive" every day. If the briefings had been shut down for absurdity or any other reason, this individual and his handful of cronies would have been first to demand they be reinstated.

Yet critics who dismissed the Follies as nothing but a pack of lies were missing the point. These daily briefings were the only forum in which reporters could hold military commanders directly accountable, on the record. And more than once, information from the field led to the discrediting of MACV's sanitized or misleading version of events. Field knowledge helped journalists to read between the lines and ask the right questions that would ferret out information that the military was unwilling to volunteer, but would begrudgingly provide when only the truth would suffice.

No aspect of the conflict was more damaging to official credibility than the so-called body count of enemy killed. Always an estimate rather than a precise tabulation, it became locked into the matrix of U.S. policy as a measuring stick of progress that commanders could neither justify nor get rid of. Allied casualty figures also were questioned, though with less reason. The Pentagon's weekly report was never "accurate" as to the number killed in the previous seven-day period; it might include some who had died of wounds from earlier actions, yet omit some actually killed during the period whose next of kin had not yet been notified. The fact that all U.S. battle losses were eventually accounted for did not deter critics from suggesting that the weekly figures were fudged to minimize adverse political effect.

There were a few in the Saigon press corps who saw the Viet Cong as a genuine people's revolution, romanticized their rice-paddy terrorism as serving a nobler cause, or simply detested all things American, and especially the military, as the embodiment of evil. At the other extreme were those who regarded the war in the simplest Cold War context— North Vietnam, a communist aggressor supported by Moscow and Beijing, inflicting its will on South Vietnam, a struggling would-be democracy whose survival depended on the United States and several token allies. For the most part, members of the Saigon press corps maintained a professional neutrality and strove to be even-handed in reporting the story, letting the chips fall, even if they sympathized privately with the American–South Vietnamese position on which side should emerge the winner. For the AP staff, there was a strong element of pride in adhering to the principle of objective journalism—an elusive, perhaps unattainable goal under any circumstances, but especially so when many critics judged deviation from the official line as disloyalty.

At the same time, a poll of journalists on that transcendent question of the outcome probably would have tilted heavily toward a communist victory as inevitable. The prevailing—if generally unspoken—view was that no result of the bloodletting was likely to favor the Saigon regime; we were witnesses to a Greek tragedy whose *denouement* was preordained. Whether based on reason or gut instinct, this verdict recognized that politically and militarily, South Vietnam was a "rotting barn," as AP colleague Carl Robinson liked to say, that would appear to be stable until the moment it collapsed. That inherent weakness, combined with the obvious limitations of the American commitment and Hanoi's evident determination to win at whatever cost, made it hard to envision either a negotiated settlement or a politically viable "third force" that would guarantee South Vietnam's future existence.

Just as the day-to-day news coverage from Saigon did not dwell in speculation on the war's probable outcome, it paid only cursory heed to the discordant dialogue elsewhere over the United States' role, or whether it should be fought at all. For better or worse, what was being said, sung, shouted, or chanted on college campuses and in American streets was only remotely relevant to the daily nitty-gritty of ground actions, air strikes, "high points," and "lulls," or the pacification program, the never-ending campaign for the "hearts and minds" of the Vietnamese. Reports involving casualties among American troops or Vietnamese civilians added fuel to the raging domestic debate, but the battlefield and the political home front became directly linked only in singular cases, such as Hamburger Hill, My Lai, or Kent State. By the time the story began shifting to the deterioration of the American military—shredded by drugs, racial tensions, and eroding morale and discipline—the withdrawal of U.S. forces was well underway.[8]

---

[8] In a 1995 panel discussion at the Freedom Forum in Arlington, Virginia, Peter Braestrup, who headed *The Washington Post*'s Saigon bureau in 1968–1969, said he could not remem-

Hunched over his typewriter, weighing the ingredients of yet another daily war roundup, George Esper would ask aloud, with a mock sigh, "What does it all mean?" The question actually was important: Facts to be meaningful must cast shadows, and everyone covering the Vietnam War tried to sort out and explain the complexities of a country and a conflict in which, it was said, everything is true—and nothing is true. Apart from the straightforward reporting that was our primary function, we gave New York editors a steady stream of news analyses, offering readers our informed judgment of the significance of recent events or those still unfolding, but such pieces were crafted in more cautious terms than the whither-the-war thumbsuckers being turned out by newspaper colleagues in Saigon and the experts who wrote, with even more assurance, from Washington, D.C.

The war—and even more so the politics—were subjects that invited wishful thinking and bad guesswork, and a great deal of both was generated—especially by the celebrity columnists and political prognosticators who came and went from the war zone. Many of these journalism heavyweights had been distinguished correspondents during World War II, the Korean War, or elsewhere. Most tended to be hawkish toward the U.S. role in Indochina, which helped to ensure that they would receive VIP treatment by U.S. diplomats and military commanders in Saigon.

MACV's red-carpet treatment for visiting Washington experts began with them being assigned, for diplomatic protocol purposes, an "equivalent rank"—usually one-star general, a considerable cut above the designation of major for Saigon's resident correspondents. The visiting scribes usually stayed in Vietnam up to a week, long enough for four-star, big-picture briefings at MACV headquarters; brain-picking dinners with diplomats, top spooks, and selected senior journalists; and meetings with South Vietnamese officials—all enlivened by trips to the field to see how the war was *really* going. They traveled by helicopter with unit commanders or high-ranking escort officers, which ensured priority for busy agendas but not much opportunity to mingle with the grunts, the Vietnamese, and Saigon's own working press.

---

ber "any dinner table conversation in Saigon where someone asked, 'Why are we in Vietnam?' Those questions seemed awfully abstract to us."

AP photographer Rick Merron, a former paratrooper, liked to tell how he once waited for hours at a remote helicopter pad on the Central Coast for a flight out—*any* flight out—and rejoiced when a U.S. Army Huey arrived unexpectedly with syndicated Washington columnist Joseph Alsop and an entourage. *At last*, thought Merron, *I can hitch a ride out of here.*

When the command briefing ended and Alsop returned to his helicopter, Merron stepped forward, introduced himself, and asked if there might be a seat for a stranded photographer. Alsop, the epitome of the old Asia hand, a superhawk on the war, and noted for his haughty view of lesser mortals, waved off the dust-caked AP man with a look of patrician disdain and whirled away, leaving Merron literally in the dust of his rotor blades. Merron eventually made it back to Saigon and told the story with great relish: "I guess he didn't realize that we war correspondents have to stick together," he said.

As the visitors departed for home filled with fresh expertise and insights on the war, we in Saigon remained acutely—if not always humbly—aware that there was much we did not know and that significant and interesting events went unreported because we didn't hear of them from tipsters or recognize clues in official statements.

The arrest of six Green Berets for killing a Vietnamese double agent—a sensational story in 1969—was disclosed by MACV in a press release routinely stuck in media mailboxes at JUSPAO. AP had a scoop of more than an hour on the bombshell revelation because George Esper had stopped by early to collect the bureau mail. MACV's daily war communiqué for March 17, 1968, mentioned several localized ground clashes of the previous twenty-four hours, including one in Quang Ngai Province in southern I Corps. The terse military language did not mention "massacre," of course, or identify the village. Neither were there any news correspondents in the area to stumble on the incident. It would be eighteen months before the name My Lai surfaced—and then it was in the United States, not Vietnam.

8 : Invasion

T he events that brought scores of foreign journalists north from Saigon in the rainy, unseasonably cold month of February 1971 had been a long time in coming. Since 1965, U.S. strategic planners at high levels had discussed the idea of an invasion into Laos to cut the Ho Chi Minh Trail and thereby seal off the flow of men and supplies to Hanoi's forces in the south. But repeatedly, the urgings of top military officials that a strike at the supply line would pay major dividends—stifling the North Vietnamese aggressors, shortening the war, saving lives—had been rejected on political grounds.

Not that there weren't arguments aplenty for it, beginning with the fact that Hanoi already was violating Laotian neutrality by using its territory to make war on a third party. Under international law, this gave South Vietnam and its U.S. ally the right to do the same thing, but the United States was reluctant to go that far. Instead, the Americans resorted to bombing, which disrupted—but could not stop—movements along the Trail.[1]

---

[1] In recent years, officials in Vietnam have blatantly revised history concerning the Ho Chi Minh Trail. In 2000, the offical Vietnam News Agency reported work had begun on a proj-

The region along the Vietnam-Laos border south of Route 9, known on military maps as the communist Base Area 611, had seen some of the war's nastiest fighting, as U.S. and ARVN forces tried to destroy the battle-seasoned North Vietnamese 325th Division that operated there, moving to and from South Vietnam on a network of cross-border feeder trails. Attacks by the allies cut into this activity, but the *bo doi* seemed to prosper in spite of it. Observers still reported the lights and sounds of truck convoys grinding along hidden routes from Laos into the A Shau, a hauntingly beautiful valley that stretched some eighteen miles, north to south, on the Vietnam side of the border, ringed on all sides by thickly forested peaks rising as high as 3,000 feet.

Beginning in January 1969, U.S. forces launched a series of new operations into the border area and the enemy's stronghold in the mystical A Shau. In the first of these, code-named DEWEY CANYON, the 9th Marine Regiment set up a chain of firebases on ridgelines paralleling the border and waged a two-month campaign, resulting in more than 1,000 NVA dead and huge hauls of captured weapons and supplies.

At Firebase Cunningham, a forested razorback ridge anchoring the southern end of the chain, the commander of the 9th Marines, Colonel Robert Barrow, welcomed a small group of reporters, briefed us on the situation, and parried our questions as to whether it was true—as rumored in Saigon—that some of his Marines had actually crossed the border in violation of the Laos neutrality agreement.

Barrow, a friendly, straight-talking officer who within a decade would rise to become commandant of the Marine Corps, could have told us—truthfully—that MACV had secretly sanctioned two cross-border forays by the Marines to ambush the North Vietnamese truck convoys they'd spotted from a distance. But, of course, he did not mention that fact. As with the open-secret U.S. reconnaissance operations in Laos, deniability was the name of the game.

In the relentless campaign by the U.S. and South Vietnamese forces to disrupt and destroy the enemy's activities in the A Shau, the

---

ected 770-mile "Ho Chi Minh Highway," which would "follow the roads and trails" of the "legendary" wartime supply route. VNA described the Trail as "Five axial roads" running along the "eastern and western flanks" of the Truong Son, with "21 lateral roads leading to the major battle fronts." In 2002, Hanoi disclosed further plans for "Ho Chi Minh Trail tourist sites" near Khe Sanh and other locations in Quang Tri province. The omission of any reference to Laos or Cambodia in these announcements clearly creates a fictional impression of a Ho Chi Minh Trail contained entirely—and always—within Vietnam itself.

most memorable effort—not necessarily for the right reasons—came in May 1969, just four months after OPERATION DEWEY CANYON.

Called OPERATION APACHE SNOW, it was a multipronged attack against a fortified mountain overlooking the northern end of the valley. The mountain was known to the Vietnamese as Dong Ap Bia and on military maps as Hill 937. It would be remembered in history as Hamburger Hill.

The operation had been cobbled together somewhat hastily after a 101st Airborne pilot, flying alone in a small OH-6 reconnaissance helicopter, inadvertently discovered signs of enemy activity. The pilot, Bruce Osborne, recalls that he was "suffering from a hangover, and vomiting out the door of the helicopter at treetop level, when I spotted a vast network of trails and steps, just barely visible through the triple canopy jungle." Further field intelligence confirmed Osborne's finding, and U.S. commanders moved quickly to exploit the situation, which perhaps explains why the operation seemed to materialize with none of the usual alerts or advance word from MACV officers to the main news agencies in Saigon. As it happened, only two journalists—*Time* magazine correspondent Wallace Terry and I—were in the immediate area when APACHE SNOW was launched on May 10 by troops of the 101st Airborne Division's 3rd Brigade, and we joined them. The plan called for three battalions of the "Screaming Eagles," each with some 600 troopers, augmented by two ARVN battalions, to attack by heliborne assault onto the mountain's growth-entangled lower slopes.

That morning we took a low-level helicopter detour down the A Shau, with Colonel Joseph Conmy, commander of the 3rd Brigade, piloting his own command-and-control chopper, seeming to dare the enemy forces to reveal themselves in the parklike greenery of the wide, flat valley.

It was the largest CA, or combat assault, that either of us had ever seen—waves of Huey slicks, used to carry troops, lifting off from a forward PZ, or pickup zone, and heading into the dense jungle hills in spectacular line formation, bound for landing zones less than a mile, in some cases a few hundred yards, from the Laotian border. The LZs had been cleared with 15,000-pound Daisy Cutter bombs that exploded above ground, wiping away trees and undergrowth—and giving the North Vietnamese clues to where to deploy in ambush.

Escorting helicopter gunships marked the way with aerial rockets to suppress enemy gunners, and Air Force F-4 Phantoms skip-bombed canisters of napalm, igniting the dark forests with orange liquid fire. En route, we were told to expect the LZ to be hot, but it wasn't—at least not at the moment we scrambled out of the Huey's cargo bay, behind troopers of the 3rd Battalion, 187th Infantry, onto a steep hillside. The Daisy Cutters had cleared more than two dozen LZs, and the NVA apparently could not cover them all.

My monthly turn in Eye Corps, the northernmost corps in Military Region I, was ending at the time, and the next day I was back in Danang to hand over the coverage to my replacement, Jay Sharbutt. Jay and I had been close friends back in the AP Washington bureau, and after I went to Saigon in 1968, he bombarded me with letters asking my help in getting him to the war zone as well. I'm sure that my personal lobbying on his behalf with the Saigon bureau chief, George McArthur, helped to bring this about.

Only recently arrived, Sharbutt talked enthusiastically about the war as an adventure, but he expressed this in a manner I found uncomfortably blasé for someone lacking any experience in covering combat. I also was concerned that he hadn't gotten off to a very good start with McArthur, and on this first trip into the field he would have to redeem himself. When he showed up at the Danang Press Center, I finished filing a long story on the start of APACHE SNOW. I briefed Jay on the operation, suggesting that he fly up the next day to see it for himself. There was nothing of greater importance going on in Eye Corps at the time.

Back in Saigon a day later, I was working the night desk in the bureau when Sharbutt called from Phu Bai, the forwardmost base for the operation that had functional telephone connections. Jay had just returned from the battle area, and over the static-marred line he dictated a story quoting U.S. officers as saying that 101st Airborne troopers were making a full-scale ground assault up the slopes of Hill 937.

After writing the story from Jay's dictation, editing it, and sending it off to New York, I phoned McArthur at his apartment to tell him what Sharbutt was reporting. Mac listened and rang off. Minutes later, he showed up in the bureau and asked, "Where's Sharbutt now?" "He's at Phu Bai," I said. "Call him back and tell him to get his ass back out there, and get hold of the commanding officer of that operation, and ask one question: What the hell is he doing, attacking a fucking mountain at this stage of the war? Tell him to keep asking that question until he gets an answer."

With U.S. troops about to begin withdrawing from the war, McArthur's profane query went straight to the heart of the Vietnam issue at that time. It was a given that even if the paratroopers captured the mountain they would not remain there long; no matter how many enemy were killed, the U.S. casualties would be seen by many Americans as a mindless waste. That was the perspective from the outside, from even so close a vantage point as Saigon.

A point that military officials and spokesmen labored regularly to get across was that U.S. troops in Vietnam were never fighting for territory as such but to destroy the adversary himself. Indeed, this had been the philosophy espoused by General William Westmoreland as commander of U.S. forces, but Westmoreland had been replaced almost a year earlier by General Creighton Abrams, who knew that part of his job would be to shepherd a respectable U.S. withdrawal from Vietnam and believed in using overwhelming firepower to limit friendly casualties as well as to kill the enemy. A frontal attack on Hill 937 seemed to run counter to that thinking.

I called Sharbutt back and relayed the instructions. The next day, he managed to wangle an interview with Major General Melvin Zais, the commander of the 101st Airborne Division, and dutifully posed McArthur's question: What was the reason for risking lives in a direct ground assault when the same results might be achieved at far less cost with Arc Light B-52 raids?

Zais, a spit-and-polish general who was known for maintaining a white-tablecloth officers' mess even in forward combat areas, replied with a variation on the classic Mount Everest response: We are attacking the mountain because it is there or, more precisely, because the enemy is there.

In a condescending manner that left little doubt as to what he thought about callow civilian reporters, Zais explained to Sharbutt that his job was to find and strike the North Vietnamese wherever they were, and in this case the enemy was on Hill 937. As for the B-52s, Zais said their results could not be guaranteed. These enemy troops were regulars, the battle-tested 29th NVA regiment, who knew how deep to dig the bunkers for protection from the bombers.

Sharbutt's vivid accounts of the paratroopers battling up the hill and being driven back, and the general's explanations of why this was happening, landed on the front pages of the *New York Times* and many other papers. It also touched a third rail on Capitol Hill. Predictably, Senator Edward Kennedy, among others, denounced the frontal assault on Hill 937—or, as it was becoming known, Hamburger Hill—as a "senseless and irresponsible" squandering of GI lives for a piece of jungle real estate that once taken would again be relinquished to the enemy. However logical and reasonable it might seem to military strategists, that idea's time had expired in the arena of public opinion.

After-action reports showed 56 U.S. paratroopers were killed and about 400 wounded in the ten-day battle, some of them the result of misdirected friendly-fire attacks by U.S. tactical bombers and the 101st Airborne's own helicopter gunships. More than 600 North Vietnamese, roughly the equivalent of two battalions, were counted dead on the moonscape of Hamburger Hill.

How the battle came to be known by that name was a story in itself. After days of international news coverage dominated by Sharbutt's reports, UPI reporter David Lamb arrived on the scene, looking for an angle that would get him into the fight for page one. On his second day, Lamb asked a young GI what he and his buddies were calling the battle. "I reminded him that other wars had names for battles, and I think I even tossed out the reminder, 'like Pork Chop Hill in Korea.' I remember that he said, 'I don't know what anyone else calls it, but to me it's like hamburger, with all this chopped-up meat.'"

Back at Phu Bai, Lamb phoned the UPI bureau in Saigon with a night lead describing "the battle for what the GIs call Hamburger Hill...." Admittedly, "I took some liberties and generalized," Lamb says today. "I really wasn't trying to recoup on Jay's jump start. I was just trying to juice the story up a little, as I did with most stories."

Not only did this "juice" help to lubricate Ted Kennedy's Senate oratory; it flowed into the pages of the military newspaper, *Pacific Stars and Stripes*, where GIs read about Hamburger Hill and began using the term themselves. The name invented by Dave Lamb became a self-fulfilling reality, and one report said it was even written on a sign tacked to a tree on the hillside.

It was one of the few occasions when the AP Saigon bureau was seriously bombarded by messages—we called them "rockets"—on a UPI story. The message from the AP Foreign Desk in New York said something like, "UPI says GIs calling Hill 937 Hamburger Hill. We hearing similar? How pls. NY Forn." We were in fact "hearing similar"—but only from other journalists who had seen or been told about UPI's story and wanted to know if we could confirm it. We were telling them we could not.

In his own calls from Phu Bai, Sharbutt told us he had known about Lamb's phoned report to his Saigon bureau and was convinced that Lamb had invented the name. Jay said he had not heard any GIs referring to "Hamburger Hill." ("Not surprisingly," says Lamb, "because he hadn't talked to the one grunt that I had.") Ed White, running the AP news desk in Saigon, fired off an indignant reply to New York, advising the editors that we had reason to believe a rival reporter had dreamed up the name as a gimmick, and we intended to continue calling it Hill 937 or Dong Ap Bia.

The editors replied by pointing out that the Associated Press, whatever the origin of the name, was by then apparently the only news organization in the world *not* using it. And because history was certain to remember Hamburger Hill, we had no choice but to join the media crowd. Hill 937 and Dong Ap Bia just didn't cut the mustard, so to speak. Hamburger Hill it was, and would always be. Dave Lamb recalls getting a message from his foreign editor, too: "It was a rather snotty telex saying AP's coverage of the battle had been superior, but I had managed to 'recoup' with a fine wrap-up piece. It made no mention of my having named the battle."

In an eerie postscript thirty-one years later, a North Vietnamese survivor of the battle would reveal that his comrades had seen the struggle for the mountain very much as the Americans had. They called it *thit bam*—the "meat chopper."[2]

Even if the battle for the mountain made sense within the Nixon White House plan for withdrawal from Vietnam, it did little to reduce the southward flow of North Vietnamese supplies and manpower. Base Area 611 was still intact; the 325th NVA Division would soon be

---

[2] As told to Denis Gray during a visit to Hamburger Hill in April 2000.

replenished and rearmed. The only way to solve the problem, if at all, would be by sending troops into Laos in massive numbers to cut the Ho Chi Minh Trail.

That idea had gained new life after the joint U.S.–South Vietnamese "incursion" into eastern Cambodia in 1970. Although that operation failed to find COSVN, the major communist headquarters, it had effectively shut down Hanoi's second supply route through the Cambodian port of Kompong Som, better known as Sihanoukville, curtailing enemy attacks around Saigon for an indefinite period.

Hanoi responded to the loss of their so-called Sihanouk Trail by expanding the Ho Chi Minh Trail, and the United States countered with an increase in bombing. By early 1971, the Trail in southern Laos was the main priority of U.S. air operations. And still the flow of men and materiel went on.

For a ground invasion of Laos, the timing was critical. Saigon needed all the time it could get for President Nixon's Vietnamization program to take hold. General Abrams, a longtime advocate of a Laos invasion, made the case: An attack in the first months of 1971, near the end of the dry season in southern Laos, could disrupt Trail traffic until the rainy season set in, closing it down for several months and probably delaying any major new offensive by Hanoi until the following year.

To complicate matters, the Cooper-Church Amendment, passed by Congress in reaction to Nixon's foray into Cambodia, barred any more cross-border adventures by U.S. ground forces. This meant that for the first time Saigon's troops would be going it alone on the ground, with U.S. units providing only air and artillery support from positions inside South Vietnam.

Even U.S. advisers, who had been at the side of Vietnamese field commanders since the beginning of the war, were barred, and there was a question as to whether a U.S. helicopter touching ground in Laos for any reason whatsoever would violate Cooper-Church. But legalities aside, the move had to be made while there were enough Americans left in Vietnam to fill those support roles.

Once Nixon's strategists reached a consensus on the feasibility of a U.S.-supported strike by the South Vietnamese, preliminary planning began in November of 1970. By mid-January, there was a perceptible increase in military activity along the northern coast of South Vietnam, just below the DMZ. Truck convoys moved north on Route 1 from Danang, through Hue, to Quang Tri and Dong Ha, and materiel was amassed at supply dumps. U.S. helicopter units in other areas of the country, including some that were getting ready to stand down, prior to departing the war zone, were ordered to put their plans on hold. They would be needed one more time, up north.

The mission itself remained for the moment cloaked in mystery, but not for long, as information leaks in Washington indicated that the next logical step in Vietnam—a massive cross-border attack into Laos—might be just weeks away.

Annoying as the security breaches may have been to the White House and military planners in Saigon, they were clues that Hanoi's generals hardly needed. The coming storm was no surprise to them. Northern spies were everywhere in the south, from the hootch maids cleaning up after GIs, to the ranks of the ARVN, to the Saigon press corps—and, as would later be reported, even inside the Danang headquarters of Eye Corps where OPERATION LAM SON 719 was being planned.

Thus as far back as October 10, 1970—a month before planning for LAM SON 719 began and four months before it was launched—the People's Army of Vietnam had created a special *binh doan* (military group) in anticipation of a possible two-pronged offensive into Laos by the Americans and South Vietnamese westward along the Route 9 corridor and northward across the 17th parallel.

By some interpretations, it was the first time that Hanoi had adopted the concept of the task force widely used by the Americans— a number of military components pulled together for a specific mission. Task Force B70, as it was known, included two experienced infantry divisions, the 304th and the 308th, and one regiment of a third, the 320th, four armored battalions, a mechanized artillery regiment, an air defense regiment, and numerous independent supporting units.

Binh Doan 70's mission in the first three months was to prepare the battlefield, and by early February 1971, as the allied buildup moved inexorably forward, the task force was put under the command of yet another headquarters, Mat Tran (Front) 702, also known as Headquarters Highway 9 Front. Once fighting began, this would serve as the combat nucleus for Group 559, the permanent military unit that managed, maintained, and defended the Ho Chi Minh Trail.

Overall, Hanoi now had some 60,000 troops in the immediate area. Lacking a road map to the enemy's complicated organizational structure, allied intelligence might have thought there were many more than that.

Within Front 702, the initial responsibility for thwarting an invasion rested with the antiaircraft artillery regiments, whose reinforcements bolstered an already formidable air defense array. Ultimately, by allied estimates, some 800 antiaircraft weapons were hidden in the area where Route 9 and the Trail intersected, aimed toward the skies that soon would be filled with U.S. and South Vietnamese helicopters.

Units of the 241st Air and 591st Air Defense Regiments would guard the critical terrain northeast of Tchepone, where Hanoi already knew the South Vietnamese planned to establish a series of mountain-top bases.

Although the press in Saigon could only speculate on intricate details of planning and counterplanning, the visible activity of the buildup toward invasion prompted a mass exodus of reporters and photographers from the capital to northern Eye Corps. There, they found rude barracks available at Camp Red Devil, the U.S. base just north of Quang Tri. Public affairs officers of the 1st Battalion, 5th Mechanized Infantry that manned Red Devil scrambled to find more space to accommodate the media locust swarm.

If short on luxuries, Camp Red Devil was at least well located. At a T-intersection a few miles to the north, Route 1 connected with Route 9, the road west to the Laos border. It was easy for journalists to hitch rides on truck convoys to Khe Sanh, the forward staging base for LAM SON 719. From the helicopter pad at Quang Tri, flights came and went regularly; journalists only had to wait for one going their way.

So the waiting began, and even in the winter's mud and dreariness there were enlivening moments. For days, the most talked-of event, other than the war itself, was the near destruction of the camp's Army-style latrine shed. A chain-smoking female reporter for a major U.S. newspaper had carelessly dropped a lighted cigarette into the hole, failing to realize that the space below was rife with fumes from the drums of kerosene used to neutralize the waste.

The resulting *whuump* nearly rocked the wooden structure off its foundation as the frightened occupant bolted clear, frantically clutch-

SPRING 1968

THE **AP** WORLD

ABOVE: AP's Saigon staff in June, 1970. "Buggery statue," Eden Building at left, National Assembly (former opera house) right background. The AP Staff usually numbered thirty to thirty-five — equally split among news, photos and technical roles. Kneeling, from left to right: Dang Van Huan, Huynh Cong "Nick" Ut, Henri Huet, Lu Xay, Toby Pyle. Standing from left to right: Jay Sharbutt, Le Ngoc Cung, Willis Johnson, Andree-Paule Mason, Tran Trung Tho, Horst Faas, Mark Godfrey, bureau chief David Mason, Huynh Minh Trinh, Richard Pyle, Carl Robinson, Rick Merron, Tran Xuan Bao, Dang Van Phuoc, Phil McMullen, Peter Arnett, Nancy Putzel, Tran Mong Tu, Edwin Q White, Hugh Van Es. Telephone represented George Esper, on leave. Also absent: Ghislain Bellorget, Holger Jensen, Max Nash, Michael Putzel, Bob Tuckman, Neal Ulevich, Terry Wolkerstorfer, Luong Ba Tinh, Tran Ngoc Bo, Truong Van Tam, Le Kim Phung, Tran Quan Hung.

LEFT: None were braver than AP photographer Dang Van Phuoc, wounded five times.

LEFT: Busy in AP bureau are Faas (left), John Wheeler, George Esper, Peter Arnett (behind Esper).

ABOVE LEFT: Huet and Pyle in Cambodia, 1970. ABOVE RIGHT: At 1969 sendoff for Tokyo-bound Huet; from left: Pyle, Van Es, 1st Cav PIO J.D. Coleman, Merron, Henri. BELOW: Rare photo of "Five O'Clock Follies" includes journalist and VC spy Pham Xuan An (2nd from left), Neil Sheehan, Keyes Beech (behind Sheehan), Seymour Topping, Malcolm Browne, Peter Kalischer (head down).

ABOVE: ARVN troops staged near border for helicopter lift into Laos.
BELOW: U.S. Marine Corps helicopters supported invasion.

ABOVE: ARVN Hoc Bao jungle fighters shown at airstrip near Khe Sanh, February 10, 1971, in this shot from Kent Potter's last roll of film. U.S. advisers were not authorized to enter Laos.
BELOW: NVA troops used all types of weapons against aircraft, as in this clearly staged photo.

FACING PAGE: In photos from Henri Huet's last roll of film, ARVN armored troops preparing to move into Laos (top) as U.S. 8-inch artillery (middle) backed the attack. Women soldiers of the NVA 33rd Field Battalion on the Ho Chi Minh Trail (bottom).

ABOVE, CLOCKWISE FROM TOP LEFT: Lt. Gen. Hoang Xuan Lam, Laos invasion commander; Maj. Jim Newman, aka "Condor Six"; USMC photographer Sergio Ortiz; AP reporter Michael Putzel; Shimamoto friend Akihiko Okamura.
BELOW: Marine Corps AH-1 Cobra gunship makes low pass at Laos border.

ABOVE: ARVN troops watch from hilltop command post near Lao Bao as enemy artillery shell explodes near troop staging point, Laos in background. LEFT: Marine Corps Cobra gunships are unscathed as North Vietnamese guns hit wide of the mark.

LEFT: ARVN wounded returning from Laotian front, in photo by Sergio Ortiz on February 10, just before photographers flew into Laos.
BELOW: Journalists at Khe Sanh included (from left) ABC cameraman Tony Hirashiki and correspondent Steve Bell; reporters Jack Foisie, Los Angeles Times (back to camera); Bob Sullivan, UPI; Michael Putzel, AP.

ing her pants while screaming, "The shitter's on fire! The shitter's on fire!" Among the few eyewitnesses was Jim Bennett, an American network TV reporter, who had volunteered to guard the latrine door against unwitting intruders and described the incident afterward as "the most unbelievable fucking thing I've ever seen."

Phase One of the Laos operation was a combined ground-air assault, beginning on January 29, to repossess the abandoned Marine base at Khe Sanh, seven miles from the border, as a staging and refueling center for helicopters, and to secure and repair Route 9—it hardly merited the term highway—all the way to the crossing point at Lao Bao.

Armored units of the 1st Battalion, 5th Mech charged west on Route 9 from Red Devil while helicopter-borne troops air-assaulted into the once notorious base where Marines had withstood a 77-day artillery siege by North Vietnamese forces in early 1968. To underscore its purpose of disrupting enemy activity in Laos, the new deployment was code-named DEWEY CANYON II, after the Marine-ARVN operation along the border two years earlier. By the time Khe Sanh was reestablished with a hastily laid temporary airstrip, supply dump, and aircraft refueling point, the only question was the precise date of the invasion itself.

In Saigon, MACV command spokesmen called news bureau chiefs and senior independent journalists to a special "deep background" briefing. There, they confirmed the obvious—that an attack into Laos by South Vietnamese forces, with U.S. support, was about to happen— and spelled out details: Some 20,000 South Vietnamese troops, the largest number ever committed to a Saigon military operation, were to strike westward, leap-frogging in helicopter-borne assaults to establish forward bases to the north and south of Route 9, then regroup for the third and last phase—capture of the Laotian district town of Tchepone, twenty-five miles west of the border.

Tchepone, which lay just on the western side of the Annamite Range, was little more than a dot on the map, but it had an importance in LAM SON 719 that was both strategic and symbolic. Most of the roads and paths that formed the Ho Chi Minh Trail crossed Route 9 east of the town. By capturing Tchepone, the invaders could claim to have sliced across the entire Trail network, severing it.

To achieve this, Saigon's planners had assembled an attack force that would include the most elite units of the South Vietnamese military: the 1st ARVN Division, its top infantry unit; plus two Ranger battalions, the 1st Armored Brigade and the Airborne Division, with the Marine Division in reserve. It would, however, be the first time that these crack outfits had taken on a major task without U.S. forces, or even U.S. advisers, beside them. No one knew how well they might perform under such circumstances.

For years, the Saigon press corps had cooperated with MACV and the South Vietnamese military in withholding disclosure of pending field operations. Most reporters recognized that even in Vietnam's rumor-saturated atmosphere operational security was a legitimate concern. No one wanted to be accused of endangering lives for a cheap headline.

Yet this honor system had some teeth. New applicants for U.S. and South Vietnamese press credentials were required to sign an agreement not to report troop movements or upcoming operations until official embargoes were lifted by commanders. Violators risked losing their press credentials, even expulsion from the country, if an offense was egregious enough. In practice, infractions of the rules were remarkably rare and usually resulted in a month's suspension of correspondent privileges—access to military facilities and transport as well as attendance at the Five O'clock Follies.[3]

The fact that the plans for Lam Son 719 had been seriously compromised by leaks elsewhere did not deter U.S. officials from imposing the customary press embargo in Saigon. Indeed, they informed the bureau chiefs that they could not even report that there *was* an embargo. Moreover, they announced that journalists covering the story in the field would not be allowed aboard U.S. military aircraft flying into Laos.

At the command briefing, we were stunned and outraged by these unprecedented departures from practice. Press embargoes were routinely enforced on military operations until actual armed contact occurred, but the embargo-on-the-embargo, as it quickly became known, meant that members of the Saigon press corps not only were subject to

---

[3] During the war, eight correspondents were temporarily disaccredited for violating the rule. Most cases were misunderstandings, with no evidence of actual damage to security. Very few knew that senior U.S. officials debated censorship proposals five times after 1965, rejecting all as impractical.

a news blackout; they could not report that the blackout itself existed. Yet our colleagues outside Vietnam were under no such impediment in reporting the story.

Just how the illogic of this arrangement eluded the policy planners was anyone's guess. Henry Kissinger would later write that the news embargo was imposed to "both protect security and prevent inaccurate and misleading reports" but "proved to be a naïve mistake," simply because the restrictions on Saigon-based journalists did not prevent them from feeding information to their colleagues in Washington and elsewhere who were free to report it under non-Vietnam datelines.

Which, of course, they did, exploiting leaks at the State and Defense Departments that left no doubt that a South Vietnamese invasion of Laos, with U.S. support, was imminent. It demonstrated an axiom familiar to U.S. war correspondents: However great the concern for security on the battlefield, it diminished with proximity to the Pentagon.

The naïveté was perhaps greater than even Kissinger realized. Rather than seeking to prevent "inaccurate and misleading reports," U.S. strategists might better have welcomed them as another way to confuse the enemy. In lamenting that the Washington press corps and U.S. television networks "treated the embargo as a major story in itself," Kissinger failed to recognize that the double whammy on reporting from Saigon was both unprecedented and unworkable—and that made it very important news.[4]

The architects of the press blackout soon recognized the futility of a situation in which news media outside Vietnam, and even non-U.S. reporters in Saigon whose work was not routinely monitored by U.S. officials, were reporting ostensibly secret information, whereas those who played by MACV's journalistic rules of engagement could not do so. On February 4, the Americans and South Vietnamese cancelled both the embargo and the embargo-on-the-embargo, unleashing a flood of pent-up stories under Vietnam datelines. "Security" vanished, with the invasion itself still four days away.

The ban on journalists flying into Laos became an even more contentious issue. In Vietnam, the press had always relied on military transport as essential to reporting from the field. MACV rules guaranteed

---

[4] Henry Kissinger, *The White House Years* (Boston: Little, Brown, 1979).

this access right to accredited correspondents, theoretically on a space-available basis, and flying on helicopters, cargo planes, and courier aircraft was routine practice for Saigon-based members of the media.

Now, suddenly, MACV officials were citing a regulation that the press had never before encountered or even heard of—nor, for that matter, had the officials themselves. Plucked from some obscure policy document, this rule stipulated that military aircraft could not carry civilians across an international border if regular commercial air service was available.

The bureau chiefs argued, with vehemence, that no such restriction had been imposed during the Cambodian incursion the previous year, although conceding that most of that border-crossing was done by armored units on the ground and that there had been very little air transport to be barred from. More to the point, we contended that it had been many years since anything resembling commercial air service existed in the Vietnam-Laos border region—if, indeed, it ever had. In the immediate area of the planned invasion, the only aircraft flying were U.S. bombers blasting the Ho Chi Minh Trail and a few helicopters on clandestine reconnaissance missions that the military itself did not acknowledge.

There had to be another reason for the ban on journalists flying into Laos. Within the Saigon news corps, the consensus was that the Nixon administration hoped it would reduce the visibility of U.S. air support in what was being officially ballyhooed as an all-Vietnamese operation and minimize negative press coverage if that operation happened to go badly.

The South Vietnamese, who were never entirely comfortable with the foreign press but generally followed the U.S. lead in dealing with the Fourth Estate, were quite content to do so this time. At the Five O'-clock Follies, the ARVN briefers announced that their helicopters and armored vehicles in LAM SON 719, unfortunately, would not have enough room for journalists, either.[5]

---

[5] Even without the embargoes, an information brownout remained in effect through most of the seven-week operation; U.S. officials refused to divulge details on U.S. helicopter operations or losses in Laos. Except for what journalists in Eye Corps were able to learn from field commanders and pilots themselves, many details on the fighting and even the heroics of U.S. air crews were never reported until months or even years later.

Thus, as the invasion of Laos began on Monday morning, February 8, 1971, the news media were literally standing on the sidelines. Reporters, photographers, and camera crews gathered at the Lao Bao border crossing could only watch as South Vietnamese tanks, armored personnel carriers, and trucks laden with troops rumbled across while, from nearby assembly areas, scores of U.S. helicopters lifted off in strung-out combat assault formation, bound for predesignated jungle objectives in Saigon's most daring and ambitious offensive of the war—a make-or-break strike at the enemy's solar plexus.

9 : Kent Potter

Born into a Quaker family in Philadelphia, Kent Biddle Potter went to work for United Press International as a photo stringer at age sixteen and worked his way up to staff photographer in little more than a year. In those early days, he tooled around Philadelphia on a big Triumph motorcycle, which he later traded for a blue-green Volkswagen Beetle with a PRESS sign in the windshield.

In some ways, Kent was a hyped-up version of the all-American boy. A lanky six-feet-two, with dark hair and pale blue eyes that gave him the smoky good looks of a young Tyrone Power, he liked cars and speed and had an easy way with girls.

At the exclusive Germantown Friends School (GFS), he was a better than average student, played end on the football team, ran hurdles and sprints on the track team, sang in the chorus of Gilbert and Sullivan's *Trial by Jury*, and liked to work on the backstage crew, handling lighting and sound for school productions. By his junior year in 1964, he and two classmates, Thomas Martin and Robert Goddard, were getting into photography, taking pictures for the school yearbook, *The Meeting*.

Run by the Society of Friends, GFS was one of Philadelphia's lead-ing prep schools, with rigorous academic standards that attracted high achievers from throughout the area. Fewer than half of the students were actually Quakers, and though the curriculum included Quaker history and philosophy, there was no attempt at proselytizing on reli-gion. The only Quaker fixture was the weekly Meeting, where students and faculty members assembled to speak on any topic as the spirit moved them.

The Potters lived in Awbury, a woodsy, parklike area in northwest-ern Philadelphia. Originally the estate of Henry Cope, a nineteenth-century Quaker shipping tycoon, it had evolved into a private enclave of graceful stone houses, whose occupants included several faculty members of GFS. The Potter home was a former gatehouse converted to a family residence. Kent told friends it had been fun to prepare meals in the great stone fireplace while the kitchen was being renovated.

Kent was part of the neighborhood group, building forts and play-ing baseball and football, but by age thirteen he was showing signs of breaking away. When his father, Lloyd, put up a basketball hoop on the Potter garage, his own son was not interested. "We played there for many hours and many days, but I have no memory of Kent's being there," says David Thanhauser, a boyhood pal. "At some point, Kent ceased to be part of our gang, but I remember no particular reason why."

But many people in sun-dappled Awbury and the tightly knit Ger-mantown Quaker community knew there was a darker side to Kent Potter and his family.

In the spring of 1961, Kent was in the eighth grade and nearing his fourteenth birthday when his mother, Blanche Lerner Potter, took her own life with an overdose of sleeping pills. Kent's grief over the death of his mother, whom he adored, was compounded by the fact that she had sent him to the pharmacy to pick up the prescription. Few things could have been more devastating, say friends who knew the story. Kent certainly had not known his mother's intentions but was wracked by guilt over having played an unwitting role in her death. To make matters worse, according to former schoolmates, his father un-fairly blamed Kent for what had happened.

Lloyd Potter was tall and thin like his son, with a leathery com-plexion, a shock of gray hair, and a carpenter's work-worn hands.

Eleven years older than Kent's mother—forty-four when Kent was born in 1947—he was a skilled carpenter who taught industrial arts in a public high school and spent his summers as a counselor and crafts instructor at a youth camp in Maine.

Kent's friends found him a taciturn, uncommunicative man. Bill Thode, a classmate at GFS, remembers the elder Potter as "old, very crusty, a quiet, stern type of guy," always sitting in a chair when Thode visited the home. Among some in the community, the father's eccentric behavior, including his treatment of Kent, led to speculation about his emotional stability.

The tragedy ripped the family apart. While Kent remained close to his sister Sherry, who was five years older and became a sort of surrogate mother, he and his father would remain forever at odds. A community veil of silence descended over the incident. The Potters, says one former acquaintance, were simply "off-limits" for discussion.

Perhaps seeking ways to channel their sorrow, fears, and hate, father and son went in radically different directions. Lloyd Potter became a pacifist zealot, away from home for long periods, taking part in peace marches and antiwar demonstrations. In the recollections of several people, Kent Potter the boy disappeared with his mother's death. He began a swift and premature transition to adulthood, driven by work, ambition, and a determination to get on with life in the real world. Except for a few close pals and girlfriends, he never looked back.

"He was pretty much a loner, a renegade, always doing his own thing," says classmate Robert Metz. Bill Thode remembers that Kent was the only one among the sixty-seven members of the Class of 1965 who did not intend to go on to college. Or, as Thode put it, "the only guy with the gonads" to chase a different dream.

"If he had a single gift, it was the ability to learn from everyone he met and everything he did—he was 'street-smart,'" says Tom Martin. "Unfortunately that kind of intelligence was respected at GFS, but not rewarded. He took what he needed from his classes and ignored the rest. While the rest of us sweated out SAT scores and college admissions, Kent lived in a world apart in which he was fast becoming master."

Eventually, Kent Potter's ambitions were to coalesce in a most unexpected way. He would join the military and embrace a kind of warrior ethic, taking giant steps to the farthest side of his father's moon.

Among the few who truly understood the depths of Kent's private anguish was Ann Bathgate, his girlfriend in their senior year at GFS. "His father cast him out," she says. "Kent was a very lonely young man. He had a lot of hurt, a deep bitterness, a mistrust. There was a lot of hate in him toward his father. Given the neglect, the parental situation ... Kent was scarred for life."

Through several years as classmates, Kent Potter and Ann Bathgate had never had much in common and were not close friends. Ann, an art student who read Kierkegaard at sixteen, was the daughter of a GFS classics professor; she "dressed differently" and loftily disdained her male schoolmates as "jerks, jocks, or idiots." She saw Kent only as a "party dude," whose interests were anything but academic. Then, at a house party on New Year's Eve of 1965, Ann recalls, "We got into a torrid game of ping pong, and just fell flat for each other."

About that time, Kent was confiding to friends that he had just broken off a physical relationship with an older woman, whose identity he would not reveal. Ann herself was on the rebound from a junior-year romance with Gorm Larsen, a Danish exchange student who had returned home. "We were both suffering from love affairs with somebody who wasn't there," she says. Although hanky-panky was not unknown at the staid Quaker school, Ann and Kent never actually engaged in sex, she says. "Of course we wanted to, but we sort of took turns backing off."

For lack of real consummation, the romance that had blossomed on New Year's Eve withered in an odd way, five months later—at the school's senior prom. As Ann remembers it, Kent refused to dance with her and "went upstairs with another girl," leaving her confused and angry.

Kent never called her again, but the day the Class of '65 sat for its formal portrait, copies of the yearbook were being passed around and inscribed with personal notes. When she got home, Ann was surprised to find in hers a cryptic message next to Kent's picture: "Don't have a good time without an impossible dream! Life is one bad break after another, with just enough good times to make you hope that things might change if only you wait a little. Don't lose that hope, kid (that is love)." Below this, as an afterthought, he wrote: "I'm sorry about a lot of things and actions, and you appear near the top of that misty, burning list. Sorry, love, luck. Kent."

Looking back, Ann sees herself and Kent as "rebels, in different ways," and Kent as having "both a tremendous need for love and a deep suspicion of it," a fear of doing anything that smacked of commitment, that might inflict more pain on him. Whatever the reason, his inscription had a tone of finality.

After graduation, Ann won a scholarship to a prestigious Philadelphia art school but decided to postpone that and move to Denmark, where she was reunited with, and eventually married, Gorm Larsen, the former exchange student. She would not see Kent Potter again for two years, when he paid a visit to their home outside Copenhagen. But she privately set aside a place in her heart for the brash, blue-eyed youth who, she says, "could look at a woman and make her knees wobble."

Kent, meanwhile, did not let broken hearts interfere with his own love life, and he had no qualms about taking risks in casual romance. A year after Ann left for Denmark, Kent, Bill Thode, and two girlfriends were holed up in a back den at the home of Kent's date when her father suddenly "banged on the door and asked what was going on" inside. "Kent was naked, and he jumped behind a couch to hide," Thode remembers. "I don't know what would have happened if that girl's father had opened the door."

It was Thode who, in a way, introduced Kent to the world of more serious photojournalism—in the person of Phil Elliott, a University of Pennsylvania student who worked part-time as a sports and on-call photo stringer for the UPI Philadelphia bureau. Elliott cut a somewhat dashing figure, driving a maroon Pontiac GTO with rumbling pipes, twin whip antennas, and a yellow flasher on the roof. Kent was already enamored of cars as well as cameras, and after meeting Elliott he became further smitten. Ann Bathgate remembers Elliott coming to the school to try out a new camera at a sporting event and Kent hovering around to see how he used it.

Through Elliott, Potter met Dirck Halstead, the UPI photo chief in Philadelphia, who soon hired the eager young man as a messenger and photo stringer. It was not long before Kent was going out on picture assignments on a regular basis. It was obvious to those around him that he had found a calling.

Tom Martin and Bob Metz tell similar stories of hanging out in the UPI bureau and riding with Kent on his assignments, ostensibly to keep notes for captions, but mostly for the fun of it. "It was an exciting, addictive life," says Martin. "We would rush to the scene, shoot it, rush to the office, then send the photos out over the wires. Affirmation was just hours away when the photos appeared in the local and national newspapers." Always competitive, Potter exulted whenever his photos "won the play" over the rival AP.

Emulating Elliott, Kent had installed a police radio in the Volkswagen that hissed and squawked with fragmented police reports of urban drama in the making. "Kent always wanted to be the first person at the scene, and he'd put himself right in the middle of things," Metz says. "And whether it was a car wreck or the sidelines at an Eagles game, Kent was not at all concerned about who was telling him to get out of the way."

Once, the two of them drove over to the Pine Barrens in southern New Jersey, where authorities were reported to have discovered a dumping ground for Mafia murder victims. Kent talked his way past the officers guarding the scene, telling Metz on his return that he "didn't see much."

Potter's first big story as a news photographer involved the holdup of a downtown Philadelphia bank. One of the bandits, fleeing from police, dashed into an underground concourse between the subway and commuter rail stations, where the UPI bureau was located. Kent rushed out with his camera and shot dramatic pictures of the robber being gunned down by the police, virtually on the bureau's doorstep. The photos later won prizes in the local press competition, and the incident became part of UPI lore: The easiest way to cover a story was just to look out the window.

But there were considerations other than work for the likes of Kent Potter. The mid-1960s were crunch time for young Americans facing the specter of combat in Vietnam. The war was an inescapable reality, intruding on lives and plans, forcing boys to make choices that were almost universally unpleasant. They could enlist, wait to be drafted, seek college or work deferments, or join the reserves and hope they wouldn't be called up. Or they could head north to Canada.

For Quakers, the question of whether and how to serve in wartime has posed a dilemma since the American Revolution, which was known in the meetinghouses of the time as "the trouble," a political crisis in which they refused to swear oaths of allegiance or take up arms for either side. In later wars, especially in the twentieth century, many Quakers became conscientious objectors—officially exempted from military service by reason of religious, ethical, or moral opposition to war and killing. For many of those, this meant alternative civilian service or serving—often heroically—as noncombatant battlefield medics.

As far as is known, Kent Potter never considered seeking conscientious-objector status as an alternative to being drafted. He was already committed to a different objective: He *wanted* to go to Vietnam—but as a photographer, not as a soldier or medic.

Sal DiMarco, Jr., a photographer at the Philadelphia *Bulletin*, and Rusty Kennedy, an AP photographer who was about Potter's age and competed with him regularly on news and sports assignments, remember Kent's interest in the war waxing to the point of obsession. It was not an enthusiasm they shared; DiMarco wanted a college degree and hoped eventually to work for *Life*, and Kennedy planned to stay in Philadelphia and raise a family. "Kent wanted to go to Vietnam because that's where the story was," DiMarco says. "He was establishing a good reputation, but he didn't have the hash marks. Vietnam was a good way to get them."

As it happened, Potter was well situated to realize his ambitions. The UPI Philadelphia bureau, already a breeding ground for young talent, would become famous as the news agency's career pipeline to Vietnam.

When UPI called on Dirck Halstead to take command of the Saigon photo operation, he turned the keys over to Frank Johnston, who soon promoted Kent to full-time staff photographer. When Johnston himself was sent to Saigon the next year, he left the energetic youth, not yet twenty years old, in charge in Philadelphia. Johnston, who later went to *The Washington Post*, says UPI headquarters in New York already was aware of Potter's eagerness to cover the war but was reluctant to make any move until his military draft status was somehow settled.

On St. Patrick's Day 1966, Kent solved that problem himself in a surprising manner: He enlisted in the U.S. Marine Corps Reserve. Joining the reserves or the National Guard was a gambit used by many young men—most notably some with future political ambitions—to avoid the draft and to keep some control over their destiny. Six years of playing weekend warrior with the Army or Air Force, with perhaps only a remote chance of being called to active duty, was far preferable to humping the boonies in Vietnam.

But the Marine Corps was hardly a place to hide out from the Vietnam War—and that was hardly Kent Potter's intention. After boot camp at Parris Island, South Carolina, he was sent to the Marine Corps photography school in Florida for training in a craft that he already knew well. By July 1966, he was back home in Philadelphia, again working for UPI and fulfilling his weekend training obligations with Marine Air Group 43, in nearby Willow Grove. Should he be called to active duty, it would be as a combat photographer for the Marine Corps.

Some friends recall that Kent's decision to join the military completed the mutual alienation of father and son. But as always, the matter remained private. Frank Johnston, his boss at the time, remembers no discussion of it. He knew only that Kent had a sister and, in Kent's own words, "didn't get along well with his father."

Shielded from the draft by his reserve status, Kent began lobbying UPI so hard for a Vietnam assignment that it seemed certain he would wind up there; the only question was when. But as the war increased in intensity in 1967, so did his anxiety. Like other young journalists hoping for a career-making assignment to Vietnam, he had to worry that the hostilities would all be over before he got there.

In 1966, just before she married Gorm Larsen in Denmark, Ann Bathgate received a letter from Kent, asking forgiveness for the "stupid things" he had done in the past. "Until I got this letter, I thought I was over him," she says. "He didn't give me any chance of getting away."

A year later, she was pregnant with her first child when Kent made a surprise visit to Denmark. It was a brief, strange encounter—the husband and the former lover, still rivals, in a sense, for her affection. But Gorm was understanding and went out of his way to make Kent feel welcome. Kent, for his part, was excited about Ann having a baby.

During the visit, Potter talked about his Vietnam ambitions—an idea that Ann did not like but tried to understand. "He needed to prove to himself that he could be different from his father, and he had discovered that he was a good photographer," she says. "He had found his calling and that was the place to be. He had to be there."

In December 1967, UPI reached outside its own ranks for the first time for a new Saigon photo chief, choosing photographer Bill Snead of the *News-Journal* in Wilmington, Delaware. Snead was no stranger to either Vietnam or UPI. The Wilmington paper had sent him to the war zone for a brief stint in 1965. Working in a city just south of Philadelphia, Snead had sold many photos to the UPI bureau there. He knew Kent Potter personally and professionally, and the younger man showed up to see him off at Philadelphia International Airport. As Snead prepared to board the plane, "the last thing he said to me was, 'Snead, you've got to get me over there. I've already asked New York and they know I want to go, but you've got to ask for me. I know you don't have enough staff, so ask for me when you get there.'"

Despite his previous experience in Vietnam, Snead wasn't sure what to expect as UPI photo boss. "Being terrified and not knowing what the hell was in store, I told him I would," recalls Snead, who went on to a later career at *The Washington Post* and *National Geographic* and is now an editor at the *Lawrence (Kansas) Journal-World*.

Snead had been in Saigon less than two months when the Tet Offensive erupted on January 31, 1968. The countrywide, coordinated series of communist attacks on district and provincial capitals and military installations caught the Americans and the South Vietnamese embarrassingly off-guard. Half of Saigon's forces had been given leave for the New Year holiday. It was the boldest stroke of the war to that time by Hanoi and its southern surrogates, the Viet Cong.

For once, reporters and photographers didn't have to go into the field to see the war; it was right up the street. As dawn broke over Saigon on that Wednesday morning, they had only to venture near the U.S. embassy to see and hear the chaos of combat. A squad of Viet Cong commandos had brazenly breached the embassy building's outer walls and was shooting it out among the concrete lawn planters with Marine guards, military police, and embassy civilian officers.

By some accounts—later vehemently denied by U.S. officials—the attackers penetrated the fortresslike building and had to be driven out by Marines fighting downward from the roof. By midday, all nineteen Viet Cong lay dead, along with several Americans, and shaken officials were trying to explain how it could have happened.

The communist troops had been told the offensive would foment a popular uprising of the Vietnamese citizenry against "the American imperialists and the puppet Thieu regime." That did not occur, but it would be years before historians came to accept General William Westmoreland's claim that the combination of a failed people's revolt and heavy Viet Cong losses had made Tet a de facto military defeat for the insurgency that in the long run would force Hanoi to commit more of its own military forces.

At the time, such arguments scarcely mattered. Coming just as U.S. officials were trumpeting great progress in the war, the Tet Offensive became a political and public relations disaster for the Americans, further undermining confidence in an already shaky Saigon government and bolstering the war's critics in the United States and elsewhere.

On all fronts, news accounts and pictures crystallized a perception of the allied side reeling under pressure. Officials had no way to minimize the psychological impact of fighting in the embassy's front yard. Eddie Adams's shocking photo of South Vietnam's national police chief, General Nguyen Ngoc Loan, summarily executing a Viet Cong suspect in a Saigon street was splashed across front pages worldwide and quickly became the seminal photo image of the war. Neither could officials give a positive twist to stories, photos, and TV reports of the grinding battle to retake Hue or the U.S. Marines under siege on the barren plateau called Khe Sanh, which some commentators compared to Dien Bien Phu.

During this period the Saigon press corps was taking casualties of its own, and Kent Potter's presumptuous remark to Snead about a staff shortage at UPI was about to be validated—in blood. On February 2, the second night of the Tet fighting, a UPI photographer named Bill Hall was seriously wounded by gunfire at a South Vietnamese Army roadblock in the city and had to be evacuated to the United States.

On March 5, days after the monthlong battle for Hue ended in its recapture by the Americans and South Vietnamese, an armored personnel carrier ran over a landmine near Phu Bai, just south of the old capital, flipped over, and caught fire. Among the victims was Hiromichi Mine, a twenty-seven-year-old UPI photographer who was on his second Vietnam tour and had won several photo awards. Severely burned in the explosion, Mine died hours later in a field hospital.

Staggered by the loss of two photo staffers in so short a span of time, the UPI bureau needed reinforcements in a hurry. And Snead knew just the man for the job—his energetic and ambitious young friend back in Philadelphia. Kent Potter was finally going to get his wish. But even as the summons came from UPI, Potter learned to his dismay that the Marine Corps also had plans for him. He was notified that he was about to be called up to active duty and sent to Vietnam. Here it was—the big chance he'd waited for, about to be sacrificed to military priority.

Fortunately for Kent, there were recourses. The record shows that he applied for, and was granted, a hardship discharge from the Marine Corps. Whether UPI aided Kent's case by applying pressure in the right places is not clear, but officials were sympathetic to the rather inventive argument that being sent to Vietnam as a Marine Corps photographer would cost him his job in Vietnam as a civilian photographer.

The hardship discharge, effective March 15, 1968, was conditional on Potter remaining abroad in the civilian job for eighteen months. Failure to do so would make him immediately draft-eligible. It was almost as if he'd had the entire scenario in mind when he joined the reserves two years earlier. And so sometime in April—the date is not certain—Kent Potter landed at Tan Son Nhut airport outside Saigon, ready to begin the adventure he had waited so long for.

Snead recalls that Kent "fit right in," getting himself equipped with uniforms and military gear at the Saigon black market and learning his way around the area. The UPI news and photo bureau was on the ground floor of a downtown building at No. 19 Ngo Duc Ke Street, with a dormitorylike room with bunk beds on the second floor and, above that, a couple of rooms where Snead lived. Potter moved in with him.

The UPI photo staff at the time included Kyoichi Sawada, a highly respected and soft-spoken Japanese who already had won the Pulitzer

Prize for Vietnam pictures, British-born Nik Wheeler, and Charles Eggleston. The latter was twenty-three, a Navy veteran who had taken his discharge from the service in Vietnam and, rather than go home to peace and quiet in upstate New York, signed on with UPI as a local-hire photographer. Eggleston behaved as if he'd never left the military. He spent much of his time in the field, especially in the Mekong Delta, where he had done his Navy service—it was his "comfort zone," Snead says—and usually carried a weapon along with his cameras.

Eggleston took Potter down to the delta to show him around and introduce him to helicopter pilots, people who could be valuable sources of information and transportation for journalists when neither commodity was officially available. Back in Saigon, Snead, Eggleston, and Potter cooked up hot chili, drank at the Melody Bar next door to the bureau, and talked about the war. "Kent didn't drink nearly as much whiskey as the rest of us, but he loved to argue, and the more he argued the louder he got, and he wouldn't get out of your face until he'd won," Snead says. That competitive fire showed in his work, as well. "He knew the importance of deadlines, and he was always pushing—'Hey, Snead—let's do this, let's do that, let's kick AP's ass!'"

Eventually, Kent was introduced at the apartment on Tu Do Street where Sean Flynn, Tim Page, and a few others stayed when they weren't in the field. Though he never became a regular denizen, Potter spent his share of time in the rooms decorated with posters and draped parachutes, sharing the opium pipe that was proffered to welcome visitors.

For all the bumptious energy he brought to Vietnam, Potter rarely talked about himself or his home life. Many acquaintances were unaware of his Quaker roots, and his Marine Corps Reserve experience not widely known. Not even Carl Robinson, an AP photo editor and declared conscientious objector who hung out at the Tu Do apartment and accompanied Potter on a trip to Singapore, ever heard him mention these things. Friends knew only that he corresponded with a sister. Mostly, the others saw a young man who thrived on his professional work and, increasingly, on the excitement of war.

Influenced by Eggleston, he began collecting guns, even keeping a rifle in his room. One evening, Snead was startled by a gunshot and rushed into the room. "What happened?" he asked. "Nothin'," replied

Potter, who then explained that he had heard a noise, grabbed a gun, and fired it by mistake, nearly hitting himself in the toe. Smoke drifted through the room, but Snead could not find a bullet hole anywhere. A few days later, while walking down Tu Do Street, Snead felt a draft and discovered the crotch area of his pants had been shredded. Inspection of the armoire where he kept the pants revealed a hole where the bullet had gone through and embedded itself in the back wall.

Kate Webb, a New Zealander who had arrived in Vietnam about the same time and became Potter's close friend, saw a softer side. The two of them spent quiet evenings sitting in cane chairs on the roof of the bureau building, Kent wearing Viet Cong–style black pajamas and sandals, watching the sun set over the red tile roofs of the old city. "We were the babies of the bureau," says Webb. "We found relief in not having to tell each other war stories. We spent quite a few evenings just talking about the world and all." But even she knew little of Kent's personal history.

If Potter had any illusions about the story he'd come to cover, they were quickly dispelled. On the night of May 4, fighting erupted again in the streets of Saigon. As during Tet three months earlier, Viet Cong squads and sapper teams had infiltrated the city, taking over neighborhoods and defying the Americans and South Vietnamese to come after them. The press corps dubbed it the "second Tet," and "mini-Tet," and donned helmets and flak jackets to cover fighting around Saigon's landmark Y-bridge, near Tan Son Nhut airport, and in Cholon, the Chinese quarter.

The next morning, a Sunday, five Australian reporters—John Cantwell, who worked for *Time* magazine, Michael Birch of Australian Associated Press, Bruce Piggott and Ron Laramy of Reuters news agency, and recently arrived Frank Palmos—climbed into one of *Time*'s "mini-moke" jeeps and headed for Cholon. Turning a corner, they ran into a roadblock manned by troops in black pajamas and carrying AK-47s. Before Cantwell could shove the jeep into reverse, the Viet Cong guerrillas opened fire, ripping the vehicle and its occupants.

That morning, after phoning AP for any last-minute updates for the magazine that was closing the week's edition in New York, *Time* reporter Wally Terry had planned to scout the situation in the city, but at

Cantwell's insistence he decided to stay with his wife, Janice, who had arrived from Singapore the day before on her first visit to Saigon.

Terry was stunned when Palmos, whom he didn't know, turned up at the *Time* villa, disheveled and blurting out a wild account of the attack. "They were ambushed. They are all dead," he kept saying. One newsman had called out *"bao chi"* and tried to show his press card, but he was ignored by the commander. To the Viet Cong, foreigners not in uniform were CIA agents.

Terry was skeptical of Palmos's story. If he escaped after feigning death, how could he know they were all dead? But it didn't matter—he had no choice but to go to the scene. With Zalin B. "Zip" Grant, a veteran Vietnam reporter who had just returned to Saigon, Terry set out for Cholon in another jeep.[1]

Blocked by fighting, they persuaded a police commander to lead an armed patrol. But the officer stopped four blocks away, handed Terry a shotgun, and told the pair they were on their own. Only after U.S. troops moved in were they able to reach the riddled vehicle and recruit an Army demolition team sergeant to make sure it wasn't booby-trapped. Laramy was dead in the backseat, arms still upraised as if to surrender. The others were on the ground, blood-caked and bloating in Saigon's heat. Every one had been shot at least fifteen times.

As they loaded the bodies into their jeep, Terry and Grant were astonished to see twenty or more young men in black pajamas trot past in ranks four abreast—Viet Cong soldiers, apparently pulling out to avoid being caught between American and South Vietnamese troops. Grant remembers the hate on their faces. "They ran right by us. I was petrified," says Terry. "I realized these might be John's killers. Why they didn't stop and kill us, I don't know." Terry and Grant handed the bodies over to a military ambulance crew, who took them to the U.S. Army morgue at Tan Son Nhut Air Base.

---

[1] Unknown to Terry and Grant, Reuters's Vietnamese reporter, Pham Ngoc Dinh, had heard a fragmentary report on the killings from a police source and headed into Cholon on foot. Nearing the ambush site, he was stopped and questioned by Viet Cong guerrillas, who told him the dead Westerners were "CIA." Prudently agreeing that it was right that they should have been executed, Dinh managed get close enough to see the bodies but had no way of retrieving them. Dinh's story appears in *Vietnam: A Reporter's War*, by former Reuters staffer Hugh Lunn (Briarcliff Manor, NY: Stein and Day, 1986).

One day later, on May 6, UPI lost another photographer. Charlie Eggleston and John Olson, another who had stayed on in Vietnam after military service and was freelancing, mainly for *Life* magazine, left downtown Saigon in a UPI jeep for a scouting trip toward Tan Son Nhut, north of the city. With them was Roger Norum, a reporter for UPI's worldwide radio service. "Radio" Roger was yet another recent newcomer, admittedly eager to experience the deep-in-the-abdomen rush of covering combat. "I wanted to be involved, see what it was all about," he says.

Shocking as it was, the Cholon ambush of the previous day would not deter others, especially the hard-core press—the wire services, the TV networks, the still photographers—from covering the war in the streets. Eggleston and Olson were good men to travel with, although Eggleston, as usual, was carrying a carbine.

Nearing the airport, the trio encountered Co Rentmeester, the *Life* photographer who was Larry Burrows's chief rival in covering Indochina. Olson decided to stay with Rentmeester, and Norum recalls that he and Eggleston left him there, continuing on their own toward Tan Son Nhut on a street known locally as Plantation Road and to the U.S. military as Rocket Alley.

At some point, Norum remembers, he and Eggleston heard shooting and hastily turned off to take cover in an empty building, a sort of garage. Some South Vietnamese troops were there, and Viet Cong were firing rocket-propelled grenades (RPGs) at them from concealed positions. The entire episode was recorded on Norum's audiotape. Amid the small-arms rattle and the blasts of RPGs, Eggleston is heard saying, "Do you have a match? It's Marlboro country, huh?" A bullet whines close at hand.

Eggleston was leaning out, trying to get a look at the situation without exposing himself too much. Norum was crouching a few feet away. Seconds later, the tape records another shot, again close by, and a thump. Eggleston was down, shot through the head. "Oh, God! My God! Charlie has been killed!" Norum cries on the tape. Of that terrible moment, Norum said later, "He didn't say anything, and blood was coming out of his mouth.... I realized he'd been shot in the head. He was dead."

After some time, the gunfire abated. Soldiers helped Norum recover Eggleston's body and take it to a U.S. military hospital. Norum then drove back into Saigon, to the UPI office, where he told his colleagues what had happened. "The romance of covering war sort of ended for me that day," says Norum, who nevertheless stayed on the job in Saigon for another two years.

The UPI bureau was shaken, Kent Potter along with the rest. But he continued to perform as if he had been at this dangerous game for years; once in it, the combination of excitement, professional competition, and even peer pressure kept one taking the risks. A week or so after Eggleston's death, he was covering a battle near the Bien Hoa Air Base east of Saigon. A small force of North Vietnamese had seized a hamlet. ARVN troops were trying to drive them out, and a group of journalists was drinking beer as they watched the action from open-air restaurant shacks a short distance away. As was often the case in Vietnam, "It could best be described as a surreal situation," says former UPI reporter Nat Gibson, who was present.

The fighting also had attracted a number of U.S. military photographers from the air base. Potter was with them, shooting pictures from the doorway of a building. Gibson was outside, trying to find a notebook he'd lost in the confusion, when the North Vietnamese launched a sudden counterattack. An RPG smashed into the building, killing or wounding several of the soldier-photographers. "I saw Kent emerge, supporting one of the wounded men, whose arm had been blown off at the elbow, nothing below it but exposed arm bone," recalls Gibson. "Under fire, he ran across the open field to safety. It was a particularly dangerous and heroic thing to do."

Some days later, at the district town of Cu Chi on the other side of Saigon, Gibson and Potter were together again—this time crouched behind concrete tombs in a Vietnamese cemetery when U.S. planes attacked. A large piece of shrapnel hit the ground between them. "We flipped for the souvenir," Gibson recalls. "I won."

Kent had been writing regularly to Ann Bathgate since their 1967 meeting in Denmark, and from Saigon he told her things that he could never say to his sister. "He told me about the black pajamas, that he kept a gun under his pillow, and one night heard a noise and almost shot himself in the foot." He wrote about Viet Cong ears being kept as trophies and claimed in one letter to have seen a prisoner tossed out of a helicopter because it was too heavy. "The letters got worse and worse,

as if he was proud of it," Ann says. "Maybe he was just trying to impress me, but with a small baby, and so far away—I was really antiwar,
anti the U.S. being in Vietnam. I thought, what is *happening* to this
man?"

By mid-1970, after covering the Cambodian incursion, Potter had
been the UPI photo manager for Vietnam for more than a year, and
the agency was worried that he, like Larry Burrows and Henri Huet,
was pressing his luck. It asked him to return to the United States for reassignment, but like Huet, he balked—threatening to resign if forced
to leave the war zone.

The result was a compromise. Potter accepted a transfer to
Bangkok, where he would run the photo shop in the UPI bureau that
was now managed by Leon Daniel, a former Vietnam reporter who
also had been reassigned to Thailand. While enjoying the unique comforts of Bangkok, the UPI men were only an hour's flight from Saigon
should things heat up in the war, which they inevitably did.

Returning to the United States for a visit in connection with his
transfer, Kent detoured by way of Denmark, rented a Volkswagen in
Copenhagen, and drove the twenty-two miles to Ann Bathgate's house.
As she went out to meet him, "He ran and leaped over the hedge and
just grabbed me as if he would never let me go," she says. "In that one
embrace I knew everything. I felt his heartbeat."

After that start, the reunion did not go well. The mood was very
different from what it had been during his visit three years earlier.
Kent was now deeply into the war, complaining about what the Americans were doing in Vietnam—operating covertly in areas where they
weren't supposed to be, for example. He said he wanted to "expose"
this, because journalists were complicit in covering it up and weren't
to be trusted. He also said the Americans were likely to invade Laos as
they had Cambodia. Such an event was not yet being planned; he
could only have been speculating.

At some point, Kent got into his rented car and drove alone back
to Copenhagen, returning to the cottage later in the evening. Ann
and Gorm knew, from what he vaguely told them, that he had gone
to buy drugs. Thus, Gorm Larsen did not give Kent the warm welcome of the earlier visit. In a heated late-night discussion with Ann,
he wanted to know how long Potter intended to stay. Although they

spoke in Danish, in the small house Kent could not help but overhear and get the message that he was not wanted. "The next morning he suddenly remembered that he had to be somewhere, and he left," Ann says. "I wanted to say, 'It's going to be all right, don't leave.' But it was too late."

The letters stopped, and Ann never saw him again.

During the same trip home, Kent went to see his father, who by then had left Philadelphia and was living in a health care facility in Florida. It apparently was the first reunion since their estrangement. They had arranged to meet at a restaurant, and Kent didn't know what to expect, but he was disappointed when his father showed up wearing a serape. He later told his old friend, Tom Martin, "I took one look at my father and went back to the bar and had a drink."

It was in Southeast Asia that Kent was reunited with Martin, the GFS classmate with whom he'd shared photography duties for the yearbook five years earlier. Martin had become a conscientious objector and left college in late 1968 to take a job in Thailand as a photographer and documentary filmmaker for the United Nations.

En route to Bangkok, he stopped off in Saigon to spend Christmas with Potter. Kent gave him a tour of the city, the obligatory first stop being a brothel. Martin did not find that surprising, but he was shocked when Kent kicked at some Vietnamese pedestrians as he steered the UPI jeep through a crowded street. "It was most disturbing. It wasn't the Kent Potter I knew," says Martin. But he, like Ann Bathgate, decided Kent was hoping to impress him with how tough and hard-bitten he had become, as if being in the war zone required that. "Kent was writing his own book from the beginning. He was always trying to yank my chain."

Over warm beers, Kent recounted for Martin the death of Charlie Eggleston, as told by Radio Roger Norum: "'One moment Charlie was standing there joking and alive, and the next moment he was dead.' Kent was angry; he said Charlie had screwed up. He repeated the photographer's maxim that no picture is worth your life. He tried to be tough and matter of fact, but the break in his voice told me otherwise."

Kent always called Tom when he passed through Bangkok, and missed no chance to impress his old friend. One day the phone rang. "Hey, Mart, I just got in from Katmandu," said Potter. "Remembering those words always makes me smile," says Martin. "They struck me then and now as the epitome of cool."

The two friends met at the Intercontinental Hotel bar, where Martin watched, awed, as Potter sent a drink "to a woman I had not noticed," and the woman, a flight attendant, quickly joined them. "It occurred to me," Martin says, "that he had modeled his life after 'Bond, James Bond,' and I had modeled mine after Opie Taylor."

Thailand was a colorful place—its temples, floating markets, monks in saffron-orange robes, and ruins of dynasties past added up to a photographer's paradise—but there was not a lot of hard news to cover. After being reassigned to Bangkok, Kent traveled around Asia on assignments, but the big story was still next door in Indochina—Laos, Cambodia, and Vietnam—and he made occasional trips back to the war zone.

In late October 1970, UPI photographer Sawada and reporter Frank Frosch were murdered on Highway 2, twenty-four miles south of Phnom Penh. Sawada was yet another who had been transferred out of the war zone for his own safety, only to return after he found desk duty in Hong Kong unbearable.

During their times together in the last months of 1970, Tom Martin saw Kent as a "chameleon," readily adopting the coloration of those around him. Doing drugs with certain friends was one example of this, he says; more important were his efforts to emulate professionals he had come to know and admire—especially Dirck Halstead and Larry Burrows. "Kent's greatest desire was to excel as a photojournalist," Martin says. "He identified with these men while expressing his contempt for the journalistic hangers-on who had come to Vietnam more for the adventure than for the work. He viewed Burrows as the ultimate craftsman and admired his modesty and courage."

Martin believes Burrows's influence, and the realization of his own professional success, was causing Potter to soften his manner, returning to "the more gentle, philosophical qualities" he had shown in earlier years. "He was losing his toughness. He was becoming a much more professional photographer and a much more decent human being."

In December, Kent flew to Bali for a brief vacation, came down with dengue fever the day he arrived, and spent the entire time in bed. He returned to Bangkok in a weakened state. Martin remembers sitting in Kent's apartment drinking a beer while Kent sipped miserably on tea. "For the first time we talked about the possibility of his death. It was a subject I had always avoided because he knew the risks far better than I. But for whatever reason, that night I was insistent that it was time for him to go home. I told him he'd done what he'd come to do in Vietnam, and reminded him that many other photographers had made names for themselves in Indochina and used it to land better assignments back home. But Kent expressed his determination to 'see the war through to the end.' He'd recently been in the States and found it boring."

As they talked, Martin says, he realized more than ever that for Kent Potter "the war was no longer just a story; he had tied his life to it. It was where his profession and his friends were. His bond to both was unbreakable."

It was the last time the old school friends would meet. Recovered from the virus, Potter left for assignment in Cambodia and was there in late January when UPI summoned him to return to Vietnam. Kate Webb, who also was in Phnom Penh at the time, remembers that the call was a rush job; Kent was told to get to Saigon as soon as possible because the South Vietnamese were expected to launch an invasion of Laos.

He had trouble finding a flight to Saigon but finally wangled a seat on an Air France flight. Kate recalls that they had no time for a ceremonious parting at the airport. They said their good-byes sitting on a curb outside the airline office. Just a quick hug, she remembers, and he was gone.

10 : Liftoff

Five UH–1H Huey helicopters, olive-green with red and yellow Vietnam Air Force markings, sat on the barren, muddy knoll at Ham Nghi, four miles east of the Vietnam-Laos frontier. Military trucks and armored vehicles roared steadily past the sandbagged tent complex, the forward command post for South Vietnam's I Corps and operational headquarters for LAM SON 719. It was February 10, 1971—day three of the invasion.

What people remember of that day exists only in fragments, a mosaic with tiles missing. For days, fog had washed the mountain ridges beyond the border to a faint gray, and lowering clouds dispensed a chilly intermittent drizzle that sequined the dark trees and turned the soil a deeper red, as if the earth's own colors were straining to escape. The weather had begun to brighten on this Wednesday morning. A pale sun struggled to penetrate the haze, and in the drying conditions vehicles were starting to kick up dust instead of mud as they rumbled west along Route 9 toward the border village of Lao Bao.

The narrow, two-lane strip of dirt and broken blacktop had been fought over in two Indochina wars. The old French kilometer markers had long since been riddled by bullets to concrete stumps. The border itself was now marked by a large, temporary wooden sign reading "WARNING. NO U.S. PERSONNEL BEYOND THIS POINT," an admonition to the U.S. troops supporting the operation that this was as far west as they could go.

Naturally, the sign itself had become a magnet; GIs stepped beyond it to have souvenir snapshots taken "in Laos," and the painted wood quickly became covered with graffiti—the names, hometowns, and units of GIs deprived of a chance to become heroes, or dead, or possibly both. Several journalists also had left their marks. Among these was a CBS News shipping sticker and, at the very top, a set of freshly scrawled letters: "LIFE" MAG—LARRY B.

The helicopters belonged to Lieutenant General Hoang Xuan Lam, commander of Military Region I and the Laos invasion force. A close friend and military-school classmate of President Nguyen Van Thieu, Lam ruled South Vietnam's five northernmost provinces in the style of a political warlord. The cross-border attack would be the most important test of combat leadership he had ever faced.

Although the Americans were the main architects of the Laos invasion, many U.S. officials had private misgivings about Lam's ability to lead a military enterprise that was bolder, more complex, and more fraught with risk than anything Saigon's forces had ever undertaken on their own. If the proud general didn't know this, he at least sensed it and was determined to prove that he and his troops—they were, after all, the best that South Vietnam had to offer—were equal to the task. By inviting some journalists on his first inspection tour of the front, Lam could show he did not fear such scrutiny and that he was quite capable of making his own decisions independently of the Americans or higher South Vietnamese headquarters, in this case by ignoring the no-foreigners-in-Laos edict.

With helicopter space for only a few, Lam wanted the top news organizations to accompany him but left it to the journalists to decide who among them would go first. There was no hard and fast rule in such cases. By tacit understanding when space or access was limited, members of the press corps generally deferred to a combination of seniority and basic journalistic requirements that gave priority to the major news agencies, newspapers, magazines, and TV networks. The right of first refusal belonged to the wire services, AP and UPI, which technically were covering the story for everyone.

Whether this convention had been invoked on this day is not clear. Although there were many journalists of all kinds in Eye Corps at the time, it may be that the handful of helicopter seats available had simply been staked out by four photographers whose credentials were solid enough to resist any challenge.

All four—Larry Burrows, Henri Huet, Kent Potter, and Keisaburo Shimamoto—were respected veterans of combat coverage, working for heavyweight news organizations. Nobody could question their right to lead the way. Moreover, it was probably assumed that if one group of journalists got into Laos with the ARVN forces, others would be able to follow. The press wouldn't even need the Americans.

The question of danger did not enter into the equation. The risks of any such venture were obvious and well known to every member of the select quartet. Journalists died in wars, along with soldiers and civilians. It was part of the war correspondent psyche to recognize the possibility of the worst, but to worry or even think much about that was to invite oneself to look for work in another field.

And while common sense said that no one was invincible, there was a sense among members of the Saigon media that journalists who reached celebrity status through repeated stellar performance could become exempt from ordinary danger, passing into a realm of immunity where the worst simply could *not* happen to them—as if North Vietnamese gunners tracking a helicopter would receive a last-second order: "Don't shoot. That's Larry Burrows up there."

A couple of hundred yards from the knoll, U.S. Marine Corporal Sergio Ortiz waited at another chopper pad, his camera bag weighing on his shoulder. The pad was close to a forward position for U.S. artillery supporting the Laos invasion. Very soon, some cargo helicopters, heavy-lift CH-53s, were due to arrive, and Corporal Ortiz's job, as a Marine Corps combat photojournalist, was to show how Marine aviation units were helping to support the South Vietnamese drive into Laos.

The clearing weather had opened the way for a massive airlift. The air was thick with the sound of idling choppers, most of them American, and off to the west, toward the border, Ortiz could see large numbers of ARVN troops milling about, waiting for the long strings of

Hueys to land and pick them up. Occasionally, impacting artillery rounds fired from beyond the border caused the troops to hunker down, but the gunners apparently were firing without benefit of forward observers, and the shells fell far away from the assembly area with negligible effect.

Shortly, Ortiz saw four men walking toward the knoll where the VNAF's Hueys were parked. Even at a distance, he could tell by their motley mix of uniforms and the gear they carried—camera bags and backpacks, with no visible weapons—that they were not soldiers but journalists. Then he recognized one of the taller ones as the famous *Life* magazine photographer Larry Burrows.

Sergio Ortiz had met Burrows twice before. Two years earlier, while still in college in Los Angeles, he had won photo and writing awards for his campus newspaper, in addition to one for himself as the top college photographer in California. One of the judges of the competition was *Life*'s Los Angeles bureau chief, Ron DePaolo, who afterward invited Ortiz to come to his office for an interview.

Ortiz was planning to boldly ask DePaolo for a job with *Life*, covering the war in Vietnam, when Larry Burrows, the magazine's staff photographer best known for that very thing, suddenly walked in the door. Struck "almost speechless," Ortiz remembers their conversation only as cordial but brief. Afterward, he recalls, DePaolo "politely laughed at my brazenness, wondering why I thought *Life* would consider sending a greenhorn, just out of college, to cover the Vietnam war when they had the likes of Larry Burrows there."

No job at *Life* was forthcoming. Instead, Ortiz worked briefly for the Los Angeles *Herald-Examiner*, then joined the Marine Corps to become a combat photographer. After a stint at Marine photography school, he found himself in Vietnam, assigned to a Marine photo unit based at the Danang Press Center. One day there, he bumped into Larry Burrows again. "He was surrounded by senior Marine Corps public affairs officers—my bosses—who were giving him the red-carpet treatment," Ortiz remembers. "I breached military protocol by interrupting a major in midsentence to reintroduce myself." Burrows apparently did not recall their Los Angeles meeting but realized that Ortiz, as an enlisted man, had overstepped his bounds; he moved quickly to head off trouble. "He shook my hand and said it was good to see me again. He showed great interest in my work and invited me to visit him in Hong Kong, if I could manage to squeeze a little R&R from the Marines." When the officers laughed, Ortiz breathed easier. Burrows's diplomatic intervention had saved him from a royal butt-chewing or worse.

Two days later, Burrows went out to shoot a story at Marble Mountain, a snaggle-toothed rock formation a few miles south of Danang, where the Marines had a helicopter base and the Viet Cong were said to occupy the crags and caves above it. Civilian journalists working out of the press camp were customarily assigned a military escort, and Burrows asked the Marines to send Ortiz with him. During the half-hour drive to Marble Mountain, Burrows talked about covering the Tet Offensive and offered advice on caring for photo equipment in Vietnam's harsh environment, such as putting lenses inside military socks to protect them from dust and humidity and wrapping exposed film rolls in foil wrappers from C-rations.

Passing one of Danang's roadside shantytowns, Burrows remarked that he wanted to do a photo essay on such a place but feared that his editors wouldn't be very enthusiastic. Emboldened by Burrows's egalitarian manner, Ortiz brought up the old story of Robert Capa's ruined D-Day film. Burrows "laughed sheepishly" and said that although he had been in the London lab at the time the culprit was someone else. "Capa took it in stride," Larry told him. "Everyone else was angry at the darkroom man, but not him."

Ham Nghi was the first time Ortiz had seen Burrows since Marble Mountain. The younger photographer hastened over to where the VNAF choppers were parked. This time, Burrows did remember him and introduced Ortiz to his colleagues—Huet, Potter, and Shimamoto. The photographers explained that they were going into Laos with General Lam and asked Ortiz what was happening across the border. "I said I didn't know—I hadn't been there, since I had orders not to cross into Laos unless it was aboard a U.S. aircraft, and then I was not to disembark from the aircraft if and when it landed," Ortiz says. A smiling Burrows replied, "Too bad. It would be great to have a Marine along." Ortiz said, "I'd give anything to photograph the ground action with you guys. It's very tempting to say 'screw it all' and go with you."

"Then do it!" said Potter, laughing. Potter, who but for the Marines' willingness to grant him a quick hardship discharge three years earlier, might well have been in Ortiz's place. The casual banter continued as they waited for General Lam to appear. Ortiz remembers Potter complaining mildly that he was hungry and that he gave the UPI photographer some rations from his own pack. As the wait continued, three of the photographers climbed into the parked Huey's cargo bay, Shimamoto on the inside, Huet beside the right-hand door, facing forward. Burrows sat opposite them, his back against the pilots' armored "chicken plate" seatbacks. Potter remained standing next to the helicopter, squinting in the pale sun.

Burrows patted the empty seat next to him. "See? There's room," he said to Ortiz. "Come along if you want." Ortiz felt himself actually tempted. It would be against orders, but maybe Burrows would stick up for him, say that it was *his* fault, not Ortiz's. But the Marine photographer knew there was no way he could risk it. He shook his head and started to walk away.

After a few steps, Ortiz stopped and turned around. "Impulsively, I raised a Nikon and shot a couple of frames," he remembers. "No particular reason. I just did it."

One of those frames shows Burrows, a white towel around his neck, looking down at his equipment. In the other picture, the last one, Burrows, Huet, and Shimamoto are looking at Potter, who apparently is speaking.

Ortiz also remembers Burrows's parting comment, "He told me to be careful, and wished me good luck." Those may be the last words that anyone yet alive heard Larry Burrows utter. The pictures are, as far as is known, the last taken of the four.

The absence of any other photos of the scene is peculiar, given the fact that dozens of journalists had converged on the staging areas for LAM SON 719, most of them probably carrying cameras. Several of them had been around the helicopter pad at Ham Nghi that morning, but they somehow managed to avoid encountering each other—as if passing through a revolving door, one visitor at a time.

Michael Putzel, one of several AP reporters covering LAM SON 719, had flown out from Quang Tri that morning. In addition to gathering information on the invasion, he had the secondary mission of delivering a message to Henri Huet. He found Huet and the others at the South Vietnamese Tactical Operations Center (TOC) in a sandbagged tent near the knoll. "Saigon photos had asked me to remind Henri that

In every child who is born, under no
matter what circumstances, and of no
matter what parents, the potentiality of
the human race is born again.

Let Us Now Praise Famous Men
James Agee

ABOVE: Kent Potter wrote
cryptic apology in Ann
Bathgate's school yearbook.
LEFT: Serious art student Ann
regarded most male classmates
as "jerks," yet fell in love with
"party dude" Kent.

ABOVE LEFT: A few years' difference — Potter (top row center) at his 1966 high school graduation.

ABOVE RIGHT: Kent Potter behind "Warning" sign at Lao Bao in 1971. Sign has notation, "LIFE" MAG — LARRY B, at top.

FACING PAGE: Always in a hurry (top), Kent discovered photojournalism in high school. By 1970 (bottom) the Quaker youth was riding helicopters in Cambodia with *Life* photographer Dick Swanson.

ABOVE: Huey lifts off;
MIDDLE: Maj. Jim
Newman (right) and
copilot John Oldham in
Newman's C&C ship;
BELOW: Crew chief fires
.50-cal. machine gun at
ground targets.

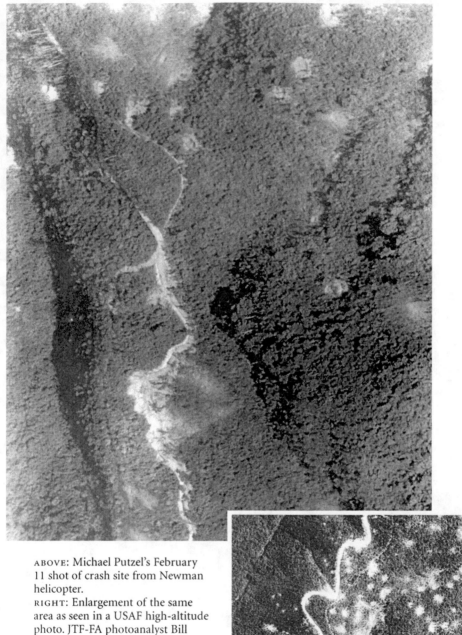

ABOVE: Michael Putzel's February 11 shot of crash site from Newman helicopter.

RIGHT: Enlargement of the same area as seen in a USAF high-altitude photo. JTF-FA photoanalyst Bill Forsyth compared these two pictures to identify crash site.

Hillside near Site 2062 where Horst, Jeff Price and Roger King found remains of anti-aircraft gun in March 1998. Jungles of southern Laos contain many crash sites, debris of trucks and weapons destroyed on Ho Chi Minh Trail, and remain dangerous due to unexploded ordnance.

his visa was about to expire," Putzel recalls. "I gave him the message and said, 'I can take your place.'" Henri declined, as he had earlier when Nick Ut volunteered to go. "He said, 'This is too big' and said he would find a way around the visa problem when he got back. He made it clear that the chance to go into Laos was too good to pass up."

Burrows, Huet, and Potter had staked out their seats on the second chopper in line. Potter, in fact, had bumped fellow UPI photographer Toshio Sakai, who was already waiting. Sakai was not pleased, but Kent, as an American and former chief of UPI's Saigon photo desk, had the right of seniority over his colleague. By some accounts, Shimamoto got a seat for *Newsweek* when another Japanese photographer, identity unknown, decided to bow out.

A fifth seat was taken by Sergeant Tu Vu, a young South Vietnamese Army photographer. Tu Vu had made friends in the civilian press corps and had confided to them a desire to become a professional photojournalist after the war. Harold Ellithorpe, a red-haired, gregarious American freelancer who ran his own small news service and often worked as a stringer-correspondent for *Life*, also climbed aboard, his intention being to write some text that could accompany Burrows's pictures. Among the other journalists coming and going at the helicopter pad was *Time* magazine photographer David Burnett. Only recently arrived in Vietnam and determined to wangle a ride into Laos, Burnett argued heatedly with the South Vietnamese major in charge, "trying every big-deal argument I could think of" to get a seat on the "press chopper." After a colleague pulled Burnett aside and warned him that he might be hurting his chances to go another day, he gave up and walked away. Burnett does not recall whether he took any pictures of the helicopter waiting to take off from Ham Nghi.

Ortiz, Burnett, and Putzel do not remember seeing each other there, like several others known to have been present at some point during the wait. These included an ABC-TV crew consisting of correspondent Howard Tuckner, cameraman Terry Khoo, and an unknown soundman. Many TV crew members carried a still camera along with their equipment and freelanced pictures to the wires.

Khoo, from Singapore, was one of the Vietnam press corps's most popular figures and had taken the last shots of Dana Stone and Sean Flynn as they rode out of Phnom Penh on their motorcycles the previous April. He was carrying a 35mm camera on this day as well, according to his friend and fellow cameraman, Tony Hirashiki. Whether he took any shots of the four photographers at Ham Nghi, and what became of that film, is not known. Terry Khoo was killed in Vietnam two years later; Tuckner also is deceased, as is the former UPI photographer, Sakai.

Shortly before noon, General Lam emerged from the TOC and headed for the helicopters parked on the nearby knoll. Suffering from a recent attack of gout, he walked with a wooden cane toward his command-and-control ship, trailed by several officers in battle dress. Normally, Lam's key staff officers rode with him in the command helicopter, but this was a special situation. "The North Vietnamese knew three months ahead that we were coming," says Lam, now retired in California. "They had put a lot of antiaircraft batteries in Laos, and we were worried about being shot down." He ordered Colonel Cao Khac Nhat, his G-3 (operations) officer, and Lieutenant Colonel Pham Vi, the G-4 (logistics) officer, to get aboard the second chopper with the photographers.

With twelve gear-laden people now on board, the pilot became concerned about the Huey's weight. He cranked up the engine and lifted the ship into the air for a quick hover test a few feet above the ground. It was overloaded; the word was passed from the cockpit to the crew chief, who gestured with his hands to indicate that one person would have to get off.

At first, nobody moved. None of the four photographers was ready to give up his seat. It was clear that Ellithorpe, the freelance writer, would be the odd man out, and Larry Burrows, ever the diplomat, resolved the matter with a deft dash of logic. "*Life* is a picture magazine," he told Ellithorpe over the sound of the idling engine. "You'll have to go later."

Disappointed but in no position to argue—and certainly not with Larry Burrows—Ellithorpe nodded, unbuckled his seatbelt, climbed down, and scurried off to the side, ducking his head in the running crouch of helicopter pads everywhere.

A minute or so later, Lam gave the order to depart, and the spectators near the pad shielded their faces from flying dirt as the five Lycoming turbines spooled up from a shriek to a full-throated roar. The pilots pulled pitch, and the dark-green Hueys lurched forward, tails up, main rotors chewing the humid air as they rose, turned in single file, and headed for Laos.

11 : Keisaburo Shimamoto

Like Burrows and Huet, Keisaburo Shimamoto had known war since childhood. Born in Seoul in 1937, during the Japanese occupation of Korea, he had returned with his family to Tokyo at some point during World War II. They were living there in 1945, as the dream of a Greater East Asia dominated by Japan disintegrated under a rain of firebombs from *B-san*, as the Japanese called the American B-29 heavy bombers.

On August 15, Keisaburo and his family, by then evacuated along with most of Tokyo's population to the countryside, gathered by their radio as Emperor Hirohito announced Japan's surrender and exhorted his people, who were hearing his voice for the first time, to "bear the unbearable." "I was choked with tears," Shimamoto would say in recalling the moment twenty years later. His school years coincided with the postwar Occupation, which he later called "the days of humiliation."

A bright student, Keisaburo was accepted at prestigious Waseda University in Tokyo, where he graduated in 1959 with a major in Russian literature. He became an admirer of Anton Chekhov, joined the Tokyo PEN literary society, and seemed destined for an academic or literary career. Always introspective, Shimamoto carried a diary-type notebook to record his thoughts and ideas. "To take a picture is a desperate undertaking," he once wrote.

His older brother Kenro, a reporter for the Tokyo daily *Yomiuri Shimbun*, helped to draw Keisaburo into a career in journalism. His big break came in 1960, when students protesting the U.S.-Japan Security Treaty attacked the Japanese Diet, touching off a melee in which a female Tokyo University student, Michiko Kanba, was fatally injured. Shimamoto was there taking pictures, and admitted later that he was surprised by the impact they had.

The pictures led to jobs at Toppu-Ya, a freelance photo agency and then a magazine. Almost three years later, on the last day of 1962, Keisaburo signed on as a reporter-photographer with Pan Asia Newspaper Alliance (PANA), a Tokyo-based news agency. Founded several years earlier by a journalist named Tokokazu So, PANA operated under the axiom "reporting of Asia, by Asians, and for the Asians." Its young, eager recruits were known as "photojournalists" and were that in a complete sense, for they wrote stories and took pictures. They also were expected to be proficient in English. But for all its ambitions, PANA struggled to compete with the wealthier, more entrenched Western news agencies on which it was modeled.

Covering the 1964 Summer Olympics in Tokyo along with other stories enabled Shimamoto to, as he put it, "frantically learn" to shoot better pictures, but he felt he was too old to relearn the English that he'd first studied in school. To succeed, he wrote later, "my only hope was my reckless mental strength and physical ability." Although his boss lamented to Shimamoto that he would have "no seniors to learn from" at PANA, as he might have at a more established agency or newspaper, there was at least one influential role model.

That was Akihiko Okamura, a freelancer who worked regularly for the agency covering major events, including the expanding war in Indochina, and enthralling the younger journalists with his swaggering, self-confident manner, unusual for the Japanese.

Shimamoto in particular was smitten by this swashbuckling character that everyone referred to by the affectionate diminutive "Oka-chan." Okamura's return from the war zone always stirred extra excitement. He would appear at the PANA offices "bringing the dust of the war and a smell of Vietnam," Shimamoto wrote later. "Young reporters, including myself, would follow his actions with enthusiastic eyes. As a contract reporter, he did not have to do what he didn't like." It was different from the daily routine that Shimamoto and the other regular staffers faced, and they wondered whether they would ever be able to emulate Okamura.

In late 1964, PANA sent Okamura back to Vietnam for a reporting stint. Watching the slouched figure going out the door, Shimamoto wished he could follow. "I felt it was something in which I could absorb myself while forgetting everything else," he said. What he wanted to forget is not clear, but at the beginning of 1965, brooding over what he called only "a certain death" and "a dark burden on my shoulders," he fled to the ancient capital of Kyoto, where he spent January 5, his twenty-eighth birthday, drinking in a small bar.

A month later, back in Tokyo, Shimamoto was devastated by a tragedy closer to home. His middle brother was killed in a motorcycle accident on a city street. Keisaburo, who was then still living at home with his mother, felt "something was really about to happen" to him. Shortly, it did. One day in May he returned from a news assignment to find a note on his desk from his editor. It instructed him to be at the nearby Alaska bar and coffee shop at five o'clock that afternoon.

Over cups of sake, the talk turned to Vietnam. The situation in Indochina was beginning to capture the attention of Japan's mass-circulation dailies. The South Vietnamese capital, Saigon, was plagued by political unrest and terrorist bombings. Nguyen Cao Ky, a flashy "air marshal" in a tailored black flying suit and purple scarf, was now the prime minister of the tenth South Vietnamese government in less than two years, and U.S. Marines, the first American ground troops, were being deployed to help defend the country against the communists.

When an *Asahi Shimbun* reporter managed to penetrate Viet Cong territory and return safely, his story made headlines. It was, Shimamoto noted, perhaps the first time since the end of the Pacific War that a war correspondent's report had played on the front page of Japan's most prestigious and pacifist-minded newspaper.

Meanwhile, PANA's own reporter, Okamura, had not been heard from for some time—not since he, too, went out to try to find his way into Viet Cong–held territory. In his absence, PANA had sent two other reporters to Vietnam on brief assignments. At the Alaska bar, the editor told Shimamoto, "If we send someone next time, it would be you."

It was not long after this that Shimamoto learned that indeed his turn had come. Although excited over being chosen for so important an assignment, he typically looked for the more cosmic message: What did it mean that he, born and raised in the midst of one war, was now about to experience another one?

In a long passage in his diary, Keisaburo noted that it was exactly twenty years since that day in August 1945 when he and his countrymen had listened to Emperor Hirohito's scratchy, unfamiliar radio voice announcing Japan's capitulation. His memories, he wrote, also were of a small friend who was killed by a strafing U.S. airplane, of "youngsters on the home front whose only hope was to become *kamikaze* pilots. B-29s were weaving through Japanese rocket artillery, which was a beautiful sight that decorated Tokyo's night sky. Small was the body of the friend who was lying just in front of the entrance to an air-raid shelter." The diary continued, "Twenty years thereafter, I am about to leave nonchalantly for the battlefield in South Vietnam. War buffets people with sufferings and smears them with humiliation. Do I want to experience such truths? Perhaps, I think so. Now I have no firm belief."

In his relentless self-examination, Shimamoto laid out two alternative formulas for reporting, which he said had been explained to him by one of his senior colleagues: "To investigate the subject in detail before setting out to do on-site reporting, or to launch into on-site reporting with clean slates and deepen knowledge in that process." He added, in what sounded like a schoolboy's rationalization for failing to do his homework, "I chose the latter. I wondered what use it would be to do a quick study of one country within a month before my departure. Moreover, since I am indolent by nature, I thought the latter approach was more fitting for me."

In Vietnam, Shimamoto was anything but indolent, performing well enough that PANA kept him there for two years. From June 1965 to July 1967, he was "Shima," a familiar, if rather reserved, figure on military operations and at the scenes of political unrest, earning the respect of other photographers for his cool courage.

When a Buddhist revolt against the Saigon government turned bloody in 1966, he was among a trio of journalists caught one day in what amounted to no-man's-land. Tim Page remembers how he, Shima, and Sean Flynn had taken cover behind a concrete porch wall, observing the action, when rebels behind the small house lobbed a grenade over the roof, nearly hitting an ARVN tank a few dozen yards from where they were crouched. Clearly assuming that the grenade had come from the house itself, the tank gunner swiveled his gun in the direction of the porch. The newsmen suddenly found themselves trapped, with nowhere to go but closer to the ground.

"We watched as that turret came around and trained straight at us," says Page. "If you're looking down the barrel of a ninety-millimeter gun, what are you going to do? There was that moment, when we thought the house was going to disappear and us with it. But Shima had an idea—he dug a white handkerchief from his pocket and stood up—slowly, very, very slowly, stood up, holding the white handkerchief in his hand." Somehow, the ARVN tank crew saw it, recognized it as a flag of truce, and held their fire.

Shimamoto returned to Tokyo a seasoned Vietnam War correspondent, looking for opportunities to further enhance his career. In January 1968, he left the financially struggling news service, signed a contract with the high-powered French agency Gamma, and returned to Saigon just as the Tet Offensive exploded across South Vietnam. After seven months he was back in Japan again, remaining there until early 1970, when he returned to Vietnam for a third tour, this time as a freelancer.

Most members of the Japanese press contingent in Saigon worked for newspapers and magazines, and while they remained a close-knit, clannish group, some reporters broke away from the cozy *kisha kurabu* (press club) habit that made journalism in Japan an exercise in controlled group-think, in which a real scoop was frowned upon because it might embarrass a competitor.

Outside Japan, the exceptions to this practice included a number of adventurous Japanese reporters who tried to cross the line to report what the war was like on the Viet Cong side. It was something that only Asian reporters dared to do—and certainly not without risk. The communist forces lived primitively and secretively, unaccustomed to outsiders. There was a danger of being killed by either side if fighting broke out, particularly if caught in U.S. air attacks or artillery barrage. Finally, those reporters who managed to pull off such a feat faced likely expulsion by the Saigon government once their stories appeared in print. Some Japanese journalists abroad also departed from the mold to freelance for top foreign news agencies and publications and as TV cameramen and soundmen.

On his return to Saigon as a freelancer in early 1970, Shimamoto found regular assignments with *Newsweek*, whose Vietnam bureau chief, Maynard Parker, took a special liking to him. After Parker moved to Hong Kong, his successor, Kevin Buckley, maintained the connection. "I didn't know him very well," Buckley says of Shimamoto today. "He was a pleasant guy, totally reliable and very well thought of at *Newsweek*. He didn't speak much English, but he delivered what we needed."

Shimamoto also had become close friends with Okamura, the PANA freelancer who had been his early model. They were often together, including during the days just prior to the helicopter shoot-down, and by virtue of having later written a book titled *He Died in Vietnam*, Okamura stands as more or less the final authority on Shimamoto. In this somewhat self-serving book, Okamura, since deceased, portrayed himself as a paternalistic guide and mentor whose advice was welcomed by the younger man he called "Kashimoto"— another foreshortened version of Shimamoto's full name—while his protégé was "inexperienced and lazy" and looking constantly to him, Okamura, for advice.

Some of this was provided, according to Okamura's account, when Shimamoto's wife, Yuko, flew from Tokyo to Saigon for a brief visit in December 1970. Okamura said that Yuko wanted to open a restaurant in Tokyo to be called Kitchen Shima, and it fell to him to persuade Keisaburo that he should go back to Japan to help her run the enterprise, saving and investing their earnings so that "he could eventually become a great news photographer." In fact, Okamura wrote, Shimamoto was ready to pack up and leave Vietnam in January 1971 but postponed his departure after learning that Yuko had landed a temporary job for several weeks on the western Japan island of Kagoshima and would not return to Tokyo until February.

Thus, Yuko's visit to Saigon would be the last time that she and her husband saw each other. But in staying on, Keisaburo still apparently intended for OPERATION LAM SON 719 to be his last combat photo assignment. In late January 1971, as press leaks in Washington confirmed that the increased military activity in I Corps was part of a South Vietnamese plan to invade Laos with U.S. support, Shimamoto, on assignment for *Newsweek*, was among the photographers who huddled in their Army ponchos at Camp Red Devil, Khe Sanh, and Lao Bao. But on February 5, he had had enough of the rain and cold and returned to Saigon for a few days' rest. Although the invasion was imminent, the sense of urgency was diminished by the continuing ban on reporters and photographers going into Laos.

Visiting Shimamoto's Saigon flat the next day, Okamura found his friend gray-faced with fatigue but eager to talk about the Laos operation. Shimamoto told of having been at the border at Lao Bao with the famous *Life* magazine photographer Larry Burrows, Toshio Sakai of UPI, and Koichiro Morita of *Yomiuri Shimbun*. He likened the coming battle in Laos to what he had seen during the North Vietnamese siege of Khe Sanh exactly three years earlier—heavy fighting, perhaps with many casualties.

During their conversation, Shimamoto also made a surprise proposal. He wanted to move into Okamura's apartment for the last few weeks before returning to Tokyo. That way, he explained, he could avoid the last month's rent on his own flat, recover the security deposit from the landlord, and settle with the Kayo restaurant, a favorite haunt of Japanese reporters, where he had run up a sizable bill. Okamura said he refused the request, even after Shimamoto "promised not to bring girls" to the apartment. That being resolved, Okamura announced his intention to fly north the next morning to cover the Laos invasion. Shimamoto replied that he planned to stay in Saigon another day before returning to the front. They agreed to rendezvous at Khe Sanh on Tuesday, February 9.

Shimamoto had dinner that night with Maynard Parker, by then *Newsweek*'s Hong Kong bureau chief, who was back in Saigon on a visit. The next evening, February 7, he went to the *Yomiuri* office. A few other Japanese journalists were there, and he cooked a meal for them. Although he was not present, Okamura later jotted down in his notebook what someone else had told him: "Kashimoto. His last night. Gingered pork."

The next day, February 8, Shimamoto himself was on a plane to Quang Tri as President Nguyen Van Thieu's palace officially announced that the invasion of Laos had begun at dawn that morning. When Shimamoto finally reached Khe Sanh on February 9, Okamura was not there as promised. Nobody knew that the resourceful Japanese freelancer had once again decided to take the big risk—this time masquerading as a South Vietnamese—to slip into Laos with the troops.

At Khe Sanh, Shimamoto did find Larry Burrows, Henri Huet, and several other photographers, and from them he learned that General Lam was considering a flying tour of the battle area the next day and might take a few journalists along. Even if space on the helicopter was tight, Shimamoto, as the camera representative for *Newsweek*, might have a good shot at a seat.

12 : Killing Zone

The five helicopters, General Lam's in the lead, headed south, paralleling the border to meet it where it abruptly angled eastward. Sitting in the open door of the second ship's cargo bay, Potter and Huet had unobstructed views of the mountainous green spine of Indochina, partly concealed in clouds and haze.

Within minutes they were circling to land at Firebase Hotel, the first of the three stops on Lam's itinerary. The artillery base had been established three days earlier on a narrow spur of Co Roc, a 2,400-foot mountain that was the area's dominant geological feature. The looming massif had been controlled for years by the *bo doi*, but this portion suddenly had become the new home of the 1st ARVN Division's artillery, whose 105mm and 155mm howitzers were supporting the forces moving west on Route 9.

On landing, Lam and his officers moved quickly to the base commander's sandbagged command post for a situation briefing. While the officers conferred, the photographers dismounted from their helicopter and wandered around, taking pictures of the gun crews in their revetments and, probably, of Lam himself. However, Lam does not remember having any conversation with the newsmen while at Firebase Hotel.

During the briefing, Lam was advised by radio that the next stop on his tour, Landing Zone Ranger South, was being subjected to probing attacks by enemy forces. The *bo doi* were wasting no time in feeling out the South Vietnamese positions. Lam, who considered the Rangers his best troops, decided he should get there as soon as possible.

Ranger South occupied another mountain ridge, fourteen miles to the northwest of Firebase Hotel. There, as elsewhere, U.S. planes had dropped 15,000-pound Daisy Cutter bombs to clear trees and foliage from the 1,600-foot ridge. Although an effective way of creating instant forward bases, the huge explosions also told the North Vietnamese precisely where the enemy would be.

Departing Firebase Hotel, Lam's Huey crossed above the Xepon River, then Route 9, thick with military vehicles. In its third day, OPERATION LAM SON 719 was already beginning to bog down. The heavy rains had turned parts of the road into a quagmire, and enemy troops were harassing the column with ambushes from thick underbrush that in some places grew right to the edge of the road. In the view of some U.S. officers, the ARVN was proceeding too cautiously, more concerned with setting up defensive bases than aggressively seeking out the enemy. It was a foreshadowing of things to come.

For reasons that remain unexplained to this day, the four other helicopters were slow in getting away from Firebase Hotel and, once airborne, lagged badly behind Lam's command ship, possibly even losing visual contact as they veered toward a more westerly heading, one that would cause them to miss their intended destination by a wide margin.

The most commonly accepted theory then—and today—is that the pilots of the photographers' helicopter, now in the lead, simply became lost over unfamiliar terrain. While conceding that he does not know what went wrong, General Lam rejects that thesis, however. "They were not lost, but the pilot may have been uncertain," he said in an interview in 1998.[1]

---

[1] Lam, who still speaks with emotion on the subject, refused to concede that the pilots might have erred and asked this author to make sure that the heroism and sacrifices of his troops in LAM SON 719 were properly acknowledged.

Hidden below the trees on a jungle slope, North Vietnamese gun crews had spent the last three days on extra-high alert. The South Vietnamese and the Americans had suddenly come to Laos in strength, with many helicopters in addition to the fast-moving bombers. But the *bo doi* were ready for the intruders, as they had been for weeks. The massive infusion of reinforcements, under the aegis of the NVA's Task Force 70, had placed hundreds of weapons of various sizes in caves, under hollowed-out hillsides, shrouded in thick jungle foliage. Out of necessity, the military units guarding the Truong Son Strategic Supply Route *had* become masters of concealment from above.

In the complex NVA order of battle, the sector of Front 702 north of Route 9 was defended by the 591st Air Defense Regiment, augmented by two companies of the 24th Battalion, 241st Air Defense Regiment. Their radar-controlled, twin-barreled 37mm guns, manned by crews of five to seven soldiers, could fire explosive shells, 150 rounds per minute, to an effective range of more than 3,000 meters, or nearly two miles.

Two days earlier, on the first day of the invasion, the regiment had claimed twenty-one helicopters shot down. That was an exaggerated figure, but there was no question that the fragile helicopters were extremely vulnerable to the rapid, devastating accuracy of the concealed guns.

Just after noon—faint at first, then growing louder—the unmistakable husky *whapwhapwhap* of U.S.-built UH-1 helicopters echoed along the jungle ridges. As the gunners stood to their weapons, they could see the dots approaching from the southeast. There were three of them, then a fourth, trailing at a short distance. Suddenly the helicopters emerged into clear view, moving from right to left across a window of sky framed by the trees.

Under the hillside, the long barrels of a 37mm, draped in camouflaging fronds, traversed from right to left, its radar console calculating the range and speed of the lead aircraft, adjusting and compensating as the target suddenly tilted into a perceptible turn to the right. The slender brass shells, linked together in the magazines, were ready for the command to fire ...

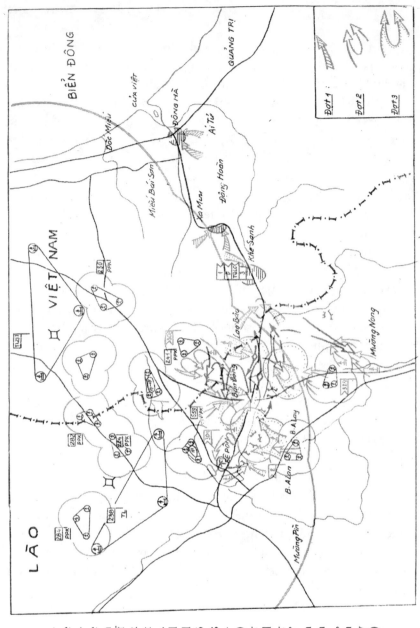

This remarkable hand-drawn North Vietnamese map of "Southern Laos—Route 9 Counteroffensive Campaign Feb. 8–March 23, 1971," shows forces of NVA's Binh Doan (task force) B70 arrayed against Saigon's invasion of Laos. Arrows mark 3-phased NVA attacks; notched pennants denote 4 of the 5 infantry divisions involved; rectangular flags are anti-aircraft artillery (PPK) regiments. In triangular gun positions, small weapons protected larger ones. Photographers' helicopter was shot down February 10 by 37-mm gunners of 241st PPK, northeast of Se Pon (Tchepone). (Map courtesy of Robert Destatte)

: :

Even without U.S. troops on the ground in Laos, the U.S. helicopter support units were keeping busy, flying the ARVN forces into their newly carved-out bases and providing the logistical and combat support necessary to keep the massive operation going. On this side of the border, too, the weather had lifted, affording a hazy visibility except where thick clouds still wreathed the higher peaks and filled the dark, jungled hollows with cottony wisps. In these improved conditions, pilots like Major James T. Newman, leading a hunter-killer team of 101st Airborne Division air cavalry, had a better crack at spotting the antiaircraft guns hidden in the forested hillsides.

Twenty-five years after its glory days as a paratroop unit at Normandy and Bastogne in World War II, the 101st Airborne had undergone a metamorphosis in Vietnam. No longer did its solders peel out from low-flying transports and float to earth by parachute. The famed Screaming Eagles had been remolded into the Army's second airmobile infantry division, an assault force built entirely around helicopters. The 101st Airborne pilots flew everything from the workhorse UH-1 Huey slicks that ferried troops into battle to the big CH-47 Chinook cargo lifters, all under a protective screen of Cobra and Huey gunships and an array of light observation craft.

Operating from a sprawling base called Camp Eagle southwest of Hue, with satellite firebases on hilltops along the Laotian border and overlooking the A Shau Valley, the division had done battle for three years with some of Hanoi's most battle-seasoned regulars in the most inhospitable terrain in Indochina. Whereas some U.S. combat units had already pulled out from Vietnam by early 1971 and others were packing to leave, the 101st Airborne was still intact and available for troubleshooting tasks. Augmented by a few aviation units brought up from the south, it caught the brunt of the mission to support the South Vietnamese invasion of Laos—and would pay dearly for that dubious honor.

The division's elite helicopter companies, with romantic and sinister names like Comancheros, Ghost Riders, Black Widows, and Phoenix, faced a battering from Hanoi's gunners in what later would be universally judged as the most dangerous sustained combat flying ever in Indochina.[2]

Leading the way in this maelstrom was the 2nd Squadron, 17th Air Cavalry, which in normal times served as the division's eyes, ears, and cutting edge and, during LAM SON 719, was additionally charged with coordinating all Air Cavalry support for the ARVN infantry, armor, ranger, and airborne forces in Laos. The Air Cav was a close-knit, swaggering, and frankly hard-drinking bunch, with various slogans that reflected their sense of uniqueness among the helicopter units. "On the seventh day the Lord rested, and the Cav flew," was one. "Out Front" was another. The patch worn by C Troop, the Condors, was a mean-looking bird on a branch above the slogan "Patience, my ass. I want to kill something."

In off-duty hours, the pilots liked to wear black Stetsons, affirming a direct line of descent from the hell-for-leather cavalry of the American Civil War and the Old West frontier. Periodically the military police would be called to some other unit's club at the Phu Bai base after a group of Stetson-wearing Condor pilots moved in and took over the bar, daring anyone there to demand the removal of their distinctive headgear.[3]

If any single individual personified this organization, it was Jim Newman, whose radio call sign, Condor Six, identified him as the commander of C Troop. A stocky, steel-nerved Georgia native who limped from bullet wounds in his left foot on a previous tour of duty, Newman flew his command-and-control ship like an outstretched

---

[2] Reported aircraft losses in LAM SON 719 have varied widely and in some cases appear inflated, partly due to confusion over those shot down, recovered, and returned to duty or written off later. Loss figures cited here were compiled from daily operational and maintenance data on orders of the 101st Airborne's deputy commander, Brigadier General Sidney Berry. By the end of the seven-week operation, the massed air defenses would destroy or damage beyond repair between 100 and 150 U.S. helicopters—nearly a fourth of the 660 choppers the Americans committed to LAM SON 719—and about a dozen South Vietnamese helicopters. Among 1,400 U.S. casualties in the debacle were 215 dead, 72 of them pilots and crewmen.

[3] C Troop operated from Phu Bai, the base near Hue from which the Hamburger Hill operation was staged two years earlier. It was dusty or muddy, depending on the season, offered minimal comforts, and was a frequent target of enemy rockets. Yet a popular slogan—"Phu Bai is all right"—expressed a GI sentiment that Phu Bai, whatever its deficiencies, was preferable to anything beyond its concertina-wired perimeter. Out there was the fabled A Shau Valley and the jungled ridges of the Annamites, all of it "Indian country."

sword; a century earlier he could have been one of Jeb Stuart's Rebel cavalry lieutenants.

He was a former master sergeant who had received a rare direct commission to officer rank. Now thirty-five, a trifle old for a combat pilot, he regularly performed feats of derring-do that left even seasoned combat veterans gaping in amazement. His easy, just-one-of-the-boys manner and soft drawl concealed a hard-core airborne gladiator who liked to do things his way and let the results answer any critics. And though Newman's sometimes rash heroics could draw mixed reviews at higher command levels, there were no skeptics among his own men, who believed Condor Six was capable of anything—except leaving somebody behind.

Charles Vehlow, a Cobra chopper pilot who commanded C Troop's gunship platoon and flew cover for Newman on an almost daily basis, remembers him as "one of the two most courageous and selfless combat leaders I ever had the opportunity to meet and serve with. He would stop at nothing to not only complete the mission, but more importantly to take care of any downed pilots or air crew members."

Says Charles Davis, a former crew chief who had no choice but to go along on some of Newman's harrowing forays, "Major Newman never asked another pilot or crew to do something dangerous while he watched." Davis still refers to the command Huey as "one-five-five"—the last three digits of the ship's tail number. "Brave leaders like Newman instill courage, even in eighteen- and nineteen-year-old kids. I believe that James Newman—and luck—are the reasons I came back from Vietnam alive."

With Charlie Troop "op conned," or placed under direct operational control of General Lam's headquarters, it was Newman who led the first flight of assault helicopters into Laos on February 8, and he would be called to attend many of Lam's daily intelligence briefings, dispensing on request his own best assessment of the tactical situation in Laos. "It was information he wasn't getting from his own people," Newman remembers thirty years later.

In the first ten days of LAM SON 719, Newman also would twice defy astonishing odds to rescue stranded fliers, earning a Silver Star for gallantry and a recommendation for the Medal of Honor, the highest award for valor. On the second occasion, he maneuvered his Huey through a storm of enemy fire to retrieve four crewmen of a U.S. medevac helicopter that had been shot down on a besieged ARVN Ranger base. Unknown to him at the time, a fifth American had stayed behind, trapped at the last moment by mortar explosions.

Rescuing downed colleagues being the leitmotif of his leadership, Newman found even the inadvertent failure to recover everyone from LZ Ranger North particularly galling—and believes it may have been the reason that his Medal of Honor application was downgraded to the second-highest award, the Distinguished Service Cross. Another former pilot speculated that this may have been because Newman was *too* good—he used the terrain features to screen his helicopter from ground fire and emerged from the episode without any bullet holes in the aircraft.[4]

But saving lives was as much a creed among the chopper pilots as was killing the enemy: Nobody was to be left behind, no matter what it took. Medal of Honor recommendations aside, "there were many Jim Newmans," says retired Lieutenant Colonel Robert Clewell, who commanded another 101st Airborne Division helicopter unit, the Comancheros, in Laos. "There seemed to be plenty of heroism, it was contagious out there, and guys couldn't seem to show enough of it."

These acts of courage were "not particularly well documented" or "well understood" at the time, Clewell believes, partly because the news media was not there to see it; also, the men of the 101st Airborne were not talking about it much when they came back from Laos. "That could have had to do with the political climate in the United States, a perception that whatever was said would only add to the controversy over this most unpopular of modern wars," he says. "Guys like us, in the 101st, bought into keeping our mouths shut because we were ordered to."

Later on, the image of South Vietnamese soldiers fleeing from Laos by clinging to the skids of U.S. helicopters would became a metaphor for the overall failure of Lam Son 719, overshadowing the courage of those South Vietnamese troops who stood and fought

---

[4] Looking back on Vietnam, and especially on Operation Lam Son 719, with the perspective of many years, Newman himself could marvel, even "get the shakes," at the official descriptions of what he had achieved and survived, as well as remember that, in that time and place, there was "no fear."

against a superior enemy, not to mention the U.S. pilots who supported them.

But all of that still lay ahead on February 10, the third day of LAM SON 719. Just after noon, about the same time that General Lam was conferring with his officers at Firebase Hotel, Jim Newman was on the airstrip back at Khe Sanh, watching his C Troop operations officer, Captain Malcolm Jones, execute a skidding, semi–crash-landing in a Huey whose controls had been damaged by a single .51-caliber bullet. It was all in a day's work, and Newman told Jones to "get another bird" and be ready to relieve him on patrol over A Luoi, nine miles west of the border and just beyond the farthest point of advance by the South Vietnamese armored spearhead. Minutes later Newman himself was airborne, heading west into Laos on his second sortie of the day. Like Mac Jones, he was almost certain to encounter enemy ground fire around A Luoi, if not beforehand. The dark-green hills were seeded everywhere with antiaircraft guns.

In the military argot of the time and place, Newman's C Troop command-and-control Huey was also the command aircraft for a hunter-killer combination known as a "pink team"—a term blending "white" for the small OH-6 Loach, or Little Bird, scout helicopters, and "red" for the AH-1 Cobra gunships.

The pink team was the bait-and-switch of Air Cav warfare: Find the enemy—by provoking him into revealing his location, if necessary—then kill him. Darting low over the rugged landscape, the teardrop-shaped OH-6 Little Bird would locate a ground target—sometimes by drawing fire from a concealed bunker or gun position—mark it with a smoke rocket or CS riot-gas grenade, then skitter away to let the death-dealing Cobras, or in some cases the U.S. Air Force fast-movers, Air Force F-4s and other fighter bombers, patrolling high overhead, hurl rockets or bombs into the jungle.

Not only did Newman conduct this lethal orchestra; he had written his own arrangement. Newman customized his Huey with side-mounted rocket pods, adding still more firepower to the formidable pink team. The forward artillery observer, riding in the cargo bay, carried explosive satchel charges and CS riot-gas canisters to fling at suspected bunkers in hopes of flushing enemy troops into the open.

Great danger was inherent in these exposed, low-level tactics, especially in Laos where the *bo doi* gunners knew their business. Their Russian-made .51-caliber machine guns, ubiquitous and made to order for knocking down helicopters, were sometimes deployed in triangular units of three that made evasive action difficult. Often these guns also guarded the larger and even more lethal 37mm and 57mm anti-aircraft guns.

Two days before, on the opening day of LAM SON 719, Newman had spotted smoke coming from a hillside and moved closer to investigate, only to find the "orange softballs"—the tracers from a 37mm—coming his way. "The major laid the helicopter on its side and dropped altitude fast," recalls Charles Davis. "The Cobras tried to cover us by firing rockets at the gun position." The enemy gunners had missed, and though it wasn't clear whether the gunships had scored any retaliatory hits, Davis remembers Newman telling his copilot afterward that only the Cobra pilots had enabled him to escape and should be recommended for medals.

Now, on his second foray of this new day, Newman's command ship and its Cobra gunship escort, piloted by Charles Vehlow, were flying west into Laos toward A Luoi. They followed the brown stripe of Route 9, staying just above treetop level, where sheer speed could minimize danger—the hurtling choppers could be over and gone before enemy troops had time to react. Below were clusters of tanks and other military vehicles, all aimed, if not actually moving, in a westerly direction. Up ahead—beyond what U.S. officers liked to call the "pointy end of the spear"—was alien territory where everything that moved or could be glimpsed under the trees was considered hostile. Fifteen miles farther on was Tchepone, the shabby Laotian district town that marked the westernmost fringe of the Ho Chi Minh Trail—the designated main objective of LAM SON 719.

It was about then that Jim Newman first observed the string of helicopters off to his left, at nine or ten o'clock. There were four of them—all Hueys—flying in single file at about eighty knots on a northwesterly course that would cross his path about a half-mile ahead. Three were flying together, the fourth trailing behind. At that distance he could not identify their markings—they could be American or South Vietnamese—but he quickly realized that if they held to their current heading they would fly directly over the ridgelines where he had narrowly dodged the antiaircraft gun two days earlier. "We didn't have any idea who they were, but we knew they were going to get shot at, too," Newman remembers.

Newman banked right to follow the unknown aircraft while simultaneously trying to raise them on the radio. Using the open guard channel that all pilots were supposed to monitor, Newman called: "This is Condor Six ... helicopters flying north, flight of four ... there's a thirty-seven-millimeter gun right in front of you ... get out of there!" For a minute or more, he repeated the warning, again and again. No acknowledgment from the mystery flight. "We kept calling on the guard channel, on all frequencies," Newman remembers. "Either those pilots weren't tuned to the guard frequency, or maybe they didn't understand English. We couldn't get them to answer."

Other American pilots, alerted by the radio hubbub, joined in a chorus of alarms. Amid the cacophony Newman recognized the voice of his squadron commander, Lieutenant Colonel Robert Molinelli, who also had seen the situation developing. Molinelli would say later that the unidentified helicopters "were heading right for the heaviest concentration of thirty-seven-millimeter guns in that part of Laos."

It was coming up on thirty minutes past noon. Now watching the four Hueys from half a mile away, Newman observed a perceptible change of course, first to a northerly heading and then to the northeast—apparently the start of a sweeping right turn. Still, no radio response.

Then, Newman remembers: "I saw smoke in the trees, and the tracers going up." The orange balls streamed unerringly toward the lead helicopter. It suddenly faltered, then vanished in a horrific bloom of yellow-orange flame. A direct hit in the fuel tank, Newman surmised. Cobra pilot Vehlow thought the rounds hit the crew compartment. The Huey "basically disintegrated," he says. Pieces of debris, momentarily silhouetted in the fireball, tumbled toward the mountainside.

For what seemed endless seconds, the other three Hueys flew on, appearing to change, even reverse course. Then there was more smoke in the trees, more orange tracers arching upward. A round smashed into the rotor mast of the third helicopter, breaking it off. The blades spun crazily away, and the Huey's tail boom separated from the fuselage, which, in Newman's words, "dropped like an egg" into the jungle.

Others remember the incident similarly but with added details. Cleve "Slim" Pickens, a C Troop pilot on an unrelated mission, remembers that his own transponder registered the *beep-beep* of a radar lock-on just before the gun fired on the other helicopters. He remembers the rotor blades whipping away as the second Huey plunged downward.

Charles Davis, in the left-side gunner's seat on the command ship, had realized, as Newman did, that the line of Hueys would pass near the ridge where they'd been fired on two days before. "At first, the radio talk between the pilots was that the gun must have been already destroyed [by the Cobras]," he says. "The helicopters did not respond to radio communications. As they came in range, the gun started firing. The first helicopter blew up in flames, the second was hit around the mast and the blades came off, and it burst into flames as it hit the ground." The Americans could hear nothing over the hammering of their own rotors and the radio chatter in their flight helmets. The whole thing was like watching a silent movie.

The hillside where the first helicopter had fallen was an instant sea of fire and roiling brown smoke. Newman, whose aircraft was now taking .51-caliber antiaircraft fire from the ground, edged as close as he dared, instructing his crew to look for signs of anyone having escaped the cauldron. "We could see helicopter wreckage but not much else—no sign of people," says Newman, who today lives in Fayetteville, North Carolina. "It was pretty clear that nobody was there. Nobody alive, anyway."

Newman radioed C Troop's command post at Khe Sanh to report the destruction of the two Hueys. No one knew yet whether they were American or South Vietnamese. Orders soon diverted Newman's team to check out the report of another crash, an army cargo helicopter several miles away. But he lingered long enough to make contact with a U.S. Air Force combat patrol loitering overhead and ask for help in taking out the gun position. Recognizing the now-familiar Condor Six call sign, the pair of F-4 Phantoms dove through the overcast and blasted the hillside. Turning from the scene, Jim Newman observed with satisfaction that the fast-movers had found the hidden menace that the Cobras had earlier missed: "They came in right under the cloud cover and took it out."

As General Lam stepped down from his helicopter at LZ Ranger South, officers advised him that just moments before his arrival "something blew up in the air." It had sounded like two explosions, perhaps two kilometers northwest of the base. It was close enough that some in the Ranger garrison reported seeing a fireball. Lam, realizing that the entourage that should have been right behind him was nowhere in sight, immediately feared the worst. "I waited four or five minutes, but they don't come," he recalled. "And then I know. They have been shot down.... We have suffered a big loss."

In minutes, the news was confirmed—two helicopters were down. Two others had escaped the area and returned directly to Ham Nghi. Lam cancelled the rest of his battlefield tour and headed back as well. As if losing two top staff officers and two helicopters wasn't bad enough, Colonel Nhat had carried a briefcase containing maps, operational plans, even the secret radio codes for LAM SON 719.

Phase One—the initial deployment into Laos—had been completed, but the possibility that the documents would fall into enemy hands meant that the rest of the plan, including the capture of Tchepone, would have to be revised. . . .

13 : "Feared Dead"

Back at Ham Nghi, *Time* magazine photographer David Burnett had busied himself for the past hour, taking shots of Vietnamese troops loading onto trucks and helicopters, as well as U.S. heavy-lift helicopters carrying slings of water and ammunition. Routine stuff, but the magazine might use one or two.

Walking past the sandbagged South Vietnamese TOC, Burnett encountered the ARVN major with whom he'd argued earlier over a seat on the helicopter standing outside. "I think your friends maybe shoot down in Laos," the major said, with a nervous laugh. Vietnamese often laughed in moments of stress, a trait misunderstood by foreigners. Burnett was confused. "What did you say?" "Your friends," the major replied, now serious. "I think helicopter shoot down in Laos." He turned and disappeared inside the bunker, leaving Burnett to make sense of what he had just been told.

My God, he thought. *Could it be true?*

Burnett wanted desperately to charge into the command center and demand more information from the major. But such places were secured against outsiders. You didn't just walk in unannounced. He decided to wait, hoping to catch the major coming out again.

About then, John Saar appeared. The *Life* bureau chief was newly returned from Saigon, where he had rushed to write the story and deliver Burrows's film of the mistaken Navy bombing attack four days earlier. Saar's first question to Burnett was, "Have you seen Larry Burrows?"

Burnett was about to repeat what the major had told him when they saw Hal Ellithorpe coming down the path from the direction of the helicopter pad. Burnett was instantly relieved. He knew that Ellithorpe had planned to go into Laos with Burrows and the others, and now they must have returned. "It can't be Larry's ship that's down," Burnett remembers saying. "There's Ellithorpe. He was on it with Larry."

But any relief was cut short upon learning that Ellithorpe had never left. Ellithorpe explained how he had been bumped from the overweight helicopter at the last moment, how Burrows had told him he'd have to get off and wait for another day. Ellithorpe knew nothing of the reported crash and was as disbelieving as the others that the helicopter could be down.

To David Burnett, there seemed little doubt that the report was solid, but grappling with the enormity of it was nearly impossible, especially without more information. They waited outside the command post, telling each other that silence was not necessarily bad news. It could just be an error, a horrible mix-up. Apparently a helicopter had crashed, but there had been five in the flight, and it was not necessarily the one carrying the photographers. Larry, Henri, and the others could be on the ground with the South Vietnamese troops, as planned.

Shortly, a group of men came from the direction of the helicopter pad. In the lead was General Lam, hobbling quickly on his cane. He was back safely; he'd know what happened. But Lam ignored them as he limped past and entered the TOC. His grim expression told them that the news, from Lam's own perspective, was not good.

Within minutes, the Vietnamese major emerged again. This time he confirmed to Burnett and Saar that not one but two helicopters had been shot down, including the aircraft that carried Lam's two staff officers, Colonels Nhat and Vi, and the four civilian journalists—eleven people in all. A rescue operation was planned. That was all he could say at the time. He did not mention what was now Lam's primary concern—not the helicopter, not his two staff officers, but the briefcase carried by Colonel Nhat. It contained the battle plans and communications codes for OPERATION LAM SON 719, a windfall to any enemy that found it.

Deciding they probably wouldn't learn more for the moment, Saar and Burnett caught a helicopter back to Quang Tri, from where they could call their Saigon office. It was important that the Burrows family hear the news from Time, Inc., not from radio news broadcasts or phone calls from other reporters.

Mike Putzel, though he was not with Burnett and the others, recalls an experience similar to theirs. "I was walking past the TOC, and someone came out and said there was a helicopter down in Laos." He could also hear a field radio inside, voices in English, "squawking that helicopters were down in Laos." It meant that the U.S. advisers to the South Vietnamese were tuned in and were discussing the still-fragmentary report. Putzel's memory of that moment is otherwise hazy; he is sure only that he decided immediately to hitch a helicopter ride back to Quang Tri and Camp Red Devil, the nearest point from which he could call Saigon. He also needed to retrieve a rucksack and a boonie hat that Henri Huet had left behind. If Henri came back, they'd be waiting for him at Red Devil.

Five hundred miles south in Saigon, in the AP bureau on the fourth floor of the Eden Building, lead writer George Esper was hammering out an early version of the daily war roundup on his typewriter; it would be updated in a couple of hours with new information from the Five O'clock Follies.

Esper was legendary among colleagues and military press information officers for his relentless reporting and his ability to solve Vietnam's idiosyncratic phone systems. His byline was a fixture atop the AP's daily war roundup, a story of record that incorporated the major events of the war, from battlefield to briefing room, woven together in 800–1,000 words every afternoon. Each day's roundup—based on on-the-record claims and denials from the Follies, reports from staffers in the field, official radio broadcasts, and information gleaned from various U.S. and Vietnamese sources—became a singular block of war activity unto itself yet flowing seamlessly from the previous day and into the next. As the anchor piece of the AP's daily Saigon report, it was as comprehensive and, we dared to believe, as accurate a reflection of the conflict's progress as could be found. It was the foundation of Vietnam coverage for hundreds of U.S. newspapers and, for many of them, the only war story they used on a daily basis.

The phone on Esper's desk rang. Through the distant hiss of static he recognized the voice of Mike Putzel, calling from the press camp at Quang Tri. Mike asked for me. I picked up the extension in my cramped office off the newsroom. It was a call we'd been waiting for with apprehension. An hour or so earlier, an officer at the MACV press office had tipped us to an unconfirmed South Vietnamese report of a helicopter down in Laos, possibly with civilians aboard. No names or other details. A call to the South Vietnamese military press office had elicited no confirmation or details. At that time we knew only that Henri Huet had delayed his return to Saigon in order to be among the first journalists into Laos.

Mike and I were both accustomed to the military phone system's fadeouts and sudden, unexpected line breaks. He spoke loudly and slowly, pacing his words so I could understand him the first time and not have to interrupt with questions as I scribbled notes:

> A VNAF helicopter ... has been shot down in Laos.... All aboard are missing and feared dead.... They include ... four civilian news pho-tographers. They are ... Henri Huet of AP ...

Although I was half-prepared for it, everything sank. The bottom seemed to fall out of my chair.

Please, no. Not Henri.

"Larry Burrows of *Life* magazine ..."

Oh, no.

The bureau secretary, Tran Mong Tu, was standing near my desk. "Tu-tu," as we called her, was still in mourning for her soldier-hus-band, who had been killed in combat just weeks after they were mar-ried. George Esper and a few others gathered in the office doorway, watching me gravely as I took down Mike's information. Only their faces spoke.

"Kent Potter of United Press International ..."

They seemed to be waiting for me to hold up a hand and say: "Wait. Hold it. It's not true."

"Keisaburo Shimamoto, of *Newsweek* magazine. ..."

That was four. Mike gave me the rest of what he knew: Seven others were on the Huey, including Sergeant Tu Vu (the Army photographer), two senior South Vietnamese colonels, and the VNAF helicopter's four-man crew. Witnesses were quoted as saying the chopper had exploded in the air. There was fire on the mountainside but no sign of survivors. A second Huey had gone down at the same time. A pilot was understood to have overflown the site and reported seeing bodies on the ground. The South Vietnamese were planning to send a search team to the site.

It was a story still in fragments, not all of which fit. We were immediately skeptical about a search. It seemed unlikely that Saigon's forces, which already had their hands full with the enemy forces in Laos, would devote resources to a single crashed helicopter in the middle of hostile territory. No one in Saigon knew yet about the briefcase containing General Lam's battle plans.

Esper was in angry denial, rejecting the whole idea of the crash, insisting that we couldn't be sure that Putzel's information was accurate. "It's only a Vietnamese field report," he said. "It could be all wrong, a mix-up." But George knew, as did we all, that the information had that special resonance of truth. It might be incomplete, and wrong in some details, but reports of that kind did not materialize from nothing.

From my office I could see across the newsroom to where three framed portraits of Associated Press staff members killed previously in Vietnam hung on the wall: Huynh Thanh My. Bernard Kolenberg. Oliver Noonan. All photographers. These things happened, and they could happen to any of us at any time. But knowing that was not the same as being ready for it.

Sometimes the person killed was someone you hardly knew, maybe someone you wished you'd known better. But, Henri Huet?

Impossible.

Henri, who was in many ways the heart and soul of the AP's Saigon bureau—the class act, the embodiment of what we all would wish to be like as war correspondents—could not just be gone in a flash.

From the distance of three decades, it seems strange that our grief could be so controlled. There were tears—tears of shock, of anger, of frustration. But no one fell apart. People were stunned into silence, or consoled each other, trying to grasp the reality of an event that had none. It was, on a lesser scale, like the assassination of John F. Kennedy: the inescapable fact, the denial that would not drive the fact away; the cold realization that all was suddenly different, a new and incomprehensible context in which life henceforth would be lived.

The sorrow would come. For the moment, the AP staff was pervaded by a strong wave of solidarity, words like "kinship" and "brotherhood" taking on sudden new clarity.

As always on such occasions, practical demands intruded. No matter what the event, our job was to report it. Four journalists missing and maybe dead; that was big news. Someone had to write the story, and by unspoken agreement, a loss of life in our own circle required a bureau chief's byline. It reflected the burden of command, just as did letters of condolence written by commanders to the families of dead soldiers.

I had never done anything like it before and have not since. It should have been difficult, writing through tears. But the words rolled out of my typewriter like any other breaking story:

URGENT

SAIGON, FEB. 10 (AP)—A SOUTH VIETNAMESE HELI-COPTER CARRYING FOUR CIVILIAN NEWS PHOTOGRA-PHERS WAS SHOT DOWN OVER THE HO CHI MINH TRAIL IN LAOS ON WEDNESDAY, APPARENTLY KILLING THEM AND SEVEN OTHER PERSONS ABOARD.

AMONG THOSE MISSING AND PRESUMED DEAD WERE HENRI HUET, 43, OF THE ASSOCIATED PRESS; LARRY BUR-ROWS, 44, OF LIFE MAGAZINE; KENT POTTER, 23, OF UNITED PRESS INTERNATIONAL, AND KEIZABURO SHI-MAMOTO, 34, OF NEWSWEEK.

As a Vietnamese operator punched the copy into a teletype transmitter that would send it by radio circuit to Manila, undersea cable to San Francisco, and land-line to New York—all in a matter of minutes—Esper was back at his typewriter, swiftly retooling his big-picture

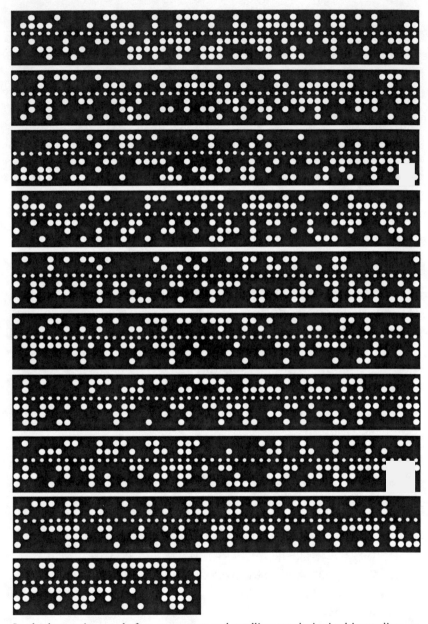

In the last major war before computers and satellites revolutionized journalism, reporters relied on the same tools used in World War II and Korea. AP Saigon's teletype operators punched news copy into perforated tape, ran it through a radioteletype transmitter to New York at then-swift 60 words per minute. At the receiving end, the coded impulses were reconverted into words on a teleprinter. This recreated tape is the lead paragraph of AP's first story on the February 10 helicopter crash. *(Perforated tape recreated by Les Glenister.)*

roundup, still leading with the Laos operation as the main event but incorporating the known details of the crash.

Other staffers were on the phones, calling military spokesmen, as well as the UPI, *Time,* and *Newsweek* bureaus. As was often true in such situations, we lacked the hard facts, the biographical data, about people that we knew well. How old *was* Kent Potter? What year was Henri wounded? When did Larry Burrows start covering Vietnam? Is Keisaburo with an *s* or a *z*? Where and who are the next of kin?

Except for some sketchy information about Henri, none of this was in the bureau files that were stored in large loose-leaf binders in cabinets under the counter that separated the news desks from the reception area. In a message to New York, we asked AP's Foreign Desk to ask *Life* magazine for biographical details on Burrows, knowing it would be hours, given the twelve-hour time difference, before anyone responded. A similar message went to the Hong Kong bureau; someone there might come up with the information sooner.

Yet another message gave the AP Radio Desk in New York the customary pronouncer for a difficult name: "Awn-REE Hugh-ET." Without that guidance, Ed White observed, rip-and-read radio newscasters would be calling him everything from "Henri Hugh-ay" to "Henry Hewitt." And because no one understood better than wire-service journalists the long reach and sudden impact of breaking news, we asked that certain people—Henri's fiancée in Tokyo, former colleagues in Maine, California, and points between, be personally notified of what had happened.

A few responses were almost instantaneous; others would trickle in over the next forty-eight hours. In Manila, AP bureau chief John Nance—the former photo editor who five years earlier had shown Henri's pictures from An Thi to Larry Burrows—summed it up for everyone, in wire-service cablese: "Sorriest."

I called Vientiane and left a message at the hotel for Terry Wolkerstorfer, a Saigon AP staffer who had gone there to backstop the Laos invasion story in the unlikely event that some operational details should come available there. Terry soon called back. Before I could tell him why I had called, he said, "It's Henri, isn't it?" Neither of us remembers how he knew—most likely by rumor circulating among the small foreign press contingent there.

In Saigon, word graduated quickly from rumor and raced through the press corps. Other news organizations, having learned of it from their reporters up north or by word of mouth in the city, were lighting up our phones, asking what we knew about a helicopter crash in Laos. From next door, NBC reporters and cameramen came in to find out details and share our grief over Henri Huet.

The normal rules of competition were temporarily suspended. The entire press corps was entitled to this story, to know what we knew. Even so, we doled out information carefully, using the customary qualifiers—the helicopter was only "missing," its occupants "apparently" killed or "presumed" dead. Without absolute confirmation, it was a time to tread softly. Everybody wanted to commiserate; nobody wanted to say there was no hope.

It was right that Ed White, who spent as much time on detached duty in Vietnam as he did at his home base in Tokyo, should be in Saigon at the time. He had been particularly close to Henri. When Henri was wounded in 1967, it was White, then the Saigon bureau chief, who had escorted him back from Danang and put him on a medevac flight to the United States.

Later, during Henri's unhappy year of exile in Tokyo, it was Ed White, the news editor there, who shored him up. It was now Ed White who volunteered to write a profile of Henri for the wire. It was cathartic for Ed White to be able to tell readers everywhere what his old friend was like.

Although some of the U.S. officers and GIs in Vietnam had trouble understanding Henri's French-accented English or pronouncing his name, Ed wrote, "They knew he had been, and would go again, any place with them—with no favors or special treatment asked." Noting that Huet had won the Capa Award for "superlative photography requiring exceptional courage and enterprise," he closed by saying: "That sums up the work of Henri Huet. He also was a superlative human being."

After leaving Vietnam the previous year, Horst Faas had taken up a new assignment as AP's roving photographer for Asia, based in Singapore. It was in that role that he had recently been with his old friend Larry Burrows in India. It was again in that capacity—and by the sheerest coincidence—that he had been flying from Singapore to

Saigon on February 10, at the very hour that the helicopter was going down in Laos.

Horst walked unsuspectingly into the AP bureau, into a scene of shock and sorrow over the loss of Henri, his former star photographer, and the others. And when Nick Ut returned a few hours later from up north, unaware of what had happened, it fell to Horst to tell Nick about the death of his idol, the man who had given him his nickname, who had gently rebuffed his offer to fly to Laos in his place. Nick took the news hard. For a time he sat in the photo office, his face tear-streaked, saying little.

That evening, Saigon photo chief Jim Bourdier, Carl Robinson, and I went to the small studio apartment that Henri kept as a private hideaway, to collect his personal possessions for safekeeping. None of us had ever been there before. We found Spartan surroundings—a bed, couch, small TV set, some magazines, camera gear, civilian clothes and field uniforms hanging in a closet. It was very much in keeping with the self-sufficient lifestyle that we recognized but no more than a sketchy outline of the complex individual who lived there.

Following his phone call to Saigon, Mike Putzel went to the daily news briefing at the press camp at Camp Red Devil and, after the military officers finished, asked to speak. To a sea of staring faces, he gave out what details were then known about the helicopter and its missing passengers. Although the information was sparse, Putzel knew more than the military did about what was, after all, a peripheral event to the main story of LAM SON 719. One of his concerns was that, in the uproar over the more celebrated civilian photographers, Tu Vu, the ARVN photographer who was a personal friend, not be forgotten.

David Burnett arrived at the press camp during the briefing—attended, he thought, by "every journalist in Eye Corps." As he recalls, "The atmosphere was funereal, and as I got to the door, Brian Barron of the BBC whispered, 'Larry Burrows is dead. Crashed in Laos.' I already knew this, but hearing him say the words just caused me to be overcome with grief." Burnett then saw Putzel, "who looked at me with the same woeful eyes I must have had. I started to say, 'How could it be? I was just with them. Henri was just here.' Before I could ramble on, Mike put his arm around me and motioned me to start walking with him. In a wonderful fatherly way he calmed me down."

In the absence of solid information, rumors flourished. There were persistent reports of bodies being sighted on the ground, even speculation about possible survivors. None of this could be substantiated, and by the next day we were desperate to know more.

From an Army friend at Red Devil, Putzel learned that there had been an American witness to the crash—a helicopter pilot named Major James Newman. The next day, Mike hitched a ride back to Khe Sanh, where he asked around and finally found Major Newman at C Troop's makeshift command post, a couple of metal Conex containers set up near the busy airstrip. Newman, in his laconic Georgia manner, related the events of the day before—the line of unknown helicopters heading into dangerous territory, the unanswered radio calls, the sudden explosion of one helicopter and the disintegration of the second.

The conversation got around to the crash site itself; Putzel wished he could see what it looked like. Newman had an idea—why not fly out there and have a look? They could go with armed escort, perhaps get close enough to take some pictures. But only on one condition, Newman added: that the reporter promise not to reveal how he got there. It would, after all, be a violation of the strict no-civilians-in-Laos rule. Putzel readily agreed; it was worth trying, even on those terms. But it also was dangerous business. The offending antiaircraft gun supposedly had been taken out by the U.S. Air Force F-4s, but there were many more hidden in the mountain slopes and hollows.

Escorted by two Cobra gunships and a Loach, Newman flew as close to the site as he dared—below 10,000 feet, by his own recollection—but still far enough away that Putzel needed a 200mm telephoto lens to get shots of the scorched hillside and what looked like traces of a roadway curling along the upper ridge. He flew back to Khe Sanh, and then to Quang Tri, with the film.

While it became clear after two days that any serious attempt at rescue or recovery was out of the question, General Lam's headquarters announced that the Hac Bao (Black Panthers), a commando unit with special training in jungle warfare, had been ordered to go to the crash site. The reason for this emerged when military sources in Saigon reported that important papers—Colonel Nhat's briefcase containing the plans and codes for LAM SON 719—had been lost in the crash. Today, Lam himself says Rangers from LZ Ranger South "tried to reach the crash site but they could not find it."[1]

Because the wreckage lay about 100 meters downhill from a section of the Ho Chi Minh Trail, it was reasonable to assume that the *bo doi* explored the site. Whether they found and buried any human remains, or recovered Colonel Nhat's secret documents, was anyone's guess. But when Hill 31, a firebase manned by ARVN airborne troops, was overrun by communist forces a few weeks later, Colonel Nguyen Van Tho, a brigade commander, and Captain Le Chau, a staff officer, were among those captured. They survived and would describe later how they had been taken to be interrogated at an NVA command bunker in the jungle, where the walls were covered with maps showing the location of every forward base and position of South Vietnamese forces—all of it chillingly accurate.

A strong indication that communist troops did inspect the crash site came the day after, from no less a source than the Viet Cong's "clandestine" National Liberation Front radio broadcasts, which we monitored regularly in the Saigon bureau and which proved especially useful during periods of heightened war activity. The broadcast claimed that two "puppet" (i.e., South Vietnamese) helicopters had been shot down in Vietnam's Quang Tri Province by "National Liberation Front" forces at 1445 hours on February 10, killing "two colonels, three majors, and many other commanding officers" of Military Region I.

Undoubtedly this referred to the Laos incident, but it was a particularly brazen mixture of fiction and fact. The broadcast credited the Viet Cong with the helicopter shootdown actually achieved by North Vietnamese gunners whose presence in Laos was not acknowledged by Hanoi. Citing Quang Tri as the location helped to perpetuate the fiction that the fighting was entirely within Vietnam and that there were no Vietnamese communist forces in Laos. In other respects, however, the broadcast was accurate—to a point. The time given was reasonably close to the truth, and it was correct that two helicopters had been shot

---

[1] The February 10 log at Joker SAR (the nickname of a U.S. Air Force search-and-rescue unit operating near Quang Tri under the U.S. Air Force Rescue Command Center), mentioned two VNAF UH-1s shot down, one with "civilian press" aboard, but it was not called to attempt a rescue or recovery.

down and two colonels killed. And whereas North Vietnam could have learned what its gunners had done by monitoring Western news reports, only from physical evidence could it have known such details as the presence of certain officers.

We concluded on our own that that the "three majors" probably referred to the photographers, whose MACV identification cards were stamped "MAJ" for major—an "equivalent rank" that was assigned to all journalists by the U.S. military command in Saigon. It was reasonable to believe that peasant soldiers examining the identity cards would not know any of that and would naturally assume that the bearers had been military officers.[2]

We could only take the Viet Cong radio broadcast at its word that there had been no survivors. At our request, the U.S. embassy agreed to try to make contact with Hanoi through a third party to seek recovery of camera gear or anything else relating to noncombatants aboard the helicopter. This idea was admittedly a long shot; predictably, it went nowhere.

On February 14, four days after the crash, all of this information went into a private message to AP's New York headquarters. It was as complete an accounting of the incident as we had at that time, including map-grid coordinates of the crash, as provided by Jim Newman. The deaths of the four photographers dominated conversations among the foreign press in Saigon for days. A framed picture of Henri went up on the AP newsroom wall, forming a neat rectangle with the other three. There was no space for another. The Japanese press contingent held a memorial service for Shimamoto at one of Saigon's Japanese restaurants. Kevin Buckley, the *Newsweek* bureau chief, was the only Westerner present. "I was very flattered," he says.

A day after the crash, the South Vietnamese provided another helicopter press trip across the border. Among those who signed on was AP photographer Hugh Van Es, a Dutchman who had covered the war for the previous five years. "The object of the exercise was to show us

---

[2] In one sense the broadcast was also "accurate" in saying that the crash occurred inside Vietnam. As opposed to standard maps of Indochina (used by U.S. and South Vietnamese forces) showing the Vietnam-Laos border as running straight north from Lao Bao, North Vietnamese Army maps showed it as a meandering line several kilometers farther west, placing the area of the shootdown on the Vietnam side.

that the ARVN controlled that part of the Ho Chi Minh Trail," recalls Van Es. "I remember very well that it was a shit ride, our pilot also got lost and circled for ages trying to find the LZ. I don't remember who else was riding on the chopper, but I guarantee you, we were not happy puppies, after what had happened." Once on the ground, Van Es and the others walked a short distance to a point on the Trail. "It was an amazing sight, beautifully camouflaged from the air, with roads wide enough for two trucks at places, bunkers, rest areas, you name it. The pictures were nothing exciting, but they got good play, since it was the first real view of the place."

As the battle of Laos continued, other small groups of foreign journalists managed to get across the border on South Vietnamese helicopters. About ten days after the shootdown, MACV organized a one-day visit for Saigon's excitement-deprived scribes, flying them in and out of Laos on a large Marine Corps helicopter for a show-and-tell briefing that portrayed the operation up to that point as a qualified success and was backed up by the usual large display of captured enemy weapons.

But no number of upbeat assessments by U.S. or South Vietnamese military officials could offset the obvious: that Saigon's forces were steadily losing control of the tactical situation against an enemy that was tenacious, better organized, and fighting on what was, to it, familiar ground. And the American pilots continued to run gauntlets of fire, first to support the embattled ARVN, then to extract them from jungle bases that were under heavy assault and, in some cases, in danger of being overrun by the *bo doi*.

Jim Newman, among them, did not miss a beat. The day after giving Mike Putzel an impromptu tour of the crash site area in Laos, Condor Six was back flying combat missions and "purposely felling trees," as the Silver Star award citation later described it, in order to rescue the two pilots of a Cobra gunship that had been hit by enemy fire over Laos and crashed on the Vietnam side of the border. Unable to gain clear access to the men on the ground, Newman used his Huey's main rotor blades to chop down several four-inch trees while crew chief Charles Davis hung out the door, making sure the tail rotor was clear of other obstructions. Despite enemy small-arms fire and exploding ammunition from the crashed Cobra, Newman managed to haul the two crewmen to safety. A photo of his aircraft back at Phu Bai showed the blades scraped and frayed but intact. "Bell Helicopter company experts advised us that a Huey could not fly with blades damaged as badly as Newman's had been," recalls Mac Jones, at the time the operations officer for the Condors.

Six days later, on February 18, Newman flew through a wall of gunfire into LZ Ranger North to recover the crew of a downed medevac chopper. Diverting from a reconnaissance mission after hearing the radio chatter of pilots who had attempted to reach the base only to be driven off by enemy rockets and small-arms fire, Newman told his Cobra escort pilots he would try and was "going in shooting." Boring in downwind at low altitude, Newman picked a landing spot away from the mortars, hoping he could get loaded and away before the NVA troops had time to readjust their aim.

Bullets ripped past the idling Huey, and mortar shells and rocket-propelled grenades exploded within a few meters as four Americans, two of them severely wounded, scrambled from a bunker and were pulled aboard by Newman's crewmates. Once assured that all were accounted for, Newman lifted the Huey off and maneuvered out through a continuing hail of fire to escape, miraculously without further casualties.

Newman's immediate superiors unhesitatingly recommended him for the Medal of Honor, buttressing the case with affidavits from ten eyewitnesses. Despite these testimonials, the application was downgraded at 101st Division level to the second-highest award for valor, the Distinguished Service Cross. A board of review and senior commanders up the line agreed, without explanation, that Newman's actions, though "exemplary," failed to meet the Medal of Honor's criteria for "conspicuous gallantry and intrepidity."[3]

---

[3] A tape recording of radio talk provides a gripping account of the medevac crew rescue at LZ Ranger North. Newman is heard telling his gunship escorts to put suppressing fire on antiaircraft positions on a nearby ridgeline, then says, "I'm going in shooting ... have you got me covered?" Cobra pilot Chuck Vehlow (Condor two-six) replies, "Roger, we gotcha." From above, Vehlow bracketed Newman's command-and-control ship with rockets and antipersonnel flechette rounds as it raced in through a beehive of hostile fire. Once on the ground, says Vehlow, Newman "seemed to be loading that aircraft *forever*." Newman's gunner, James Locke, and First Lieutenant Katysis Miller, the onboard artillery observer, exposed themselves to the enemy fire to help the two medevac pilots, who were badly wounded and crawling toward Newman's idling ship. Locke pulled the pilot aboard and

In the end, LAM SON 719 fell far short of Saigon's and Washington's hopes and expectations. The ARVN made only a token move to seize Tchepone, and even though military spokesmen insisted that the seven-week operation had achieved its objectives and ended in "orderly retreat," the spectacle of panicky South Vietnamese troops fleeing Laos by clinging to the skids of U.S. helicopters became its defining image.

Even Henry Kissinger conceded that those pictures "destroyed any prospect" that the White House could sell the public an upbeat version of LAM SON 719. "It clearly did not realize all our hopes, nor did it fail completely," he would write later of the ambitious operation. "As always in Vietnam the truth lay somewhere between the claims of the Administration and the abuse of the critics."[4]

---

held him by the belt while using his other hand to fire his M-60 machine gun. In his witness statement, Locke said that Newman asked, "Do we have them all?" and one of the wounded men replied that yes, all were aboard. Ending nearly a minute of tense silence on the tape, Newman is heard saying, "Okay, I'm coming out ... I've got three U.S. aboard ... taking fire, taking fire...."

Only after he had maneuvered the helicopter out through another storm of bullets—even flechette rounds from Vehlow's Cobra guns were coming close—did Newman discover that he had four, not three, survivors aboard. And only after that did he learn, to his considerable dismay, that a fifth man, Specialist Five Dennis Fujii, had stayed behind, unable to get to the helicopter because of mortars exploding outside the bunker. Years later, Newman's crew chief, Mike Feucht, told him he had feared that Newman, upon learning that one man had been left behind, would turn around and go back for him.

Dennis Fujii was trapped at LZ Ranger North for two more days, tending to wounded ARVN soldiers and calling in U.S. air strikes to prevent the North Vietnamese from overrunning the base. When he finally escaped aboard a rescue helicopter, it, too, was hit by gunfire and made it as far as LZ Ranger South, a few miles away. Eventually making it to safety, Fujii also won the Distinguished Service Cross. The commander of the medevac helicopter died a few hours after the rescue from shrapnel wounds suffered as he tried to recover code equipment from his crashed aircraft.

[4] Perhaps the most scathing criticism of OPERATION LAM SON 719 came from a participant. In a written commentary, Colonel Hoang Tich Thong, who commanded a South Vietnamese Marine brigade, blamed General Lam—whom he described as "someone who made his way by supporting the right political factions"—for inept planning and leadership. Thong also said that faulty intelligence had caused Saigon to grossly underestimate enemy strength in the target area (two divisions as opposed to the four or five that actually were present). Thong bitterly accused the Western press of undermining the operation by "playing up ARVN failures" and repeated a charge that the BBC, by prematurely reporting an attack on Tchepone, tipped off the enemy to South Vietnamese intentions and forced the ARVN to hastily mount the assault "in an attempt to save face." However forewarned, the North Vietnamese pulled out of Tchepone, then struck back with such force that an orderly withdrawal turned into a chaotic rout.

14 : Aftermath

For more than twenty years, there was no change at the Laos crash site except that wrought by nature.

No record of the crash existed in the case files of the Joint Casualty Resolution Center, the agency then responsible for attempting to recover POWs and MIAs. Even if it were not impeded by a lack of cooperation from host governments, the JCRC had no reason to include the loss of a South Vietnamese helicopter in Laos with no U.S. military personnel involved.

The jungles of the Laos panhandle remained inaccessible to other outsiders. The only prospect for any kind of systematic searches being done in that region depended on a change in the diplomatic realities—the leaders of Vietnam, Laos, and Cambodia consenting to let the vanquished return, seek out, and reclaim their dead.

The pain of our loss, as friends and colleagues of the fallen four, was in no way comparable to that of families whose loved ones were lost and missing during the war. Although families could cling to hope that loved ones would eventually turn up alive as POWs, our absence of knowledge allowed no corollary of hope. There were no vaguely comforting niceties in Jim Newman's description of the helicopter exploding in a fireball. Survival was not an option. There would be no change, no further developments, no resurrection, so to speak.

Inevitably, at the time of the helicopter crash, there had been those, even in the Saigon press corps, who expressed the view that the deaths of Larry, Henri, Kent, and Keisaburo had been pointless, a total waste. This I could not accept, not then or ever. Vietnam had been a place where men could learn to love each other in a collegial way, where friendships were formed in the crucible of shared experience. Passing the test of reliability and competence under stress was crucial to acceptance by one's peers.

No one had defined the ephemeral quality better than that war correspondent of an earlier era, Ernest Hemingway, with his coinage of "grace under pressure," and no one embodied it more than Henri Huet and Larry Burrows. It was impermissible that men of such professional aplomb and generosity of spirit could die without meaning. Yet some people were quick to declare the loss of the four lives a stupid, mindless waste. In the Saigon bureau, where Henri's photo now hung with the others on the newsroom wall, we did not concede this. Stepping into the street and being hit by a bus—that might be a pointless death, but it was not applicable to someone who had committed himself so fully to a life's mission and lost that life performing it.

Explaining this to ourselves and to each other was not simple. We all knew what there was to know. Most of us had been through similar experiences before. Being bureau chief did not make me any wiser than anyone else, yet I felt that some colleagues were looking to me for an answer. I found it in a kind of syllogism:

> Henri Huet believed deeply in what he did, Henri Huet was the best at what he did, Henri Huet died doing what he believed in, and did better than anyone. His death, therefore, had meaning.

Of how many people could such a thing be said?

: :

After a vast sigh of relief in the world that it was over, the Vietnam War took root in history, another piece of the twentieth century that would be talked and written about, taught in college classrooms, and end-lessly parsed and analyzed. The Laos helicopter crash would be a few paragraphs in the chapter on how the press covered the conflict. Most of us, in our twenties and thirties during the war, had been educated, molded, and aged by the Vietnam experience. It had been a club. Whether one had been a TV celebrity-journalist doing the career-en-hancing cameo turn, or a wannabe freelancer arriving at Tan Son Nhut with a blank resume, the membership roll had been open, and it was now closed. You either had been there or you hadn't. You either understood what it had been about or you didn't.

Horst Faas said he had stayed on in Indochina as long as possible "because we all seemed convinced that we played an important role in history, telling the story as it was," and "because it gave the winners in that very, very competitive business of news reporting from Vietnam the opportunity to be on page one, day after day, year after year." But once the war was over, he said, "I did not want to look back on those years. The war that I—and, I believe, many of my colleagues—wanted to be won, was lost. Rather than the satisfaction about career achieve-ments, I shared a feeling that we, the journalists, too, had in a way abandoned the people whose struggle and suffering we had covered—the South Vietnamese—and had left them to an uncertain and often awful fate. Many of them had become close friends and had worked for us for many years."

Horst had even hoped to "wipe out memory," but "the mind was not a computer," and when the time came to work on *Requiem*, a book about all the photographers killed on both sides of the war in In-dochina, he discovered not only that the past had not vanished but also that "through benefit of time we could now see much more clearly what we had achieved, or failed to achieve." Thus, as time reshaped the events and emotions of those years into memory, and members of the former Saigon press corps went on to other things, the network of friendships remained loosely intact and surprisingly vibrant. Hearing from someone for the first time in twenty years was not necessarily a surprise.

The occasional reunions of former Vietnam journalists were not given so much to swapping war stories—the description invariably given in news reports—as catching up on each other's subsequent lives and careers—who was where, whatever became of this person or that. But the past would raise its voice, and eventually the rambling path of conversation would lead to that helicopter crash in Laos back in 1971—"the one that killed Larry Burrows and the other photographers, remember?"

Fortunately, time had leavened the sadness, but it was intriguing, for those of us who had been there at the time or had known the victims, to recall the details—how we first learned about it, how we had reacted, what had happened next. And then the questions: Could there have been survivors? Was the crash site ever located? Had anyone ever been there? Was there a chance that anyone might go? After so many years of exposure to the tropical elements, what would be left of human remains, wreckage, any hard evidence of the incident and the lives lost?

Questions—always questions—but never answers.

Returning to Asia in the late 1970s, living in Japan and in closer proximity to Indochina, I found myself thinking more often about the crash. At the Foreign Correspondents Club of Japan, a wall plaque in the lobby listed the names of journalists killed or missing during the wars in Korea and Indochina. Henri Huet's name was there, with an asterisk indicating that he had been a club member. And there were many old hands around the club's Shimbun Alley bar who remembered the friendly Frenchman from his year of exile in Tokyo.

In those late 1970s, even as the Khmer Rouge ravaged Cambodia, a faint wind of change was fluttering diplomatic curtains in Vietnam and Laos. It was during that time that the idea of making a pilgrimage some day to the crash site in Savannakhet began to take shape in my mind as a real possibility, something to be pursued in earnest should the opportunity arise, as it almost surely would.

While they grieved separately and in private, the families of the four photographers had in common with those MIA families—and with us—those same unanswerable questions. They could not know what actually had occurred, could not know for a certainty that everyone had died, could not know when, if ever, the truth would emerge.

The political obliteration of what had been the Republic of (South) Vietnam meant simply that there was nobody to ask.

Larry Burrows's son, Russell, was twenty-two and nearing graduation with a business degree from the University of Southern California when his father died. He rushed back to Hong Kong to join his mother and sister, Deborah, then fifteen, and to begin a life that was not at all what he had been planning for. Russell did not need reminders of his father, yet he found them everywhere in the years that followed. Turn the page of a magazine, there would be a Larry Burrows photo. Open up a box, there would be papers, perhaps pieces of camera equipment that had been his.

Life magazine remained a support group bordering on second family. Russell even married into it. His wife, Bobbi, was a *Life* magazine picture editor. Together they discussed the idea of someday establishing the details of Larry's death, maybe even recovering his remains. It was always a hope, never an obsession, but Russell saw it clearly: "However certain you are of something, you are obliged to prove it conclusively if you can, to fill in that fraction of the decimal point. You have no choice but to go as far as you can."

Russell had all the basic information that was known about the flight into Laos, including news reports from the time and the personal recollections of *Life* and Time, Inc., staffers who had been at Khe Sanh and Ham Nghi. There was even a piece of paper with grid coordinates indicating the probable location of the crash. That had come from military officials via John Saar. Russell saved all these items for the day when they might become useful, that is, should the political circumstances change and the area become accessible to foreigners.

Perhaps because that prospect was so remote, the other families seemed resigned to their loss.

:: ::

In life, Henri Huet had seemed to his friends and colleagues a man virtually without faults. In death, this was even more true. Although it was too late for him to become a household name, news-magazine stories on the crash had given Henri's work its due, and there was a spate of posthumous tributes by the AP and others. Joe McGinniss, a columnist for the Philadelphia *Inquirer*, wrote a thoughtful column, drawing on his impressions of Huet during two visits to Vietnam.

Just two weeks before the shootdown, Henri had volunteered to take the pictures at the wedding of his fellow AP photographer, Dang Van Phuoc. McGinniss, who went along to observe the event, described Henri thus: "He worked carefully in the pagoda, never intruding but always getting exactly the picture he wanted." It was a snapshot in words of Henri Huet.

He was remembered also by soldiers. Henri might have been surprised, and surely gratified, to know how many Americans he had met in the field remembered him and sent messages. In Saigon, the government issued an official statement of condolence at the loss of an eminent native son.

In France, the Huet family remembered well, and apparently with great fondness, the handsome, smiling middle brother who as a young man had played soccer and aspired to be an artist before he returned to Indochina in military service and stayed on as a civilian. Although there was very little in common between his career as a combat photographer and the quiet, middle-class domesticity of his brothers and sisters, Henri wrote letters home, and his occasional visits were always welcome. "He was our prodigal child," said older brother Paul. "He was very charismatic, and in our little village he was very popular."

Paul was in his office when David Mason, the former AP Saigon bureau chief who had subsequently returned to Paris, called on him personally with the bad news about Henri. "It was a sad moment, but we knew that he was always in danger and we were not surprised," Paul said. Other than a Mass, there was no memorial.

Left hanging was the mystery of Henri's children, Joelle and Sandrine. Paul said Henri's former wife, Sonia, had brought them to live in Saint-Malo in 1967 for about a year, then moved to the south of France, then to Morocco, and later to New Caledonia. After that the trail disappeared. Apparently she did not care much for the Huet family, and it is possible that she stopped using the name for the children, said Paul. "We lost contact. We never stopped searching for the children. Everything is very distant now."

In Tokyo, Inger-Johanne had weathered the initial shock of Henri's death to find herself the accidental curator of his interrupted life. In the year they had known each other, he had shared a great deal more of himself with her than he had with others, allowing her to see beyond the modest, happy-go-lucky demeanor, into the private soul of the boy of mixed blood who had endured schoolyard taunts, into the depth of pride that he felt in his achievements and reputation as a war correspondent.

This was revealed not in Henri's words while alive but in the fat compendium of personal papers that he had left in Inger-Johanne's care. There were clippings of news stories written by other AP staffers in Saigon from Henri's meticulous notes, under his byline; letters and messages of congratulations for awards he had won; and good wishes for his recovery from wounds.

There were photos not only by Henri but of Henri—as a baby; in a group shot with his brothers and sister; Henri with troops; with a Montagnard and a baby elephant; with South Vietnamese politicians; Henri holding up a plasma bottle for a wounded soldier; Henri himself lying wounded, legs blood-spattered, in a dugout trench as others called for a medic.

There were letters that he had written in French and in his flawed but fearless English. The job inquiries spawned by his days of frustration in Tokyo were all there. Inger-Johanne also was dismayed to find in her mailbox, a few days after the shootdown, the last four letters she had written to Henri, returned unopened. For whatever reason—probably because he had been away from Saigon a great deal—he had not found time to read his mail.

Yet eerily, there also was a last letter *from* Henri, dated January 24 in Saigon. If Henri Huet had any premonition of life ending in seventeen days, there was no hint of it in the chatty, single-spaced page of fractured English; one searches the letter in vain for phrases dripping with ominous portent or throat-catching irony. Henri wrote of the possibility that he might have to go to Phnom Penh the next day, saying he hoped instead to get word that his services would be needed at a preview of the Winter Olympic Games at Sapporo, enabling him to get back to Japan briefly. He also described for Inger-Johanne a "stream of flowers" in Saigon's street market for the upcoming Tet holiday, when "all the old debts must be paid before the beginning of the new year, or that may bring bad luck for the rest of the coming year." He admitted

that in all his years in Vietnam he had never photographed the Tet fes-
tivities. "Shame on me!" After promising to send money because "I do
not want you to eat dry fish any more," he closed: "I love you ... I love
you ... I love you."

Letters of consolation poured into Inger-Johanne's mailbox, many
of them from people she had known in Philadelphia and other points
along the way but who had known Henri only by reputation. One letter was from John Gruenberg, with whose family Inger-Johanne had
lived in Bala Cynwyd, a Philadelphia suburb, while studying at Penn.
In expressing condolences, Gruenberg mentioned that by a curious
coincidence he and his wife, Anne, had also known Kent Potter's family. He even remembered Kent as an infant and had seen him once
during Kent's brief career with UPI in Philadelphia. "What a world,"
Gruenberg remarked.

Others, who had known and worked with Henri, spoke glowingly
of his skills and character. James Bourdier, who had replaced Horst as
AP's Saigon photo chief the previous September, wrote: "I imagine
that I looked at every negative Henri shot, and I cannot recall seeing
one that was not technically perfect—exposure, composition, everything that makes a good photograph. Singularly, his most important
trait, to me, was his sheer, utter devotion to duty, and in this case the
duty was his photography. Henri took it more seriously than life itself."

To assuage her grief, Inger-Johanne embarked on a two-track cru-
sade of letter-writing. In some, she proposed photo exhibits, magazine
articles, and books as fitting memorials to her lost lover. Some responses were sympathetic and initially encouraging, but little came of
them, mainly for lack of money. In other letters, she spoke of a "strong
feeling" that Henri was still alive, and in the weeks after the crash she
tried to make any contact that might help determine whether there
had been survivors or bodies recovered.

One letter went to a French restaurant owner in Bangkok who supposedly had "some contact with the Pathet Lao," the Laotian communists. In another, she asked "the leader of the Pathet Lao" to "check
through your prison camps to see whether my fiancé, Mr. Henri Huet,
is still alive." Others went to various diplomats, at least one in Hanoi.

Whether or not she understood the futility of these efforts, they
were doomed from the start. The Pathet Lao had little more than a to-

A Legacy Not Lost

Selected work by the four photographers

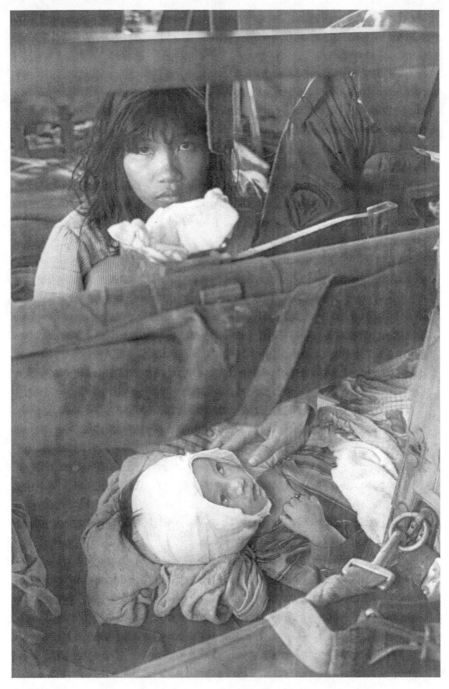

Kent Potter photographed injured Vietnamese children awaiting evacuation
by helicopter.

Body of U.S. paratrooper killed in War Zone C is lifted to medevac helicopter in 1966 photo by Henri Huet. Professionals were careful to avoid photographs in which dead could be identified visually.

Some pictures took on tableau quality, such as Kent Potter's photo of ARVN soldiers helping wounded colleagues.

ABOVE: Spending days and even weeks in the field, Huet produced many scenes like these Marines with a downed helicopter, after three-day battle near DMZ.
BELOW: Larry Burrows, with USMC artillery unit in jungle, also captured essence of war.

ABOVE: The war's impact on civilians is seen in this Potter photo of a war-wrecked Catholic church.
BELOW: Keisaburo Shimamoto's photo of woman mourning over bodies wrapped in plastic.

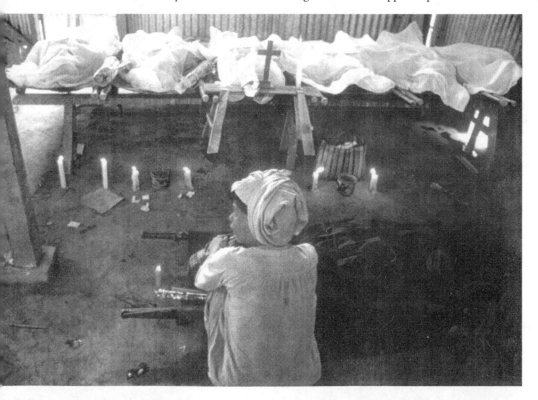

ABOVE: An artist's eye and feel for Vietnam's moods enabled Huet to capture scenes like U.S. 173rd Airborne Brigrade troopers wading a river in the rain.

RIGHT AND BELOW: Henri swam a Mekong Delta Canal on cover of AP magazine in 1968, and depicted GI keeping M-60 machine gun dry.

THE
AP
WORLD

Summer 196

Burrows' 12-page *Life* essay on Yankee Papa 13 shows Marine helicopter crew chief James Farley after rescuing two wounded colleagues. Burrows braved crossfire for this seminal Vietnam photo story that won the Capa Award.

Huet's Capa Award series on the 1966 battle of An Thi included this photo of wounded 1st Cav medic Thomas Cole (right) helping a wounded sergeant. Burrows urged his *Life* editors to use Huet's pictures.

LEFT: A thoughtful Green
Beret advisor to South
Vietnamese Special Forces
near Cambodian border,
by Potter.

BELOW: Yankee Papa 13's
Farley weeps over day's
events. Burrows worried
about intruding on privacy
but called it necessary to
show "what others are
going through."

ken presence in the embattled panhandle where the helicopter crashed, although the propaganda turned out by Hanoi tried to make it appear that they were the only communist forces in the area. The North Vietnamese, who actually controlled the region, had never acknowledged their own presence in Laos and were not likely to do so to help a grieving foreigner.

Discreetly, Inger-Johanne asked mutual friends in Hong Kong whether Vicky Burrows also was holding out hope that her husband might have survived. One replied on March 31: "A friend who knows her well assures me that she does not entertain any hope that he is still alive. If he should show up one day, she would consider it a miracle." The writer also discouraged Inger-Johanne from trying to publish a magazine article suggesting there was a real chance of someone having lived through the crash. An editor who was consulted, he said, did not think it would be right to "raise the hopes ... of the people close to the four journalists."

In letters to close friends, Inger-Johanne revealed many details of her relationship with Henri, often closing with a comment making clear she had not given up. "Henri was really the first man in my life who was really good to me ... unreservedly giving love and moral support galore," she wrote to a Norwegian friend. At the bottom of the typed page, she added in longhand, "If nothing happens, I am going to find him myself."

In another letter a week after the crash, she described the long-range plans that she and Henri had made. She had intended to move herself to Singapore to be closer to Henri in Vietnam, retrieve his son and daughter from their unreliable mother, and bring them to Singapore as well. Eventually, they would live as a family in Australia or southern California. "I feel a deep obligation to continue things the way he would want me to ... until he comes back," she wrote.

: :

Kent Potter's obituary appeared in the Philadelphia *Inquirer*, a brief item that recalled his local background but said little about his later life and career. The Potter family grieved in silence. The fact that Kent had broken away, first to join the military, then to go off to war on his own, was impossible to reconcile. Kent's sister, Sherry, to whom he had remained close, became the keeper of the flame, but even that glowed only in private.

Ann Bathgate, Kent's last high-school girlfriend, had not heard from Kent since his last, less-than-satisfying visit to Denmark in 1970, and she knew nothing of his death until a year after it happened. Her parents arrived in Denmark for a visit, and Ann and her husband, Gorm, met them at the airport in Copenhagen. "Getting off the plane," Ann recalls, "the first thing that my mother said, totally out of the blue, was, 'Did you know that Kent is dead?'"

Ann was, in her own words, "thrown completely off balance." "I kept saying, 'What did you say?' I couldn't believe it." She had remembered that last visit as "heaven and hell, all in one," and had never attempted to contact Kent afterward. Although he was in Vietnam, and presumably in danger at times, she had never given thought to the idea that he might be dead. Surely, if that happened, she would somehow hear about it.

Yet on reflection, she was not surprised at the news. Based on his earlier letters and that last visit with its mingled emotions, she already had felt that Kent would not survive for a long time in his chosen profession. "The war took over his life and changed him completely," Ann says now. "He had to have it, like a drug." She also came to believe, and still does, that Kent was hurt so deeply—first by his mother's death, then by his father's cruel reaction, and finally by the loss of the woman he really loved—that he had developed something akin to a death wish in Vietnam. It was a feeling, she thinks, of becoming immune to any more pain, of being, in effect, bulletproof.

Kent's death plunged Ann into a depression that would last five years, assuaged only by her husband's understanding presence and what she describes as "notebook after notebook" of therapeutic poetry. For a time she was hospitalized, and when her second child was born, she fantasized that it was Kent's.

In 1982 Ann and her husband divorced, and seven years later she married another Dane, whose dark hair and blue eyes reminded her too much of Kent Potter. That marriage, "to a ghost that is not there," did not last. She remained close friends with Gorm, her first husband, kept a place in her heart for Kent, and liked to quote the Danish writer Ib Michael:

You touch something, and time stands still ... you fall into vague observance, while the mind is filled with figures whose lives are another today. If they live at all. Memory moves with the delay of light. Stars we see, no longer exist ... space is empty of everything but echoes.

Yet just as Inger-Johanne could not readily accept the reality of Henri's death, Ann clung to a vague hope that Kent had somehow gotten off the helicopter before it crashed and was still alive, growing old in a different life, somewhere in Southeast Asia. "I went for years," she says, "thinking that that guy was just going to walk in my door one day. You keep hanging on as long as there is nothing definite. Maybe, someday ... "

In Bangkok, Tom Martin, the old school chum who had last seen Kent during his bout with dengue fever two months earlier, received the awful news in a call from UPI's bureau chief, Leon Daniel. At first he focused on the words "missing in action" as offering hope, "as if Kent and the others had simply taken an unexpected side-trip on the road to some great adventure."

But within days reality set in, and Tom found himself sadly cleaning out Kent's apartment above the Chinese noodle shop. There was not much there other than clothing and cameras, Martin recalls, until he stumbled on an "unexpected treasure" of contact sheets and prints. It was his first real look at Potter's war photographs, and he was amazed by their depth and quality. "Back in Philadelphia, Kent had shot news much as everyone else did—flat lighting, subject in the center," Martin says. "These photographs showed maturity far beyond that. In Vietnam, he had mastered composition and lighting. He blended art and content to tell a poignant and lasting story."

In Saigon, where there were no illusions that Kent Potter was going to turn up on anyone's doorstep, UPI took charge of the camera gear, photos, and other personal belongings. In death it became even more clear how far Kent Potter had traveled from his Quaker roots. In his increasing enthrallment with things military, Kent had become a habitual collector of souvenirs. Former UPI reporter Robert Sullivan remembers being delegated to "get rid of the guns," a duffel bag filled with weapons of various kinds, even hand grenades, that Potter had left behind when he moved to Bangkok.

The UPI bureau boxed up Kent's more benign personal effects and sent them along to his sister in Philadelphia.

One day in the late 1970s—he does not remember the exact date—Jon Falk, a Philadelphia newspaper photographer, was shooting a routine assignment at a public library when he was approached by a well-dressed, well-spoken woman he had never seen before. As Falk recalls the experience, "She introduced herself, and asked if I had known her brother, Kent Potter. I replied that I had not, that he was before my time in Philadelphia, but I knew of him by reputation and through mutual acquaintances. She then told me she had boxes of Kent's stuff in the attic that she had never opened and now wanted to find somebody knowledgeable about cameras and so forth to inventory the contents and help her dispose of them."

Falk thought over the unusual request and agreed to it. On a Saturday, he and his wife drove out to Germantown. Sherry, he remembers, had brought the boxes down to the dining room where he opened them and sorted and catalogued the contents. There were cameras, lenses, electronic equipment. Falk made a list and, with Sherry's concurrence, agreed to sell or give away the most valuable Saigon souvenirs. She did not offer much in the way of explanation. "During the time we were there, she stayed in another room," says Falk. "The only thing she said was, 'We are a Quaker family, and we never understood why he went there.'"

Sherry later remarried and moved to Colorado, where she has steadfastly refused all requests to talk about her brother or the crash. In 1996, she told this author in a brief telephone conversation, "It happened a long time ago and the government has said there was no hope of ever finding anything. It would be a waste of time and money to even try."

There were, however, some fitting memorials to Kent Potter. The cameras he once used were doled out to people who could use and appreciate them. Jon Falk had one. Rusty Kennedy, Kent's old friend and AP rival, had another—a Leica whose black enamel was worn away to reveal the burnished brass underneath. One day when Kennedy was covering a story at City Hall in Philadelphia, the mayor noticed the camera and remarked on its well-used appearance. Says Rusty, "I told him, 'This camera has a lot of history.'"

: :

Keisaburo Shimamoto was memorialized a year after the crash in a photo book, *He Died in Vietnam*, published by the *Yomiuri Shimbun*. The book was the inspiration of his wife, Yuko, and contained a chapter detailing his last days by Akihiko Okamura, his friend and former mentor at Pan Asia Newspaper Alliance.

While he wrote of being deeply saddened by his friend's death, Okamura focused on their relationship in the five months preceding the crash. He clearly intended this as an object lesson, "For Those Young People Who Follow Shimamoto Keisaburo." Okamura told of their last meeting in Saigon on February 7 and their pact to meet again at Khe Sanh two days later—a rendezvous that did not occur because Okamura, on that day, had managed to smuggle himself across the border in a South Vietnamese military vehicle.

Okamura later denied widely circulated reports that he had disguised himself as an ARVN soldier. Rather, he claimed to have more or less conned a U.S. military adviser at the border. "I did not use magic to break through the checkpoint, nor did I hide in an empty box and evade the eyes of the guards. I only used the international passport that freelance photographers covering international news must always carry—that is, 'the smile the adversary cannot resist'—and politely thanked an unknown U.S. colonel, saying, 'I will never forget you,' shook his hand and boarded the truck." Thus, Okamura was inside Laos, and out of touch, when the helicopter carrying Shimamoto and the others was shot down. There was no reason the troops he was with on Route 9 would have known about it. Helicopters were being shot down all over the place. It was a full week before Okamura learned, from a Vietnamese newspaper, that the press helicopter had been among them. On February 25, he returned to Saigon and got the full story from correspondents at the *Time* office.

In his book for "those who follow Shimamoto," Okamura argued that freelancers had "different goals in life" than staff photographers and should follow different career strategies. Shimamoto, he concluded, should not have gone into Laos aboard the helicopter but instead should have done as he, Okamura, had done—wangling a secret trip to get exclusive pictures rather than merely duplicating the work of staff shooters for AP, UPI, and *Life*. But this overlooked the fact that Shimamoto was not working on his own but under contract to *Newsweek*, which meant he had to get into Laos and out again in time to meet a deadline in New York. There was no room in that for a wandering minstrel with cameras, spending a two-week sojourn with the troops.

Yuko Shimamoto said, after a year of "continuing to pray for a miracle," that she had become reconciled to Keisaburo's death and decided to try to have the memorial book published. Its intended purpose was similar to Okamura's—to help teach young people aspiring to the photographer's craft that the road was not easy. "What I strongly hoped for was not only to publish the photographs left behind by a photographer who died unaccomplished despite his great talent, but also to preserve his struggle and deficiencies as they were for young people following his steps," she wrote in a wistful postscript to the book. "I hated to see my husband's death being reconstructed into a beautiful fiction. I only wish he would remain forever an ordinary husband, a dictatorial husband, and a lonely husband who would occasionally drink and amuse me or trouble me by self-conceitedly saying, 'perhaps I am a genius.'"

Yuko said the book "represents very closely the way he was" and imagined her husband "scratching his head and saying, 'In spite of myself, this Shimamoto made a little mistake this time.'"

15 : Discovery

One day in April 1995 I was sitting at my office desk in New York. It all began with the buzz of the telephone, and the caller introduced himself. It was Bill Forsyth, an investigator-researcher for the Joint Task Force–Full Accounting, the Hawaii-based Pentagon agency whose mission was searching for American MIAs in Indochina.

Forsyth explained that he had been given my name as someone who might be able to help him track down some information about a case he was then pursuing. He asked whether I remembered the South Vietnamese invasion of Laos back in 1971 and whether I remembered a helicopter crash during that operation in which four civilian photojournalists had been killed.

By coincidence, Forsyth's call came just weeks before the twentieth anniversary of South Vietnam's defeat, an event that was to include a reunion in Saigon of former wartime journalists. It was to be my first return to Indochina since the war, and the mind already was astir with thoughts of the past. It took me a few seconds to realize that Forsyth's call was not related to the anniversary reunion. Sure, I replied, I remembered the invasion—Operation Lam Son 719, it was called—and I certainly had not forgotten the helicopter incident. Three of the four men killed had been personal friends, and the day that it happened was vividly recalled.

To my considerable surprise, Forsyth informed me that the case already had been under investigation by the JTF-FA for several months; JTF survey teams had visited a number of possible crash sites without positive results. The agency had exhausted all leads, and any further exploration would depend on new information. Ideally, Forsyth said, he hoped to find the map grid coordinates of the crash site. Did I perhaps have this information or know where it might be found?

The JTF-FA inquiry, I would learn, had reached this point by a very convoluted path. In 1994, an Ohio woman, looking through the belongings of her late mother, had come across a yellowed newspaper clipping concerning her father—a U.S. Army pilot who had perished twenty-three years earlier in the crash of a CH-47 Chinook helicopter during Operation Lam Son 719. The big, twin-rotor cargo chopper, carrying a slingload of fuel, had overshot its destination in Laos, was hit by 37mm antiaircraft fire, and exploded in midair, killing all six men aboard. The news clipping, an AP story datelined Khe Sanh on February 15, 1971, described the incident as witnessed by other U.S. pilots and mentioned an aerial search for the wreckage led by a Major James Newman.[1]

Eager to learn more, the pilot's daughter called AP headquarters in New York. There, an editor located the original story in the archives. It carried the byline of Michael Putzel, who in the interim had left the company and joined the staff of the *Boston Globe*. When she finally located him at the *Globe*'s Washington, D.C., bureau, Putzel remembered the story. He agreed to look into his own Vietnam files, collecting dust in the attic. "She wanted to get whatever details she could because of conflicting information," he says. "That night, I went up to the attic and found a box of stuff, including my old notebooks from Lam Son 719." He sent the woman what information he could find that seemed relevant.

---

[1] In an odd echo of the February 10 crash, the U.S. pilots, like their South Vietnamese counterparts, had lost their bearings over Laos and failed to respond to frantic radio calls from their own gunship escorts.

At the JTF-FA offices in Hawaii, meanwhile, Bill Forsyth already was on the hunt for information about the 1971 Chinook crash, laying the groundwork for a possible search for remains of the six crewmen, who were officially listed as killed in action, bodies not recovered. Tracing the dead pilot's next-of-kin to Ohio, Forsyth made contact with the same daughter, and she steered him to Mike Putzel as a possible source of further information. Forsyth then called Putzel to ask what he might be able to add.

The matter of grid coordinates came up in conversation, and that led to yet another subject—the crash of the South Vietnamese helicopter carrying the photographers. Putzel gave Forsyth details of that incident, based on Jim Newman's eyewitness version, and told how Newman had taken him on a daring reconnaissance flight over the crash site the next day. He suggested that Newman, by then retired from the army and last known to be living in Texas, also might have useful information.

Bill Forsyth, who prided himself on a comprehensive knowledge of Vietnam War aircraft losses, especially those in Laos, was amazed to learn for the first time about a helicopter crash that had killed eleven people, among them four foreigners whose bodies had never been recovered. "He couldn't understand why those missing people weren't on his list," says Putzel. Most puzzling to the veteran JTF researcher was that one of the four civilian journalists, Kent Potter of United Press International, apparently was American yet did not appear on any list of MIAs in Indochina.

Forsyth knew that in the absence of an obvious U.S. military connection there was no reason that a South Vietnamese helicopter shot down in Laos would necessarily be on record at Joint Task Force headquarters. But if Potter was indeed a U.S. citizen, that would be sufficient grounds, even at such a late date, to add his name to the MIA list and to qualify the VNAF helicopter loss for an official inquiry. Now in full sleuthing mode, Bill Forsyth managed to track down Jim Newman, who in the meantime had moved to North Carolina. In a phone conversation, the former air cavalry commander confirmed what Putzel had already told him and elaborated on his own role in the two crash incidents—the U.S. Army Chinook and the VNAF Huey with the newsmen aboard.

Forsyth next visited the Hawaii State Library, where, in the micro-film pages of the *Honolulu Advertiser* of February 1971, he found de-tailed news accounts of the shootdown of the four journalists. They identified UPI photographer Kent Biddle Potter as a native of Philadelphia. Based on these findings, Forsyth wrote a memo recom-mending that Potter be added to the list of Americans missing in In-dochina and that the crash of the South Vietnamese helicopter be marked down for future investigation.

On April 1, 1995, the incident was assigned Case Number 2062. Kent Potter officially became the forty-fourth civilian on the roster of Americans "dead, body not recovered." Thus, on the slender reed of one man's Yankee birth, a process would go forward that might clarify not only his fate but that of ten other people who happened not to be Americans.

JTF investigators found their preliminary efforts to locate the VNAF crash site limited not only by a dearth of information but also by contradictions in what records did exist. Even simple clerical errors led down blind alleys. Two decades after the shooting stopped, the fog of war still lingered over the Annamites.

Although the most "official" record—the VNAF list of aircraft losses for 1971—correctly recorded such details as the time, tail num-bers, and casualties in the February 10 incident, it inexplicably gave grid coordinates indicating that the two Hueys in Lam's entourage had been shot down on opposite sides of the border, the first at XRay Delta 677447 in Quang Tri Province of South Vietnam, and the second at XRay Delta 565520, several kilometers to the west, in Laos. Neither of these locations was correct.

Compounding that confusion, a log entry for February 10 at the U.S. Air Force Rescue Command Center, better known as Joker SAR, said: "VN lost two helos 1230h, 4 American [sic] members of the press on board, position XRay Delta 677477 on VN-Laos border." The "477" appeared to be a misreading of "447" in the VNAF report. And though it was closer to the actual location in Laos, the Joker SAR record also was wrong.

Entries in official Southeast Asia Loss (SEAloss) records dated Au-gust 1, 1971, and December 1, 1971, further muddled the question of whether the helicopters had gone down in Laos or Vietnam. Significantly, a JTF document noted that SEAloss data "has been found to be inaccurate in other cases, and this bears out its inaccuracies."

In a monograph, "Lam Son 719," that he later wrote for U.S. Army historians, former South Vietnamese Major General Nguyen Duy Hinh reported correctly that both helicopters had been shot down near LZ Ranger South in Laos, but he erred in putting the newsmen and the two ARVN staff officers on different aircraft. That contradicted the eyewitnesses at Ham Nghi, the casualty figures in VNAF's loss list, and General Lam's personal recollection.

Despite such widespread misinformation, Joint Task Force officials put Case 2062 high on their list, and the unit's State Department liaison office reached out to the known next-of-kin to advise them that the long-ago crash was under investigation.

In January 1995, an eight-member JTF survey team led by Captain Timothy Thurmond visited four villages in an area where the SEAloss record indicated the two VNAF Hueys might have crashed. One site, three kilometers northeast of the village of Ban Ta-Lai, had been scouted the previous year by a team working on an unrelated case; it offered nothing new. A second site, to the southeast, yielded bits of burned helicopter debris. In interviews, nine villagers said most of that wreckage had been scavenged and sold to scrap collectors. Shown a pair of eyeglasses and a 35mm camera, the villagers said they had seen nothing similar at the site.

Near Ban Charin village, the Americans examined a crash site originally found by villagers returning to the area in 1974. They said an orange parachute recovered there had been cut up and the pieces doled out to eleven families. From that information and its own discovery of jet-engine remnants, the JTF team deduced that a fighter-bomber, not a helicopter, had fallen there. The search for Site 2062 would have to move elsewhere.

When he picked up the phone three months later, Bill Forsyth knew it was a long shot that anyone would still have a record of the grid coordinates—if they ever did. Surprised to learn that an investigation of the crash had been launched, I had to tell Forsyth that I did not have the information and wasn't sure where it might be found. But even as I did so, something tugged at my memory. I promised to think about it.

: :

The return to Vietnam in late April was an emotional occasion for all of us who took part, but especially for me, as I was traveling with others on a special lecture schedule that allowed only one day in Saigon before moving on to Hong Kong. My wife, Brenda, who had never been in Vietnam before and was traveling separately with a friend, arrived the same day, and we turned our one night together in Saigon into a romantic rendezvous.

Brenda's perspective on Vietnam had always been one of an American deeply opposed to the war, regarding the entire subject of Vietnam with animus. Suddenly, now, she found Vietnam no longer a negative abstraction but a country of real people, sights, smells, and noise, a cacophonous Southeast Asian assault upon the senses. From the window of a postwar high-rise hotel, we looked out across the tile and tin rooftops of the city now renamed for Ho Chi Minh, a place entirely new to her and in some ways now unfamiliar to me.

We had not recognized that Vietnam actually had been an obstacle that stood between us, one that in the sharing of the moment had disappeared.

Brenda's new connection to the place, and to its turbulent history, deepened on the strength of her visit to an aircraft crash site southwest of Danang, where she watched a JTF team search for the remains of a Marine Corps pilot whose A-4 Skyhawk had gone down in April 1967. Returning home after ten days in Vietnam, she wrote a freelance story for *Archaeology* magazine about the search, Case 0642. I envied her that experience and hoped for something similar in regard to the Laos affair.

With no further word, the situation drifted, and I had put the matter aside. Then, in early July, Bill Forsyth called again. He brought me up to date on Case 2062. Though he admittedly had little to report that was new, I was impressed by Bill's obvious sincerity in wanting to find that lost helicopter. What I had not come to appreciate was his persistence. He wanted to know whether I had come up with any more ideas about those grid coordinates. This time, the answer clicked. I still didn't have that information, but I now remembered suddenly where it might be found.

Back in 1971, when Mike Putzel called the AP Saigon bureau to report on his flight over the crash site with Jim Newman, he also had supplied us with grid coordinates of the location, most likely obtained from U.S. military officials, perhaps Newman himself.

The information was of no value at the time because there was no way for anyone to reach the crash site. But it obviously was worth having on record for the future, and with that in mind I had included the grid coordinates in a five-page memorandum to AP headquarters, spelling out everything we knew, a few days after the crash. With luck, I figured, that memo should still exist in the old Saigon bureau files—which, by a combination of foresight and good fortune, had been carefully preserved and were not very far away.

Among the former Vietnam hands who had traveled back to Saigon for the anniversary reunion was Peter Arnett, who had parlayed his record as a Pulitzer Prize–winning AP war correspondent in Vietnam into a second career as the globetrotting star of CNN. During the transpacific flight, I had outlined for Peter the details of the Laos crash investigation. Naturally interested, Peter remarked that if the original AP Saigon bureau files could be of any value in the case, they were available—safely ensconced in his basement in McLean, Virginia.

Until then, I had all but forgotten that the day before Peter left Saigon in 1972 we purchased several metal footlockers at the Saigon central market, packed them with the dozens of loose-leaf binders that held the bureau's raw files, and shipped them out of the country as Arnett's unaccompanied baggage. The papers already had been deteriorating in Saigon's tropical climate, and we were dismayed to find that a few important pages were missing—a hazard, we learned too late, of trusting a couple of researchers for private authors to have unsupervised access to the loose-leaf binders. Our purpose in shipping the documents had been to preserve for posterity a uniquely original history of the first ten years of the Vietnam War—how it was reported at the source before being trimmed, shaped, homogenized, and streamlined into the final version of stories that would move on wires to some 1,500 newspapers and hundreds of broadcast subscribers in the United States and countless more around the world.

Peter's expressed intention had been to donate the files to a college journalism library, where they could be used by scholars. But as he also had mentioned the idea of writing a book on his career—a project for which the raw files would be an invaluable resource—we had no illusions of this happening very soon. However long the Arnett autobiography might take, we knew the files would be in trustworthy hands.

As soon as Forsyth rang off, I dialed Arnett's number in northern Virginia. Kept in almost perpetual motion at CNN, he was rarely at home. But this time he answered on the second or third ring. When I explained my purpose in calling, Peter remembered our conversation during the Saigon trip. He recalled immediately the memo that I was describing; in the course of writing his book, he had plumbed the same pages of the files many times and knew them intimately.[2] My memo to New York had been written within a few days after the crash on February 10, 1971. Finding it should be a simple matter—and it was. In minutes, Peter was back on the phone. "I've got it. Five pages. I'll fax it to you."

Watching the pages roll out of the fax machine, I was struck by how ridiculously easy it had been, after twenty-four years, to find exactly what I wanted. Score one for careful recordkeeping. The words were ghosts, floating up from the page. The memo was all there—untouched, unsullied, unwrinkled by time or the elements. The tight, semicablese jargon, the hand-edited strikeovers, insertions, and deletions, all were as familiar as if written the day before. Recognizing the idiosyncratic typeface of the old Smith-Corona that I had used in Saigon, I wondered if it might still be in use, in some rabbit-warren office of a Communist Party functionary or government bureaucrat, in that city of a different name.

All the thoughts and emotions of that long-ago week had been limned into my terse, fact-packed report to Fifty Rock:

Five [sic] ARVN helicopters left Ham Nghi forward command post inside South Viet border about noon 10 Feb, departure witnessed by several other newsmen ... pilots of trailing choppers lost track of Lam and continued north while he landed at 2nd firebase ... as chop-

---

[2] Arnett's book, *Live from the Battlefield*, was published in 1994 (New York: Simon & Schuster).

pers flew past at about 1,000 feet, the gun fired on lead ship ... Major
Jim Newman, who supplied these eyewitness details, said he ordered
his pilot and crew chief who could also see it happening to watch for
anyone jumping out or escaping ... to the best of their knowledge,
nobody did ... consensus of opinion is that only by the most remote
chance could anyone have escaped either helicopter alive.[3]

And on page four:

Location of first crash site is XD563524 and second crash site is
XD565552. Both are about 12 kilometers (seven miles) west of the
Laos-Vietnam border and approximately same distance north of
route 9. The terrain is mountainous and jungle-covered, with many
open areas on hillsides and is laced with the roads and trails that together make up the Ho Chi Minh Trail.

The memo went on to describe the antiaircraft fire intensity, the
indications that North Vietnamese troops might already have reached
the crash site, and our request to the U.S. embassy to "begin a private
diplomatic effort" through international third parties to retrieve remains and personal effects of the photographers, even as the South
Vietnamese commandos supposedly were trying to get to the scene:

It is not known how long it may take Hac Bao to reach the area, considering terrain and presence of hostile forces. Estimates range from
a week, to two weeks, to never.

Like a second baseman turning the double play, I relayed the memo
from Peter Arnett in Virginia to Bill Forsyth in Hawaii. Less than an
hour after Forsyth's call, the information he wanted was in his hands.

: :

---

[3] Lam's entourage was reported at the time to consist of five helicopters, a figure used in writings then and since. In a 1997 interview, Lam asserted that a total of four helicopters left
from Ham Nghi; thus, there were only three in the group that was attacked. But Jim Newman and other airmen who witnessed the incident are for the most part firm in recalling
that they saw four in that group, of which two—the first and third in line—were shot down.

Almost simultaneously, the search for Site 2062 was moving into another phase. In the same month I supplied Forsyth with the grid markers, a JTF investigating team reached the location in Quang Tri province of Vietnam that had been mentioned in the South Vietnamese Air Force loss listing for "10.2.71." Although this was miles from the more likely sites in Laos, JTF policy mandated that all potential sites be surveyed, no matter how tenuous. That Quang Tri site, a hill called Ta Puc, turned out to be an abandoned U.S. artillery base, still littered with shell casings and other flotsam of war, including a two-wheeled water cart, what the GIs called a "water buffalo." Nearby was aircraft debris, evidently from a Huey helicopter, on what may have been the base landing pad. There was no sign of human remains. The team reported that it could not correlate the wreckage to any one of the known aircraft losses in that area.

The focus shifted back to Laos, where it belonged, but the process moved slowly. The Laotian government had the final say on the scheduling of MIA searches and, for reasons of its own, was insisting that the Joint Task Force's field activities be conducted systematically from north to south, effectively putting Savannakhet Province, an area especially rich in sites awaiting inquiry, well down the list. The U.S. officials, wary of doing anything that might antagonize the Vientiane bureaucrats, raised no objections.

Thus, it was not until six months later, in January 1996, that another JTF-FA team finally was able to inspect the ground at both of the map coordinates that Mike Putzel had obtained twenty-five years earlier. In a phone call from Hawaii, Lieutenant Colonel Roger King, public affairs officer, informed me that both surveys had come up empty on helicopter wreckage or other crash evidence. Yet the foray hadn't been totally in vain. At the northernmost site, XRay Delta 565552, investigators had found the rusted debris of a Russian-type 37mm antiaircraft gun and ammunition, scattered in a streambed.

Although it was now clear that the locations we were given in 1971 were not the crash site itself, it was intriguing that one would turn out to be a former North Vietnamese antiaircraft position—one that, judging by the evidence, had been taken out of action by U.S. bombers. The enticing question, of course, was whether this could have been the gun that shot down the VNAF helicopter.

Considering the extensive array of antiaircraft emplacements in the area, there was no way to tell. At the very least, the discovery suggested that the search was now focused in the right area. If this was the same 37mm gun, the crash site itself would be close at hand—probably within a radius of about two miles, the effective range of the weapon. But that was by itself a lot of ground to cover, especially in such densely overgrown terrain.

Once again, the search was at a dead end. Roger King called to say that unless more new information came to the fore Case 2062 might be shelved, consigned along with scores of cases to a kind of limbo status—not closed but with no further action pending.

Then, suddenly, again there was new hope.

Even as the JTF team was finding the wrecked gun in Laos, Mike Putzel was going through papers again in his Washington, D.C., attic. While looking for something else, he came across a manila envelope. To his surprise, it contained the photograph he had taken of the mountainside from Jim Newman's helicopter. It was the evidence we'd been waiting for.

: :

Bill Forsyth grew up in Placerville, California, site of the historic Gold Rush—somehow fitting for someone who would devote a career to mining secrets from the earth (or at least from its surface). As a young man, he had enlisted in the U.S. Air Force and was trained as an aerial photo interpreter. In twenty-seven years, based mainly in Hawaii, he had become intimately familiar with the face of Southeast Asia—its rivers and streams, mountain passes, the rocky karsts rising from the jungle, and the infrastructure of civilizations that were strewn unevenly across it. To Forsyth's expert eye, any change in the landscape from one day to the next could be a clue to something happening in the military situation—a troop movement, an increase in truck traffic, a new road being built under cover of darkness and triple-canopy jungle. Armed with such skills, Bill Forsyth could treat his deadly serious task as a sporting challenge. "It was something I really enjoyed," he says. "Us against the bad guys—they hide, and we find."

Retired from the Air Force, Bill Forsyth had found a way to apply his expertise to a second career as an analyst and investigator for the

Joint Task Force-Full Accounting. Its demands and his abilities were a perfect match. He became a sort of one-man detective agency, equally adept at researching documents and library microfilm and tracking down hard-to-find witnesses and MIA-POW relatives.

But no one was as good as Forsyth at aerial photo analysis. In that capacity, his knowledge of Indochina from above enabled him to spot the anomalies in the landscape, especially of Laos, that could indicate where an aircraft had crashed, perhaps even where bodies were buried. The man who had once told the U.S. Air Force where to find the enemy was now helping to resolve the mystery of what happened to some of the pilots that the enemy had found instead.

So it was in April 1996, when Bill Forsyth, alone in a borrowed office at the Defense Intelligence Agency in Washington, D.C., placed a picture on a photo lightboard and turned the switch. It was the black-and-white photo of the crash site taken by Mike Putzel. Illuminated from beneath, details of the scene emerged with almost three-dimensional clarity. There was the ridge with the dirt road winding along the top, an apparent burned area on the slope below it. Murky shadows became jungle foliage shading a ravine.

Forsyth placed another photo beside the first. Taken in May 1971, three months after the crash, it showed the Vietnam-Laos border region through the high-resolution cameras of a U.S. Air Force SR-71 Blackbird photoreconnaissance plane, flying a computerized track at 70,000 feet. From that altitude, a pilot could see very little through the tropical haze, but the cameras could pick up amazing detail if the weather was right—though not, as was sometimes claimed, the numbers on a car's license plate.

A squiggly white line meandered across the photo from upper right to lower left, passing through white splotchy areas that to the untrained eye resembled the lights of cities and towns. Forsyth recognized the line as Route 1032, an old French-built secondary road that began in Vietnam, crossed into Laos through the Ban Raving Pass just north of the former DMZ, and ran southwest through the mountains. During the war, it had served as a key section of the Ho Chi Minh Trail.

The bright splotches were bomb craters—some, randomly scattered, were the work of fighter-bombers; others, in broad, streaky patterns, were the signature of the high-flying B-52 strategic bombers fly-ing out of Guam and Thailand. Somewhere along that road, Forsyth was certain he would find the same distinctive curves that were visible in Putzel's photo. "It was a fairly easy piece of imagery research," Forsyth says. "I had to look at several SR-71 missions before I found one that was clear over the area. We had the grid coordinates that put us in the general vicinity. It wasn't very long before I was able to match up the bends in the road. I knew immediately that we finally had the right place."

Acting on Forsyth's findings at the first opportunity, the Joint Task Force dispatched another team into the same area where the first search had been conducted in early 1995 and the gun wreckage had been found a year later. On June 18–19, 1996, the team surveyed the ridgeline and the burned area shown in the Putzel photo. On a slope below the hogback they found shreds of a vest but nothing else of interest.

Convinced they were on top of the crash site despite the lack of physical evidence, the team members returned to the ridge the next day, this time with Mr. Leu, the chief of nearby Ban Ta-Lai village. Leu, who had been away hunting when the MIA survey team previously visited the area, looked at the burned area, shook his head, and led the Americans up and over the top of the ridge, then pointed down the east-facing hillside.

"There," he said.

Rocky, thick with bamboo, the hill sloped away from a fairly gentle thirty degrees near the top to fifty degrees and finally a precipitous seventy-degree drop to a rocky streambed. After returning to the area after 1974, villagers had scavenged this site, as they had others. Any large pieces of metal were long ago sold or used for building. Based on the witnesses' account of the flaming crash, there probably had been relatively little such material to collect.

Clambering about the wooded slope, the searchers found several unexploded cluster bombs. They also turned up the first solid clues to the crash: shreds of cloth; a badly crushed U.S.-type steel helmet; a tooth; a possible bone shard; and bits of metal and plastic that the team's aircraft expert diagnosed as having come from a Bell Aircraft Corp. UH-1 helicopter. Most significantly, they recovered a few shreds of 35mm film—the emulsion was long gone, but otherwise it was intact after twenty-seven years. It was the type of film used by news photographers, not something normally found in significant quantities at crash sites.

In the carefully modulated, one-step-at-a-time procedure employed by JTF-FA for all crash sites, the evidence was left in place and photographed. The team's report would be the basis for any decision to return to the site. And in his report, the team's equipment analyst, Sergeant Thomas Cherro, called the film "a strong indicator [that] this is probably the crash site associated with Case 2062." His superiors concurred, signing off the report with their own recommendation that would take the search to the next and crucial level: "Excavate."

∷

Once again, a call from Hawaii. It was late June 1996, and the caller was Roger King. In the previous two years I had developed a telephone friendship with Roger and with Major (later Lieutenant Colonel) Barbara Claypool, the public affairs officers at Joint Task Force headquarters, talking to them about various MIA cases that might one day be turned into an interesting story. Any one of them had that potential, of course, but I was primarily focused on two—the midair collision of two B-52 bombers over the South China Sea in July 1967, in which a two-star general was among the missing, and of course case 2062, the Laos helicopter crash. Every time we spoke, I reminded them of my special interest in the latter incident, and my desire to be on the scene, with a companion, if the Laos mountainside was ever to be excavated.

In this call, Roger got right to the point. "I've got some good news on 2062. We think we've found the crash site." I listened with growing excitement as he told me about what had been discovered on the hillside—the tattered vest, part of a helicopter skid, and pieces of windshield Plexiglas "consistent with" a Bell UH-1 Huey, a bashed-in U.S.-type steel helmet, and shards of film.

"Film?" I asked, incredulous. "They actually found film?"

Roger replied that the searchers indeed had found strips of 35-millimeter film scattered about the site. Even though the emulsion was worn away after twenty-seven years, the importance of the film could not be overestimated. It was true that some American helicopter crewmen carried small personal cameras in their flameproofs; I always thought it somewhat ludicrous to see a pilot or door gunner flying into danger suddenly whip out his little Olympus and start taking snapshots. South Vietnamese pilots generally didn't do this. People were always ready to question their military prowess, but tourists in their own country they weren't.

Still there was no indication of when an excavation might take place. Every MIA-related foray, or "joint field activity," was subject to a schedule set by the host government. American teams could not simply fly in and poke around. The searches were preplanned, approved by Laotian officials and carried out in batches of several at a time, four times a year. To complicate matters, the Laotians were then insisting that the sites be given priority on a north-to-south basis. As there were scores of crash sites still awaiting investigation in northern and central Laos, it could be a long time before the teams worked their way down into the panhandle and Savannakhet province.[1] Even so, it was the most encouraging news we could have had at that time. I sent an e-mail to Horst Faas in London, advising him of the discovery of film, and the now-near certainty that the site would be excavated.

In the hoping and the planning for this endeavor, Horst had been my first—and only—candidate for a partner. Given his Indochina experience, his general savvy about the jungle, and his personal commitment to preserving the memory of those who had covered the Vietnam War with cameras, there could be no better choice. When I proposed the idea to Horst, he was immediately enthusiastic. We began laying plans, tentative though they were, toward the day that we might actually walk on the mountain and touch the past as no one had ever done.

We agreed that it was important not to advertise our intentions too broadly. For one thing, there was no assurance that any of this would ever happen. For another, we did not want to stir up interest among other journalists. We could foresee a nightmarish swirl of reporters and TV crews, people with no stake or real interest in the story beyond its fleeting news value, clambering about the hillside, intruding on the

---

[1] As it turned out, further field work on Case 2062 was postponed three times over the next eighteen months.

Laos plan. Moreover, the infusion of more British flavor meant only one thing: The BBC production was to be all about Larry Burrows, with the other three dead photographers reduced to minor background figures.

With due respect to Larry, the story as Horst and I envisioned it was not about one man; it was about all of them, four individuals from different places who, whatever their relative accomplishments in life and career, were united in sharing danger and who, in death, became brothers. We heard nothing more about the BBC project until months later, when the producer sent word that the network had decided against a staff project and had turned the proposal over to a freelance producer. After one or two contacts, he also bowed out of the picture. Once again, we were on our own.

16 : Return to Laos

After months of on-again, off-again delays, word came suddenly in February 1998: A Joint Task Force team would be going to Laos in March to excavate several sites, and Site 2062 was on the list. If Horst and I wanted to be there, we had to act fast.

Visas were necessary, of course. But a passport and cover letter sent to the Laos embassy in Washington languished on a functionary's desk for two agonizing weeks. Increasingly worried that the long process might collapse at the last minute because of an indifferent bureaucrat, I appealed to contacts at the Joint Task Force in Hawaii for advice. They understood the problem and referred me to a U.S. embassy consular official in Vientiane who was known for her skills in cutting through red tape. Gambling on her assurances of help, I retrieved my passport from the Washington embassy.

Travel plans were complicated as well. Yet amazingly, everything fell into place. By prearrangement, Horst and I would rendezvous in Bangkok and fly to Vientiane. Horst flew from London to Bangkok, then booked into a hotel room at the airport. Six hours later, I arrived in Bangkok on a twenty-six-hour flight from New York via Seoul.

At midnight, I knocked on the door at the airport hotel. Horst opened it, expressing his predictable annoyance at being disturbed. "Where the hell have you been?" Hearing the familiar accent, I knew that this project, so long in the wishing, so difficult in the planning, was finally to become reality.

Vientiane's Wattay airport was its old, somnolent self on the bright Saturday morning that we arrived from Bangkok. A couple of small commuter-type aircraft in the livery of Lao Aviation squatted on the sun-seared tarmac. Where once the vintage C-46s of Air America, the CIA airline, took on cargoes of rice for the villages and weapons for the mercenary armies in the northern mountains, there was only empty concrete. I wondered if a camera could somehow capture the latent thermal image of one of those planes, like the cars whose ghostly outlines were photographed in supermarket parking lots back home.

: :

Surrounded by Thailand on the south, hermetic Burma on the west, China on the north, and the battling Vietnams on the east, the Laos of precommunist days sat uneasily in its mountain cockpit, a place apart in a multitude of ways. It was known in those times as the Land of the Million Elephants and the White Parasol, a phrase that did justice to the quaint charms of the mountain kingdom but belied the undercurrents of political treachery and violence flowing through its history.

Except for the Buddhist temples that shaped its exotic image, Vientiane during those years could have been a dusty river town anywhere in the world—a Hannibal, Missouri, on the Mekong, where even the clock lost its urgency in the lazy afternoon heat. In languid, bougainvillea-scented evenings, tinkling laughter and a promise of carnal pleasures drifted from tiny bars on unlit, unpaved side streets. After midnight, the silence might be broken only by the creak of a *samlo* bicycle taxi heading back to the hotel.

It was probably the only country where the official press spokesman for the U.S. embassy was a former Polish submarine captain. Most members of the American community at that time lived in Kilometer Six, a suburb of homes, lawns, backyard barbecues, and tricycles-in-driveways that looked as if it had been airlifted intact from the outskirts of Kansas City, circa 1965. Vientiane also boasted the world's only known Arc de Triomphe built with stolen cement. The Patuxai, or Victory Gate, a garish Southeast Asian version of the Paris landmark, had been erected in the 1960s with concrete originally intended by the U.S. aid agency for airport improvements. The local people, we would learn, still called it the "vertical runway."

The government then had been a masterpiece of political accommodation, in which the Pathet Lao, a homegrown communist insurgency vaguely comparable to the Viet Cong, was both a part of the neutral coalition and its enemy on the battlefield. The Pathet Lao leader, Prince Souvanaphong, was the estranged half-brother of the pro-Western prime minister, Souvanna Phouma, and lived in armed exile in the mountains. But Pathet Lao troops had their own compound in the city and went shopping in the morning market like everyone else—except that they wore uniforms and rode in military vehicles.

The first test for a newly arrived correspondent in Laos was to get a grip on all this; the second was to make it plausible to readers. As Laos was not a regular fixture on front pages, major news organizations paid part-time stringers there to keep track of daily events, sending out alerts when the need arose for heavyweight reporters to come rushing in from Saigon, Bangkok, or Hong Kong. Once on the scene, these visitors followed a basic routine—making the rounds of briefings with U.S. and Laotian officials, following up with brain-picking sessions with key foreign diplomats, local journalists, and others who stood to be well informed even if outside the official loop.

The secret war waged by General Vang Pao's CIA-financed Hmong army against the Pathet Lao and the North Vietnamese in the 1960s and 1970s was just that—secret. Vang Pao's mountain redoubt at Long Cheng, northeast of Vientiane, was officially off-limits to visitors and, except for occasional glimpses by enterprising journalists or trekkers, was as phantasmic as Shangri-la.

The best way for journalists to see any of northern Laos—and, if lucky, something of the conflict—was to hitch a ride on an Air America "rice-drop" flight. These aged but sturdy C-46 cargo planes droned deep into the mountains, skimming low over isolated villages as native "kickers" shoved wooden pallets of bagged rice out the door. It was understood, though not officially admitted, that weapons were delivered to sympathetic tribal groups the same way.

In Vientiane, foreign journalists were generally regarded by the embassy and Air America people as the equivalent of bubonic plague carriers. Only privileged outsiders, and very few reporters, gained acceptance at the Purple Porpoise, the bar where the pilots of the CIA airline put their hand-tooled cowboy boots on the rail.

Journalists relied for most of their information on military attachés and analysts at the U.S. embassy. By their account, the war was an endless spinning of dry-season offensives, forever threatening strategic road junctions near the Plain of Jars, a high-mountain plateau northeast of Vientiane that was littered with ancient stone jars of uncertain purpose, left there by a long-lost civilization. The fighting never seemed to resolve anything, and the embassy briefings, always on a nonattributable background basis, were purposefully opaque on the U.S. role. The United States supported the neutral coalition government, but questions about the alleged delivery of weapons and drug smuggling were dismissed as having no basis in fact.

: :

With time to kill, Horst and I set out to find what remained of the old Laos. Much of Southeast Asia lay under a pall of haze from fires as far away as Indonesia, and along Vientiane's riverfront the air was especially acrid with smoke from the fires of the late dry season. The normally swift-flowing Mekong River was reduced in places to only a trickle between undulating dunes of exposed riverbed. There we found Vientiane's most visible postwar civic improvement: a bridge spanning the Mekong, connecting the city with the Thai town of Long Khai. One of only two bridges in the 2,600 miles of the world's eighth longest river, it stood as a symbol of true economic progress under Lao-style socialism but sorely lacked the cheeky panache of the previous government's misnamed Victory Gate.

The more we wandered about, looking for the past, the more we found things had changed—yet remained the same. There was little to suggest that a war was once fought here, almost nothing to indicate that the country was now under a socialist regime. The U.S. embassy, the onetime hotbed of high-tech espionage and military intrigue, looked about the same, but the current ambassador, Wendy J. Chamberlin, bore no resemblance to the succession of tough cold warriors who had managed the clandestine struggle three decades earlier.

This was not because Chamberlin was lacking in the Laotian experience. Back then, as she explained to us in an interview, Chamberlin had been a member of International Voluntary Services (IVS), a Peace Corps–like organization, jointly funded by private and government sources, that operated in several Southeast Asian countries.

The IVS volunteers were mostly idealistic young Americans—many of them conscientious objectors—who performed good works but did not hesitate to express pacifist and sometimes radical anti-establishment attitudes that earned them few friends in U.S. diplomatic and military circles. The ambassador was quick to acknowledge that as the daughter of a career Marine Corps officer she probably had not fit precisely the mold of the sandal-shod youth brigades in wartime Laos.

In our meeting, she said that being on the losing side had not diminished long-range U.S. interests in Laos, which she defined as economic and agricultural development, the ever-troublesome narcotics trade, and efforts to deal with unexploded ordnance, a leftover problem for which the United States bore special responsibility.

Other than a glancing brush with its foreign ministry bureaucracy, we saw little evidence of a nation under communist-style iron rule. "We haven't even seen a policeman," said Horst. Was this a police state with no cops? Not exactly, Ms. Chamberlin explained; although it had only one political party and a flag with a hammer and sickle on it, the Laos government did not consider itself a communist state but one in transition to a more democratic model. Ninety percent of local enterprises had been privatized, and the United States, former enemy and citadel of capitalism, was Laos's second largest source of foreign investment after Thailand. Laos, she said, was pledged to a future as a multiparty state "when it becomes appropriate."

Vientiane's several new hotels reflected the apparent confidence of the foreign investors, and in design and comfort they were a long way from the stolid architecture, surly staff, and grudging amenities that are the hallmarks of totalitarian hospitality. At the Lao Plaza, blazing tiki torches invited guests and passersby to an outdoor beer garden where waiters served large frosty pitchers of Heineken. Noisy, smoke-belching motorcycle taxis had largely replaced the pedal-powered *samlos* as the people's transport, but these, too, were barred from the hotel driveway where official-looking black Mercedes-Benzes arrived and departed in a door-slamming bustle worthy of Hong Kong.

The new regime hadn't gotten around to paving the streets, and, as we expected, the city's fabled night life was gone. For nostalgia's sake we went looking for the former site of the White Rose, an Indochina saloon-bordello once legendary among journalists, spooks, and government officials. Unable to find the White Rose on streets that all looked the same, we sought refuge in a small bar where a bored young woman served beer before going back to watching Thai music videos on a TV set above the bar.

Vientiane's other famous after-dark emporium, the legendary Madame Loulou's, also was history. For years, Loulou, central casting's version of a French brothel-keeper, hair coifed high and face garishly made up, had presided over a shabby bungalow on a quiet side street, where the house specialty, indeed its only service, was oral sex.

I thought back to 1970 when Kent Potter, visiting Laos for the first time, was introduced to Loulou's. The grande dame, who was said to train all her girls personally, took one look at the tall, handsome Potter, announced "he ees mine," and led him into her boudoir with its rococo-lampshade decor. Memory ends there; presumably Kent came away from his first encounter at Loulou's another satisfied customer. When the war ended, so did Loulou's career as proprietress of the brothel that was at once the most notorious and the most secret establishment of its kind in Southeast Asia. Loulou, who had spoken of her wish to someday return to France and perhaps run a small *tabac*, left Vientiane and vanished into obscurity.

Walking back to Thong Nhat, Vientiane's main street, Horst studied a white-fronted building, the Asia Pavilion Hotel. Although much changed, we recognized it as the former Constellation Hotel where, back in the 1960s, owner Maurice Cavallerie, an expatriate Frenchman who also held the franchise on imported Heineken beer, had played host to most of the foreign journalists visiting Vientiane in hopes of plumbing the mysteries of Laos. One of these was the plumbing of the Constellation, whose bathrooms were so small that one could sit on the toilet, take a shower, and brush one's teeth at the same time. In a daily afternoon ritual, visiting and resident correspondents would gather in Maurice's lobby bar to compare the latest information and try to figure out what it meant. The lobby of the Constellation may be the place where the word "surreal" became a cliche.

I remembered my first visit to Laos and that circle, probably in early 1969. The embassy press officer of that time, who was dominating the discussion before what seemed a rapt audience, had seemed familiar. When someone called him Jerry, the realization dawned that he was Jerome Doolittle, who had been a friend of my brother's when they served Army duty together at Fort Myer, Virginia, in the late 1950s.

Horst and I moved on to the Lao Revolutionary Museum, housed in the onetime French governor's palace. Among the hodge-podge of flyspecked exhibits of Laotian history, mountain culture, and military souvenirs was one that featured some early 1960s-vintage photos that Horst, to his considerable amusement, recognized as his own work. They were black-and-white pictures of U.S. military advisers whose names he was even able to recall. The captions were heavyhanded propaganda rhetoric and, of course, gave no credit to the photographer.

Like most authoritarian governments, the Laotian regime requires that visiting journalists travel with official escorts. Their responsibilities range from facilitating transportation and opening official doors to explaining to the local official in his native tongue why he does not want to be interviewed, and spelling out the "safety concerns" that prevent the visitor from wandering into sensitive or unauthorized areas. Dusadee Haymond, the U.S. embassy consular officer who had hacked through the bureaucratic bamboo to help us obtain Laotian visas and personally steered us past airport immigration formalities, now arranged to introduce us to our minder at the press department of the Ministry of Foreign Affairs.

Over tea in his office, we found Soukhasavan Sanapay to be a young man with a pleasant manner and an uncertain command of English. We were not sure that he understood the exact nature of our mission, but he knew his job when it came to spelling out the rules. We were not allowed, he said, to take pictures of "military installations, bridges, or hydroelectric plants." *Cold War paranoia dies hard*, I thought.

When Horst assured Soukhasavan that we had no interest in such things, he seemed satisfied, and we parted with an agreement to rendezvous at 4:30 A.M. for the one-hour flight to Savannakhet, a southern province capital. From there it would be 125 miles by road on the next-to-last leg of our journey. There were only six passengers on the small, twin-engine aircraft, but even at that hour Lao Aviation felt it was necessary to provide entertainment. Almost from takeoff to landing, the shrill voice of Whitney Houston knifed from a loudspeaker directly above our seats. No amount of pleading could get the lone cabin attendant to turn down the torture, but fortunately we landed before Horst's annoyance reached critical mass.

At Savannakhet's run-down wooden terminal we encountered our American escort-to-be, Army Lieutenant Colonel Roger King, who was seeing off three Americans, officials of the Veterans of Foreign Wars, who had been on their own guided tour of crash sites. "You're going to be very impressed," one of them said. I was struck by how much these men of the Vietnam era resembled the World War II generation that one usually associates with veterans' groups. Time was creeping in its petty pace.

Our final staging point in Savannakhet was the Phonepaseud Hotel, whose proprietor, Somphone Bounphakom, exemplified capitalist genius run amok in a socialist economy. Not only did he own and manage a combination motel-restaurant-discotheque with "the best swimming pool in southern Laos"; he also owned the local drinking-water plant, producing an unending parade of white plastic bottles of potable water. "Mr. Water," as some called him, also had the contracts to provide lodging for various international organizations operating in the area. This included the Joint Task Force's MIA search teams, which used his hotel as a regional base.

For the overland leg of our long journey, Somphone was ready with an almost-new Toyota Land Cruiser and driver. The price was $100 per day—expensive by Laotian standards but well worth it considering the deplorable state of Route 9 for most of the 125 miles. Our destination, Sepone, was eight hours away, over the crazy-quilt of dirt and broken asphalt that the old French highway had become. Traffic was all but nonexistent, but road hazards included cows, water buffalo, goats, dogs, and children. In some places, brush fires raged along the shoulder of the road, as if seeking a way to leap across.

Sepone, twenty-five miles west of the border, had been the final objective of OPERATION LAM SON 719. The name then had been Tche-pone, although both spellings still appeared on regional maps. All but destroyed by bombers before the invasion, Tchepone's strategic value was its location, close to where the main north-south roads of the Ho Chi Minh Trail crossed Route 9. Once Saigon's forces reached the town, they could claim to have cut across, thereby severing the entire Trail.

As we drove eastward, the open, undulating terrain turned into forested foothills, and the dark shapes of the Annamites loomed be-yond. Reaching Sepone, we searched in vain for the government guest-house; even our minder had no idea where it was. Eventually we found it, on the grounds of an agricultural research farm. The facilities, in that spirit, were rustic. It was a small building on cinderblock stilts—a safeguard against snakes and other pests—a main room with four bunks, each equipped with a mosquito net. (Though we had been warned in advance about voracious, malaria-carrying mosquitoes, they proved to be nonexistent in the late dry season.)

There was no electricity in the guest house, and the bathroom consisted of a large cement tub that was kept filled with cold water when it ran, intermittently, from a single tap, with several plastic buck-ets for self-dousing. It was primitive but gloriously invigorating, and we found ourselves being immersed—not just in the bath but in Southeast Asia itself.

As reconstituted from its wartime shambles, Sepone still was not much more than a string of ramshackle wooden buildings along a mile of the highway, but it was nevertheless the main population cen-ter of the area. There were a few shops and coffeehouses, a large morn-ing market, and a smaller black market that required a little effort to locate, behind a row of shacks. The town had no heroic statue or gran-ite memorial to fallen heroes; the only monument to its wartime or-deal was a large bomb casing standing erect beside the highway, painted with a skull-and-bones and the letters "USA." Sepone, as a dis-trict capital, also was a regional center for education on the perils of unexploded ordnance (UXO)—leftover bombs and shells that were, as we would discover, in plentiful supply in the jungles of the Laos pan-handle.

Sepone's UXO Center produced a variety of posters and warning signs geared to the local population, and one coffeehouse had decorated its walls with them. The posters showed various types of explosives and peasants being blown up by objects they had found or inadvertently stepped on. One poster warned farmers not to wield a scythe closer than ten centimeters to the ground, lest it cut into a hidden cluster bomb and blow off a leg.

Among the town's few commercial establishments we found a restaurant that looked more promising than the others and turned out to be ideal for our purposes. It was a sort of open-air Laotian truck stop—open from early morning until very late at night and catering almost exclusively to Vietnamese drivers hauling cargo overland between the South China Sea coast and Savannakhet on the Mekong.

Anyone who drove that rocky road called Route 9 on a regular basis certainly deserved a good meal. The owner, Madame Me Tao, served up a hearty bowl of the breakfast soup called *pho*, in addition to other Vietnamese specialties. Stocky and gray-haired, Me Tao was a native of Saigon who had lived in Sepone since 1950. She had stubbornly remained through the worst of the war days—and had a shrapnel scar on her face to show for it. We ate all our meals there for three days—almost always in the company of the truckers, who took little interest in our presence, as if camera-toting foreigners were everyday customers at their roadside eatery. We presumed that they presumed we were tourists.

After an early dinner on the first evening, we drove east, across the Chinese bridge, toward the Vietnamese border. The country beyond the town was deserted, the road itself a narrow track whose shoulders were covered with scrub growth—the same thick foliage that had helped the North Vietnamese lie in ambush for the South Vietnamese tanks coming from the other direction twenty-seven years earlier. Six miles east of Sepone, we found what we were looking for: the Ban Alang base camp, a cluster of blue tents in an open field just off the highway. We weren't expected until the next morning but were welcomed by Lieutenant Colonel James Ransick, the commander of JTF's Detachment Three, responsible for all MIA investigations in Laos.

There were, at the time, eighty-four MIA crash sites still to be explored in Laos, thirty of them in the area, and most near the Ho Chi Minh Trail. The majority had been fighter-bombers carrying one or two aviators. That sounded easy compared to a helicopter with eleven victims, seven of them Vietnamese whose personal records probably had been lost. Ransick conceded that Site 2062 posed special challenges, but "there is no such thing as an easy crash site."

In our case, the area's villagers had been willing to forgo the special demands they sometimes made as a condition for allowing the intrusion of MIA search teams. Frequently, Ransick said, the excavation of a site could not begin until the spirits were appeased in the traditional manner of the Bru tribe, that is, by the sacrifice of a water buffalo or a pig. "There are always cultural sensitivities. Cultural beliefs dictate the way we do business," he said.

Returning to Sepone, we bedded down at the guesthouse in pitch darkness, with the cowbells tinkling gently in the pasture outside. The next morning—after a waking dream and an early bowl of *pho* at Me Tao's—we set out again for Ban Alang and our first flight to crash site 2062.

17 : "A Handful of Soil"

When Horst and I stepped off the little French helicopter at Site 2062, the first order of business was typically military—a briefing. We sat on crude wooden benches under the blue tent as Captain Jeff Price, the commander of the nine-member Joint Task Force–Full Accounting team, gave us our bearings on a map tacked to a tent pole, and explained the procedures used in excavating.

Price was a thirty-three-year-old career soldier from Springfield, Oregon, and like all team members was a volunteer for this duty. He knew the history of the crash, the names of the known victims, and other details. We were struck at the outset, and would be again, by the deep personal commitment that these people—none of them more than children when the Vietnam War ended—manifested toward the task at hand.

The local Bru villagers, not demanding animal sacrifice to placate the gods, may have been appeased themselves at the prospect of being paid to help with the digging and screening of dirt. The standard rate was $24 per day. On paper that seemed a princely sum for the average Laotian subsistence farmer, but under the diplomatic agreement governing Joint Task Force operations, the money was paid directly to the Laos government, to be distributed by it to the hired workers. The American team members admitted they didn't know how much of it actually reached the laborers scrabbling in the dirt for bones and artifacts.

As team commander, Price shared the decision-making with the team's only civilian member, anthropologist Lisa Hoshower. She was in overall charge of the recovery operations, deciding when and where to dig—and, ultimately, when to declare the job done. The other seven team members were a military mix, mostly career men, and most of them experienced in this work—collectively, some forty-four MIA search missions.

The oldest member, at thirty-eight, was U.S. Air Force Master Sergeant Ralf Hawkins, of Fort Smith, Arkansas, the team's medic; the youngest, U.S. Army Specialist and photographer Michael Harsch, twenty-four, of Salt Lake City. Others included a Marine Corps explosives expert, two Army mortuary affairs specialists, a linguist-interpreter, and an Air Force life support technician trained to identify aircraft parts and equipment.

The second day of work—the first full day of digging—had just begun when Horst and I arrived. Looking down the slope from the ridgeline, we could see Laotian workers formed in a bucket brigade, passing pails of dirt to a screening station. Others were busy lashing together another platform of cut bamboo. These *Kon-Tiki*–like structures resembled pictures of bridges built by the North Vietnamese to carry troops and supplies over streams and steep ravines during the war. How many of these workers, we wondered, had honed their construction skills in the service of the *bo doi?*

On the previous day, before any digging began, the Americans had chopped away the bamboo, leaving only stubble, and swept the entire area for UXO—any bombs or other explosives that were readily visible on the ground. Finding and clearing explosives was a requirement at every MIA excavation site in Indochina, but it was especially important in this part of Laos, where the land was littered with cluster bombs, dud bombs, and shells—the lethal leftovers that the posters in the Sepone coffee shop warned about.

We noticed that on opposite sides of the ridge lay the rusted halves of a large steel pod, one of the bomb casings that had spewed the

CBU-26 cluster bombs over the hillside where we stood. Each such bomb could cover a space the size of a football field with 200–600 of the fiendish area denial weapons. Roughly 80–90 percent of them would detonate on release, but the rest might lie in wait for months, even years, before some disturbance caused them to explode.

A few steps below the hilltop, Jeff Price showed us a shallow pit, marked with a red warning sign and containing a dozen or so of the gray, baseball-sized globes that were capable of killing a person if kicked, dropped, or even tilted the wrong way. Jeff said the local people called them "bombies" and had learned to leave them alone. Numerous Laotian villagers had paid the price for not doing so; the amazing thing was that no Joint Task Force member or site worker had ever been injured.

Once the UXO was dealt with, the team surveyed the terrain, setting a base marker on the upper slope from which to measure off a grid of squares, 5 meters on a side. From the crest, the east-facing hill inclined downward about twenty-two degrees for some 50 meters, where the tape marked the crash site's upper boundary. From there it tilted to a steeper thirty-two degrees and finally to a sheer forty-five degrees about 150 meters down, where it ended in a shallow, rocky streambed. Climbing naturally was difficult everywhere on the hill; one slip and a person could be impaled on a truncated bamboo stalk. We needed makeshift walking sticks to keep our feet. The team also rigged ropes from trees on the lower hill, there being no other way to negotiate that part of the slope without sliding down the rocky, loose-clay surface into the creek.

The hill looked like an archaeological dig anywhere—small red and blue plastic flags marked locations where an initial survey had turned up metal and plastic shards, bits of film, a couple of boot soles. Yellow pennants marked potentially explosive items yet to be policed up.

The search was moving downward with amazing speed and efficiency. As each grid square was scraped with shovels and hand tools to a depth of ten to forty-five centimeters, the dirt was passed up to the screening stations, dumped into wood-framed boxes, and sifted through quarter-inch screen. Whatever remained on a screen after the sifting was then examined by an American team member; if it was not a stone or something else common to the hillside, it was added to the growing collection of clamps, bolts, and other items to be examined further.

The holy grail could be a bit of bone, a human tooth—numerous identifications of MIAs have been made through a single lonely bicuspid. But everything that didn't fall through the screen was potentially interesting, and at each station one of the Americans hovered behind the sifters, peering over their shoulders like prospectors looking for glitter in the pay dirt.

Halfway down the hill, Jeff Price introduced us to Lisa Hoshower, a forty-one-year-old tomboy with clear green eyes, bushy, sun-bleached hair under a well-worn baseball cap, and a mordant wit, nurtured and honed in earlier careers, which included police work and a stint as a security guard at the Three Mile Island nuclear plant in her native Pennsylvania. In the latter role, Hoshower happened to have been on duty the night in 1979 when a radiation leak from the number-two reactor triggered a partial meltdown and the biggest crisis in the history of the American nuclear industry. That experience, she said, "convinced me that being a guard in a nuclear power plant was not what I wanted to do with my life." She returned to school, earned her Ph.D., and traded her cop's badge and sidearm for an archaeologist's trowel, working in Turkey, Peru, Spain, Egypt, Chile, and Illinois before CILHI hired her in 1994 to lead MIA excavation teams.

Even as we talked, Hoshower was directing that the work shift from the upper hillside, where few interesting items were being uncovered, to the gully that ran down the north side. Years of erosion had caused considerable slope wash down the ravine into the streambed, she said. "During the monsoons, they tell us, it's a whoosh—a rushing torrent. We're going to find a lot of stuff down there." Almost certainly, she added, that would include some human remains.

Roger King bantered with Hoshower over this. "How would you like to find a twenty-one-inch femur?" he asked. The anthropologist shot back, "I could live with that. I'd get a bottle of Jack Daniel's over that!" Like characters from *M*A*S*H*, the team relied on the irreverent humor that helps to sustain people engaged in essentially grim enterprises like searching for the violently dead. The work was hot and arduous, and Staff Sergeant Michael Swam, thirty-one, of Largo, Florida, called frequent rest breaks. An Army mortuary specialist by training, Swam on this dig was the senior team sergeant—in effect the straw boss. Everyone sat down and drank from the white plastic bottles from Somphone's bottling plant back in Savannakhet. There was no rationing of water; pallets of the white plastic containers were stacked in the command tent and handed out freely among the workers. After ten minutes or so, Swam would bellow an order and the workers returned to their tasks.

Though burdened with cameras, Horst was negotiating the steep hillside with the same big man's agility that had got him through countless ordeals in the wilds of Africa and Indochina, but he was skeptical of the wanton consumption of water. "In Vietnam, we always took salt tablets," he groused. Times had changed, Jeff Price told him; the field doctrine of the New Army was constant liquid replenishment.

During a midday lunch break, the American team members trudged up the hill and gathered in the blue tent, breaking out rations of crackers and cheese, cans of tuna, and Dinty Moore stew. Among the last to arrive was Air Force Tech Sergeant Aaron Carpenter, who brought along the morning's take of intriguing artifacts. Carpenter, thirty-two, from Los Angeles, was the team's life support technician, whose first task at most crash sites was to determine whether a pilot had ejected or ridden the plane down. Remains found close by the wreckage indicated the latter. But bodies also could have been removed; finding ejection-seat parts in the debris was the more reliable clue. If they weren't present, then chances were that the pilot got out before impact.

Obviously, none of this mattered in a helicopter crash; here, Carpenter was looking for items that would confirm the aircraft as a UH-1 Huey helicopter—and, with luck, a metal data plate with serial numbers traceable to a specific aircraft. The materials recovered thus far, though just fragments, were consistent with a Huey, but that was as far as it went.

In addition to the morning's harvest of "BAS," or broken aircraft shit, as Joint Task Force members called it, Carpenter had two items of special interest: a pair of U.S.-type steel helmets. They were badly smashed, rust-caked, and showed signs of having been in a fire—the plastic liners were almost fused to the steel. After some discussion, we agreed that the helmets probably had belonged to the two South Vietnamese colonels, Nhat and Vi, who had boarded the helicopter at the last minute. This was a process of elimination; the helicopter's two pilots, crew chief, and door gunner would have worn standard flight helmets, and pictures of the four photographers before takeoff do not show any of them wearing helmets. Photographer-Sergeant Tu Vu does not appear in the pictures, but there was no reason to think he had a helmet, either. They were an encumbrance that most photographers preferred to do without. The two colonels would have been in combat gear, including helmets. This was the first of several discoveries that fell neatly into place—supporting, or at least not contradicting, known facts of the incident.

Though MIA search policy only rarely allowed for an official ruling without forensic identification of human remains, the finding of 35mm film shards was already solid proof, at least for our purposes, that this was indeed the hillside where the photographers' helicopter had come violently to earth. Some U.S. helicopter crew members in Vietnam carried personal snapshot cameras, but the South Vietnamese were not known for that. Jeff Price noted astutely that a helicopter on a strictly military mission would have no reason to have so much film aboard, and Lisa Hoshower concurred. "It really guarantees that we're looking in the right place," she told us.

But Lisa's frustration was beginning to show. The absence of remains where she was convinced they should be found was a puzzle. An aircraft crash that killed eleven people ought to yield something in the way of bones or teeth. Once, when a promising nugget turned up at the screening station, a team member called urgently for Lisa to come and see it, but she took her time, refusing to get excited. "Whatever it is, it's been here for twenty-eight years, and it's not going any place," she said. On close examination, what at first resembled a tiny bit of human bone turned out to be a shard of plastic. "There is no bone shaped like that in the human body," Lisa said, returning to the ravine where she had been digging out a bamboo root with a pickaxe.

We took note of the fact that the nine Americans did not simply stand around directing their forty-two Lao laborers but set an example by doing the heavy work—chopping out roots, moving rocks, wielding shovels. When Hoshower spotted a pair of Lao workers taking a break by themselves, she confronted them: "You two, sittin' on your butts. You only stand up when I come around." The verbal message was lost on the two workers, but her forceful manner seemed to get the point across, as the two men turned glumly and looked for something to do.

It was clear that Jeff Price was not alone in his personal commitment to this task. All the team members seemed to approach it as if looking for their own long-lost relatives. In a way, that was true. Most of those who died in Indochina had been about the same age and were mostly military—people that the team members themselves could relate to. "This is probably the most honorable thing we are doing right now," said Master Sergeant Hawkins, who, in addition to his job as medic, was a sort of self-appointed goodwill ambassador to the workers.

Even so, Hawkins, on his eighth search in Laos and thirteenth overall, was the only member of the team who had ever actually met an MIA relative—the son of a tail gunner whose B-24 Liberator bomber crashed in southern China during World War II. "It just made me feel good to see him there," Hawkins said. Generally, the team members seemed to think it was enough—perhaps better—to perform the work anonymously. All MIAs and their families were equal; the passion was in the work and the discovery.

Late in the afternoon of the first day, small forest fires began erupting on nearby hillsides, blazing furiously for minutes, then dying out, only to burst forth again on another slope. Price got on the radio, and for a time it looked as if he might have to call in the JTF's two Squirrel helicopters to evacuate the fourteen nonnatives from Site 2062. The fire abated before getting that close, but when we finally returned to the Ban Alang base camp, we found the Americans there exhausted from having just fought and defeated a serious fire of their own. Driven by a dry wind, the flames had crept to the edge of the helicopter landing area but were thwarted by backfires before burning into the tent area itself.

Day two began with a breakfast of *pho*, bananas, and coffee at Me Tao's cafe, after which we drove again out to Ban Alang and climbed aboard the chopper to Site 2062, where we found Jeff Price and his team already at work. Lisa Hoshower was doggedly repeating her optimistic prediction—human remains, she pledged, would be recovered this day. Work was now being concentrated in the ravine, which for excavation purposes was divided into three shallow pits dubbed, in descending order, R7, R8, and R9 (*R* meaning "ravine"). Part of the stream course running down the gully, they were marked off with rocks and sandbags, although the water at this stage of the dry season was barely a trickle.

We spent time at the hilltop, where I wanted to do some interviews while Horst, Jeff, and Roger King took a hike down the vague remnant of old Route 1032, a/k/a the Ho Chi Minh Trail or, as I liked to think of it, Bill Forsyth Boulevard. About 100 yards south of the crash site, under an overhanging ledge, they came upon the remnants of what obviously had been a gun emplacement. From there, the gunners would have had a clear shot at the helicopters, framed by the trees like ducks in flight. Jeff coined a phrase for it. "It was a kill-de-sac," he said. Roger agreed; any aircraft that flew past the gun location as the three Hueys had done "would have been in a death trap."

There was nothing, however, to prove that this gun was the one that shot them down. As Colonel Molinelli and others had noted, the area was studded with scores of antiaircraft guns, any number of which could have zeroed in on the wandering flight. The three explorers decided to cut their expedition short when they discovered the area where they were walking was a sylvan minefield, littered with half-buried cluster bombs.

During their absence, and with the help of the team's twenty-nine-year-old linguist and interpreter, Army Sergeant Don Anongdeth, of Los Angeles, I interviewed Mr. Leu, the village chief who had first shown another team of JTF investigators the mountainside back in 1996. This wizened, sunburned man, who looked older than his fifty-four years, confirmed that the road we were standing on had been part of the North Vietnamese supply route during the 1960s: "I never saw any trucks, but I heard the noises at night that must have been trucks."

Leu recalled how he fled his home village of Ban Ta-Lai in 1968 to escape the U.S. bombing and walked for two and a half days to another village. There he waited out the war until 1974, when Lao officials asked him to return to the village, where he was later elected chief. Leu, who could neither read nor write and supported his wife and four children as a subsistence farmer, said he was always looking for new places to plant rice and had decided the hillside was a likely place. While hacking away bamboo and undergrowth, he discovered pieces of metal and other debris indicating that an aircraft had crashed there.

But he was not the first to find it. "Many people had been to this place before, and the wreckage had been scavenged except for many small pieces. They were all burned," Leu said. The large pieces were sold at a trading center in the village of Ban Dan. Leu said he had never met anyone who had seen the helicopter come down or anyone who claimed to have seen bodies or to know whether the North Vietnamese might have buried any. At this point he seemed nervous, apparently mistaking my questioning on these points as some sort of official inquiry. "He wants you to know that he is poor but honest," Anongdeth translated. "He didn't see any of that."

Later on that second day, team members made a discovery that further confirmed the site, if any was needed. Digging between rocks in the ravine pit known as R7, Army Staff Sergeant Bill Adams, twenty-eight, the team's other mortuary specialist, from Buena Paris, California, suddenly stood erect, calling out "EOD man!" The Laotians nearby didn't know that "EOD" meant "explosives ordnance disposal," but they could see what Adams saw—a strange, round object protruding from the stones. "Bombie!" cried one, and they all dropped their pails and scrambled away, some of them slipping and sliding on the steep side of the gully.

Marine Staff Sergeant Carl Holden, of Wilson, North Carolina, made his way down to where Adams stood. Holden, twenty-eight, was the team's EOD specialist, responsible for sweeping the crash site for UXO before digging began and handling any that turned up later. After the site was closed, he would destroy all of it in one big controlled explosion. Holden bent down to study Adams's discovery in place, then gingerly dug it out and held it up for all to see. "It's a camera lens," he announced.

"They found a lens!" Horst called over to me, from his perch on the hill above R7. He was grinning in triumph.

We examined the lens closely. The crusted dirt of nearly three decades had frozen its focusing ring, and the filter was broken, but the maker's data was legible: Nikkor-H 35mm Auto T3 F=2.8 cm No. 315907 Nippon Kodaku Japan. Although the serial number offered search process, distracting the local workers, demanding briefings and on-camera interviews with the American team members.

In truth, I knew that if the word spread and other journalists or organizations took an interest in the story, there was nothing we could do about it. Television in particular had a way of disrupting an event. The very presence of a TV camera could change the dynamics of the story it set out to cover. We already had too much invested in the Laos project to let it become a staged, packaged-for-the-audience version of reality. My apprehension about this suddenly deepened with a telephone call from London. A British Broadcasting Company television producer had learned of our project—how, I did not know—and was proposing that a BBC crew be present to cover the excavation at the site if and when that might occur. I replied that it was the military's place, not ours, to say yes or to object, but we were determined that the story not be distorted or twisted into something other than what it was—a search for four people and, for us, a gesture of respect to their memory. I suggested that if BBC intended to cover it, perhaps it could do so as a documentary of our effort. In that case, BBC might also be willing to cover our expenses as part of the deal. The BBC man was thoroughly agreeable to this. He assured me that he understood our concern about maintaining the story's integrity and promised to send me an outline of the project as he envisioned it for broadcast.

In a week or so, the draft arrived in the mail. I read it over in amazement. The story line was laid out in elaborate detail, even down to describing our actions and the very thoughts that would be in our heads as we watched the excavation of the crash site where our friends had died. "In this documentary, Piles [sic], Faas, and [Tim] Page are principal characters obsessed with Vietnam and the glamour of war," it said. "Their memories paint a vivid picture of Vietnam's past and the events surrounding Burrows' death."

There it was. Bad enough, I thought, that they're willing to call this preimagined event a "documentary." Not only did they want to fill our made-for-TV minds with claptrap about obsession with war and its glamour; they intended to add a character to a story in which he had no real-life role. Friend that he was, Tim Page had no direct connection to the original event—the helicopter crash—or to our return-to-some hope of tracing the owner, it didn't matter all that much. A 28mm lens for a Nikon F camera had been standard equipment for Vietnam War photographers; it was a safe bet that some of those on the chopper, including Tu Vu, had carried one. Owner's name or not, it was another important piece of circumstantial evidence.

That evening, we looked ahead to one more day at the crash site. Already, the experience had been so intense that it seemed as if we'd been on the mountainside for weeks.

Earlier, Horst had said, "We ought to leave something behind." As it happened, we had the perfect answer; Horst had brought a copy of *Requiem*, the book about Vietnam War photographers—all of those who had died, on both sides—that he had coedited with Tim Page. It included a chapter on the Laos crash that I'd written, as well as many pictures by the four, particularly Larry Burrows and Henri Huet. We decided the book should be buried at the crash site, so we proposed the idea to Jeff Price.

Returning to Sepone, we dined as usual at Me Tao's. Some Vietnamese drivers were finishing their meal as we four arrived—Horst, Soukhasavan, our driver, and myself. As usual, they gave us only a cursory once-over as they paid the bill and roared away in a clashing of truck gears.

After dinner we drove back out to the Ban Alang camp, where we'd been invited to talk to the troops—not only our own team but also members of two others that were using the base for excavations at other MIA crash sites in the area. Before the assembled group of perhaps forty people, we told the story of the helicopter crash and its photographer-victims and how we came to be there. The soon-to-be-interred copy of *Requiem* made for a great visual aid.

Horst did most of the talking, rambling eloquently, as he tends to do when talking about his profession and the people in it. He spoke movingly of our dead colleagues. There was an affectionate humanity in the words that I had not heard previously from the practical genius I had known for thirty years.

Larry Burrows, he said, "incorporated all the good things about the British, but he was a citizen of the world." Henri Huet was a man loved and admired by all who knew him, a man with no detractors, and there was a special sadness in the fact that only after his death—many years after—had the quality of his work come to be fully appreciated. "What would Henri and Larry think about all this?" Horst asked, referring to the activity now associated with their deaths. "They'd have a joke about it. But we hope they wouldn't make a joke. We'd hope that they'd understand what was going on, they'd understand what all these Americans are doing, disturbing something that doesn't need to be disturbed."

He added, *sotto voce* to me, "Henri would have liked these guys. Maybe that's why he is letting them do this."

Horst mentioned the finding of film at the crash site, film that had been long ago exposed to the light and then exposed to years of weather, so that the entire emulsion was worn away, leaving nothing. "The film is the essence," he said. "We'll never know what was on it ... a mystic message. Put it in a scanner and get an abstract pattern of decay." He seemed to be suggesting there were ghosts on the film, if only they could be seen.

Finally, he said, referring to the search team at Site 2062, "We are glad that they are not finding bone. Sometimes you have to put rationality aside and believe in spirits for a little while." In so saying Horst spoke for both of us. Although recovering remains was the central point of the exercise for the JTF team, it was not so important to us. If the bones could not easily be found, perhaps it was just as well that they not be found, that the hillside remain the natural repository that it had been for nearly thirty years.

At the crash site for the third day, we discussed the business of the *Requiem* book burial with Jeff Price. He offered to keep the book and have the team bury it in an appropriate spot just before they closed the site, which was scheduled to happen on April 5, two weeks hence. We settled on a spot halfway down the hill, where the steep slope leveled off briefly before plunging on to the streambed. Roger King had dug a shallow test hole there on the first day, and with a little more spadework it would be perfect for a ritual interment.

Jeff Price produced his hand-held Global Positioning System device and in a minute or so had linked to four satellites, fixing the spot down to its one-square-meter location on the earth's surface. It was ideal. The book could be wrapped in plastic and placed in the ground upright, facing east, toward Vietnam—Henri's home country and the place where all four had experienced their greatest professional moments.

Remote as it was, there was always a chance that in some future century, or millennium, archaeologists would discover this underground tombstone. If so, they would find it inscribed:

In memory of our friends and colleagues
Larry Burrows
Henri Huet
Kent Potter
Keisaburo Shimamoto
Tu Vu
and the South Vietnamese soldiers
who died together at Site 2062
10 February 1971

For Tim Page, Horst Faas, and Richard Pyle
We thank the men and women of JTF-FA
Detachment 3 for their efforts
To recover their remains

For the rest of the story, future investigators, if any, would have to rely on the book itself. The story was there, on page 278.

Later, Horst and I walked as far as possible down the rock-strewn ravine to where it dropped off sharply to a lower level. In the monsoon, this probably would have been a raging waterfall. We wondered whether the physical evidence that Lisa Hoshower could not find had merely gone over the edge.

Before our final departure that afternoon, we assembled the team on the hilltop for a group portrait. In contrast to the cheery banter and jokes that had leavened their labors during the previous three days, the camera caught them all looking very serious.

The search at Site 2062 continued for another two weeks after we left. During a stopover in Bangkok, I filed a story to AP in New York, describing the events up to that point. It quoted Lisa Hoshower as saying the finding of film "guarantees that we're looking in the right place" and expressing again her hope that the ravine eventually would produce the human remains she was looking for.

In Bangkok, we also discovered that despite our efforts to keep the

ABOVE: Along Route 9, Laotian houses on stilts are safe from snakes and other dangers.
BELOW: Villagers lay out tools for cutting bamboo at Ban Mang.

ABOVE: Hired by JTF-FA at $24 a day, Laotian villagers form bucket brigade to carry recovered artifacts at Site 2062. Tape divides site into sections for excavation.
BELOW: Steepness of hillside makes work much harder.

ABOVE: JTF-FA team with authors at Site 2062; from left to right, Don Anongdeth, Michael Swam, Aaron Carpenter, Ralf Hawkins, Carl Holden, Lisa Hoshower Leppo, Michael Harsch, Horst Faas, Bill Adams, Jeffrey Price, Richard Pyle.
BELOW LEFT: Lisa examines artifact; RIGHT: T-shirt logo of JTF-FA.

CLOCKWISE FROM UPPER LEFT: Bucket of soil reaches sifting station; Lao workers cross bamboo bridge; boy uses support rope to climb hill; JTF-FA team member swings pickaxe.

ABOVE: Using archeological method, Americans, Laotians sift dirt through screens, leaving artifacts.
BELOW: View of Site 2062 shows terraced area already excavated.

THIS PAGE, FROM TOP: Jeff Price with lens and film; Lisa Hoshower Leppo and Aaron Carpenter examine steel helmet; truck debris on the Ho Chi Minh Trail; unexploded cluster bombs.

FACING PAGE, CLOCKWISE FROM TOP LEFT: Bill Forsyth at work; Johnie Webb with Site 2062 artifacts at CILHI lab; "Burrows Leica" at CILHI.

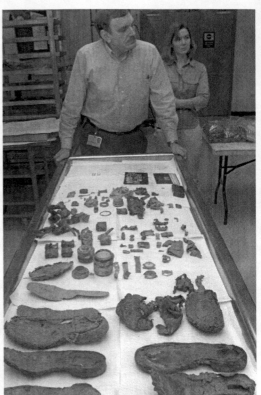
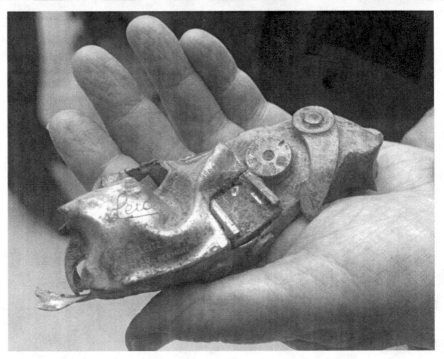

ABOVE: Yomiuri Shimbun reported on Kenro Shimamoto's Buddhist ceremony for his brother at Site 2062 "after 27 years."
BELOW: Birth medallion reading "Cecile, nee 16-6-1947" is believed to have been Henri Huet's.

Laos project from attracting attention we had come dangerously close to being overrun by other news organizations. Unknown to us, and apparently spurred by our visa applications, the Laos Ministry of Information had circulated a news release about the excavation among the Bangkok press corps, inviting reporters, photographers, and TV crews to Laos to cover the story. I was grateful that we hadn't known about this at the time. The last thing Horst and I had wanted, or needed, was a parade of latecomers, with little knowledge of the original incident and none of the more recent series of events, traipsing over the crash site. In retrospect I could imagine on-site news conferences interrupting the work at Site 2062, Laotian workers gawking at the cameras—any number of intrusions that could compromise the nature of the search and, therefore, our story.

Fortunately, none of this had happened. Whereas the BBC had decided on its own not to get involved in the story, this time the gods had ordained an economic and political crisis in Indonesia. Many Bangkok-based foreign journalists were off in Jakarta, and those who stayed behind apparently saw no reason to chase after a shred of history from the Vietnam War era. In the final analysis, the Bangkok press corps had been a no-show.

After returning home, we received further reports on the progress of the search. Important and interesting items continued to turn up—among them a dental bridge, a part of a Leica camera body with a serial number, two more lenses with numbers obliterated, a key with a lion motif, and a religious medal, the Virgin Mary on one side and a name and date inscribed on the other: "*Cecile nee le 16-6-1947.*"

There were belt buckles, shreds of fabric, several size-nine military boot soles, two Seiko watches, a gold Rolex watchband and fragments of others, two Nikon nameplates, "probably from a camera bag," a total of thirteen rolls of 35mm film, a film canister with film inside, a boom microphone mount, a flare launcher, uniform buttons, a padlock key, a survival knife, a .38-caliber pistol (probably carried by a pilot), data plates, a door latch, and seat and lapbelt hardware from a Bell helicopter.

The only item that could be ascribed to a specific person was a Vietnamese military dog tag. It bore the name of Le Trung Hat, in service since 1969, a Buddhist with type-O blood. There was no indication of rank that could tell us whether he had been a pilot, crew chief, or door gunner. But we now knew the names of all but three of the eleven victims.

There also were possible human remains, including four teeth without restoration. Matching these through DNA was a long shot—considering the number of people on the helicopter—but one that remains to be taken. The finds that Lisa Hoshower was looking for did not materialize, even in the creek bed where she had predicted remains would be recovered.

By April 1, the JTF team had covered 90 percent of the site and had seven days left before the deadline decreed by the Laos government for that phase of MIA investigations. As digging was concentrated in the creek bed, Lisa swung a pickaxe and inadvertently chopped a buried cluster bomb in half. Fortunately, it did not explode, and the incident spurred a closer examination of the rocky ditch, revealing that it was rife with undiscovered explosives. This was the stream that Horst and I had explored on our last day at the site. Hoshower called a halt to any further work and declared Site 2062 officially closed.

There it ended, at least for the immediate future.

: :

Comparing our feelings about the experience, Horst and I found that we had arrived more or less independently at the same conclusions. If a crash victim's family could only be satisfied by the positive identification of remains, that was that family's private business. We didn't require that for the fulfillment of our purpose. Many questions probably were never going to be answered, but they didn't have to be. As Horst had suggested in his remarks to the assembled JTF-FA team members, the circumstantial evidence gathered at Site 2062 was strong enough to reveal the truth, as far as it could be known, of what had happened there. The objective of our pilgrimage—to seek out that truth—had been accomplished.

It would take some time before I was able to fully grasp the experience in its whole, to realize what Horst and I had managed to achieve in a world that for journalists is too often dominated by managed events and prepackaged information. This had been the real deal—a speculative journey conceived, planned, and carried out, every element of it our own doing, right down to the military rations that I had bought for $20 in an Army-Navy store on West 42nd Street. There were no public relations news releases, no staged photo ops. Perhaps only journalists who had seen so much of those things could truly appreciate an adventure that was so random, so pure in its uncertainty.

A day after the site was officially closed, another outsider visited the hillside. After reading a newspaper report—perhaps mine—about the search, Kenro Shimamoto, the older brother of Keisaburo, had flown from Tokyo to Laos on a trip arranged by the Japanese embassy in Laos and the Bangkok bureau of the *Yomiuri Shimbun*, the Tokyo newspaper from which he had retired. The Joint Task Force detachment in Vientiane provided escorts for the Japanese visitors, happy to accommodate a close relative of one who had died at Site 2062.

On the hillside, Kenro Shimamoto conducted a private Buddhist ceremony, pouring sake and collecting "a handful of soil," as he put it, in a small urn, symbolic of his brother's remains, to be buried in Japan. Kenro said afterward that while at the site he had heard, on the hot wind, Keisaburo's voice, calling him "*O Nii-chan*," or dear older brother.

I found a special resonance in Kenro Shimamoto's story. On that third day, a few minutes before we climbed aboard our helicopter for the last trip back to the Ban Alang base camp, I had stood for a minute at the top of the ridge, looking down the steep slope, trying to absorb the scene in a way that would become an indelible memory, one with enduring clarity despite the inevitable tricks of time. I became aware of something indefinable. Not a voice, certainly, but a sense, a thought, perhaps a presence: *We are here.*

I told Horst, unashamedly, that the hill had spoken to me.

There is no way to know whether such experiences are driven by some telepathic force beyond knowledge or are simply the product of wishful imagination.

Before this journey, I would have thought only the latter. But in that final moment, gazing down the plunging slope to the rocky stream and the tall trees that pierced the sky like the spires of a cathedral, it was easy to understand why the people of the mountains believe that spirits dwell in such places.

We could never say otherwise.

18 : Epilogue

On April 17, 1998, Kenro Shimamoto, his ninety-five-year-old mother, and other immediate family members held a private memorial service for Keisaburo, and the urn containing the symbolic remains was interred in the family tomb at Tanega-Shima, a small island in Kyushu in western Japan. "I went to the jungle in search of his shadow," Kenro later wrote. "The soil must have absorbed the spirit and blood of his final moments."

In June, a letter arrived from Captain Jeff Price, who told how he had gone on, after Case 2062, to another MIA recovery mission in Papua New Guinea that "resolved several WWII cases" and soon would be off to yet another job in North Korea, whose government had finally consented, after lengthy negotiations, to allow Joint Task Force teams to search for American remains from the Korean War on its territory. The work of the organization was continuing in Indochina, but there were many other Americans still missing from wars around the globe.

Jeff added, "I want to report to you that in the manner that you and I agreed, on 1 April 1998 at 0930 hours we buried the book at [grid coordinate] at an elevation of 1076 feet. I ensured that the book was standing up with the cover facing Saigon on a 178 magnetic degree azimuth. Only the American team was present, and each team member was honored to be able to participate."

There have been no other ceremonies as yet.

Kent Potter's sister, for private reasons, declines to have anything to do with the case. When a representative of the U.S. State Department's POW-MIA office called her in early 1998 to advise her that the excavation of Site 2062 was about to be undertaken, she replied as she had to this author two years earlier: So much time had passed, there was nothing to be gained by such an effort.

The physical evidence gathered at the site leaves no question that a UH-1 Huey helicopter fell there and that it carried a number of people with cameras. Although that evidence remains maddeningly shy of the standard of proof that forensic science demands for identification, the circumstantial evidence is more than persuasive. The four photographers were seen, and photographed, getting on the chopper at Ham Nghi. In response to questions in the days after the crash, South Vietnamese officials had told us that all the journalists were in their seats when the Huey departed from Firebase Hotel on the second leg to LZ Ranger South, and there was no question that all were killed when the Huey was shot down. And though the Nikon camera lenses found at the site could not be traced to their owners after so many years, the broken Leica camera body almost surely had belonged to Larry Burrows.

Horst could find no picture of Larry in which the serial numbers of his cameras were visible, and Russell Burrows's search of his father's personal papers turned up no insurance or customs records. But the serial number enabled Leica company officials in Germany to trace records showing that that particular Model M3 camera body had been sold by its Leitz London retail outlet on July 7, 1960. There was no record of the purchaser, and the store no longer exists. But Burrows was a regular customer of the Leica outlet at that time, and only he, among the four, was in London in July 1960.

Horst and I already had concluded that the camera was Larry's— and Leica officials had concurred—when, in the course of a casual conversation over lunch in New York, Russell suddenly remembered something that offered even stronger circumstantial support: On July

1, 1960, while covering the independence celebration in the Congo, Larry Burrows was caught in a street riot, and his cameras were smashed by the mob. He managed to cobble together a workable camera to finish the assignment, Russell said, but on return to London, he would have needed to buy new equipment.

Russell's recollection seemed to end any doubt that the camera recovered at Site 2062 was indeed Larry's, probably one of those seen in almost every photo of the *Life* photographer at work.

Even more tantalizing was the mystery of Cecile. From the first word that a religious medallion bearing that name and a date of birth had been found at the crash site, we believed that it must have belonged to Henri Huet, who was the only Catholic among the four photographers.

Although the Joint Task Force investigators initially reported the name on the medallion as "Ceciley," I guessed from the start that it more likely was "Cecile," a common French name. But who *was* Ceciley? The name meant nothing to members of Henri's family in France. Among his Vietnam acquaintances, former AP colleagues George Esper and Eddie Adams said they recalled hearing him speak of someone by that name, but they don't know—if they ever did—who she was.

No pictures of Henri show him wearing the medal, but he could have carried it elsewhere, perhaps in his camera bag.

The connection was not made until early 1999. In a telephone conversation, Inger-Johanne Holmboe had told me that she had no knowledge of the medal, or of anyone in Henri's past named Ceciley, or Cecile.

A few days later, as I was rereading through some old letters and other materials that Inger-Johanne had previously sent to us, a name suddenly leaped from the typewritten page. In an essay of remembrance that she had written in 1971, shortly after the crash, Inger-Johanne had mentioned that during his recuperation from wounds in New York in 1967, "Henri met a girl, Cecil ... "

Ceciley ... Cecil ... *Cecile.* ...

Another call to Stockholm followed. This time—her memory triggered by what she had written twenty-eight years earlier—Inger-Johanne recalled what Henri had told her about that previous love affair.

He had described how he met a Belgian photo model while convalescing from wounds in New York in 1967, a whirlwind romance in which they traveled to Cuba and Mexico, and became engaged to be married—a plan that would come to naught with the *"Cher Henri"* postcard that landed by mistake in Inger-Johanne's own mailbox in Tokyo on New Year's Eve, 1970—and inadvertently brought Inger-Johanne and Henri together.

In April 2000, en route back to Vietnam to cover the twenty-fifth anniversary of the war's end, I stopped off in Honolulu and spent a day visiting the CILHI laboratory and the Joint Task Force headquarters. Lisa Hoshower—by now married to Jeff Leppo, another CILHI forensics expert—was at the laboratory. So was Jeff Price, now a major. I met several others who theretofore had been only names or voices on the telephone.

En route to the JTF-FA compound at Camp H.M. Smith, in the hills overlooking Pearl Harbor, photographer Ronen Zilberman and I could see small airplanes circling and diving above the harbor, and we heard occasional explosions. The film *Pearl Harbor* was in the final stages of shooting.

At Camp Smith, we were well received and sat for a briefing on the agency's operations, with which, as it happened, I was already very familiar. Down a corridor in a rear office, I found the person I was most eager to meet. The amazing Bill Forsyth, the man who had been at the core of this story, who in a real sense had made it all possible, was hard at work at his desk, solving other crash-site mysteries with his documents, maps, and photo lightboards.

Neither agency could have been more hospitable to a visitor. One drew the impression that the researchers and forensic experts carry the knowledge of many, if not all, pending MIA cases around with them, as if in a mental briefcase.

At CILHI, tucked away in its corner of Hickam Air Force Base, the visit began with conversation over coffee and the requisite military-style briefing by its commander, Army Colonel David Pagano, and his civilian deputy, Johnie E. Webb Jr. Afterward, we walked back to the main examining room. It was a large open space, brightly lit, with rows of white-topped tables, each containing the bones and other artifacts of a specific case under study.

One table held the skulls and bones recovered in 1996 at Koh Tang Island off Cambodia's western coast, where a Marine Corps effort to rescue the crew of the hijacked U.S. cargo ship *Mayaguez* in May 1975 had ended in disaster—two helicopters down and forty-one Americans dead—in a bloody, bizarre postscript to the Vietnam War.

Johnie Webb, a tall, Texas-born retired Army colonel, had arranged for all the artifacts from Site 2062 to be laid out on another table. Most of those items, of course, Horst and I had never seen, as they were collected after we left Laos. On the table were three camera lenses, all from Nikon cameras; several rolls of 35mm film; the key with the lion device—it looked like an apartment key; several fragments of watchbands and pieces of watches; belt buckles; shoe soles; and an array of small pieces of metal and plastic from the helicopter. Amid all this were the two centerpieces of the recovery effort—the Leica camera body and the medallion.

From an office, somebody produced a copy of *Requiem* and laid it on a table, open to Roger Mattingly's photo of a tired and grimy Larry Burrows the morning after the friendly-fire air strike on Route 9 and three days before his death. The camera body, set atop the page, rested at the exact angle as one of the two Leicas in the picture. While it was no surprise that the hardware and fittings matched perfectly, we reacted in amazement at seeing the picture of the camera and the real thing precisely juxtaposed.

The gold medallion was smaller than I had expected, about the size of a fingernail. On the front was the bas-relief of the Virgin Mary; on the reverse side the name "Cecile," etched in script with a flourish beneath, and below that, "*nee le* [born] *16-6-1947.*" I could see that the engraved curlicue had caused JTF examiners to misread the name as "Ceciley."

The French words, not mentioned in the previous reports on the medal, indicated that it had been given to Cecile as a birthday gift and that she was twenty-three in 1971, certainly old enough to be charmed by the dashing French war photographer. It was another small clue to who she was but no help in proving what we believed and wanted to believe—that the "Cecil" of Inger-Johanne's writings was the "Cecile" of the medallion. Spelling aside, there was simply no other logical explanation for the name appearing in both contexts. Cecile's last name, and whereabouts, remain unknown.

I picked up one of the watches, its face still intact enough to be readable. It was a Seiko Sportmatic. The hands were stopped at three minutes past twelve, the date also at twelve. I showed it to Lisa, saying,

"This watch ran for at least two days after the crash. Something was still ticking on that hillside." The idea of this seemed to hit both of us with a sudden force. Lisa's eyes sparkled with tears. "My God," she whispered.

Behind a sliding wall were the shelves of boxes containing human remains and other key artifacts from the field, some nine hundred in all. Some were part of cases under study; others were awaiting corroboration by new information. Some were simply fragments of missing persons cases that would never be solved.

Johnie Webb opened a storage box to show me the dental bridge of five gold teeth, which we also believed to have been Larry Burrows's, and the single bone shard recovered from the Laos hillside. The shard, he explained, was so small that it would be destroyed if submitted to DNA testing.

The CILHI laboratory was still hopeful of identifying some human remains from Case 2062, but the forensic process was hampered by the paucity of recovered material, the lack of dental records for any of the eleven people who perished, and the very fact that seven of them were Vietnamese military men, for whom no records are known to exist.

Lisa told again how she had ordered the crash site closed, a few days ahead of schedule, after she unwittingly sliced the cluster bomb with her pickaxe and discovered that the rocky creek bed at the bottom of the hill was full of UXO. It was the place that Horst and I had explored on our own last day at the site, trying to find where the creek led. "I don't know why you guys didn't step on something," Lisa said.

She confirmed our suspicions that the jungle growth had concealed a ledge, a sheer dropoff of many feet that in the rainy season would become a rushing cataract, carrying remains and other materials to oblivion downstream.

Site 2062 was officially closed on April 5, 1998, but the case is still technically open—meaning that at some point a Joint Task Force team might return to excavate the 10 percent of the site left unexplored. JTF-FA officials say a full sweep of the area for unexploded ordnance would be required before the site could be reopened. That had not been ruled out.

Although no American or local citizen had ever been killed or seriously injured during the MIA searches in Indochina, the sundry dangers—ranging from unexploded ordnance buried underfoot to flying into inhospitable places aboard aging, creaky Soviet-built helicopters—made it unlikely that such a run of luck could last forever. And it did not. On April 7, 2001—three years almost to the day after Site 2062 was closed—word flashed across the AP wire from Hanoi that seven Americans and nine Vietnamese were missing, presumed killed, in the crash of a helicopter in Quang Binh province, 280 miles south of Hanoi, near the former DMZ.

Reading the same first reports in London and New York, Horst and I both knew the helicopter must have been on a Joint Task Force mission when it plowed into a fog-shrouded mountainside, and we feared that some of the friends we had made at Site 2062 might be among the casualties.

A quick call to a friend at CILHI in Hawaii confirmed that the Russian MI-17 helicopter indeed was carrying a JTF-FA team, but he allayed our apprehension that anyone we knew was aboard. The overall impact of the crash was devastating, however. The victims included the soon-to-depart commander of the Hanoi detachment, U.S. Army Lieutenant Colonel Rennie Cory Jr.; his designated successor, U.S. Army Lieutenant Colonel George D. Martin; the deputy commander, U.S. Air Force Major Charles Lewis; and Nguyen Thanh Ha, deputy director of Vietnam's MIA search group. Those deaths would prompt JTF-FA to postpone six MIA excavations scheduled to begin a month later.

"It is strange, but this loss brings it home to me even more than being on one of the sites," Roger King messaged from Fort Bragg, North Carolina, where he was now based as a senior public information officer. In Washington, President George W. Bush offered appropriate words of condolence to the families of those killed: "Although not lost in a hostile act like those for whom they search, they, too, have lived lives of great consequence, answering a calling of service to their fellow citizens."

And so they did, as did those that they had gone there to find.

∷

Among the many postscripts to the story of the four photographers, none was more welcome than a letter to the authors from Tom Martin, Kent Potter's high-school classmate and, years later in Thailand, the collector of Kent's possessions after his death. What it said had application, in some form, to each one of the four, and resonated deeply with our own feelings, Horst's and mine, about what had taken them—and us—to Indochina, to war, and to the mountainside in Laos:

> Those of us who were his family and friends feel a deep guilt that we were not able to talk Kent into returning home, but as I look back on his life, I believe that from the moment he took his first news photograph back in Philadelphia, Kent had found his destiny and could not deviate from it. In the beginning, he had been attracted by the lifestyle, but soon he became committed to the life.
>
> It was inevitable that he would have been on that helicopter, on that day, in the company of the best combat photographers of that era, doing the thing he did best. If someone had been there to warn him of the risks, he would have answered that some chances are necessary to live life to its fullest. If his death was tragic, the life that led him to be there was a triumph.
>
> It gives me some sense of closure to know that someone has visited that crash site that I have tried for so long to picture in my mind. But it also gives me comfort to know that nothing of Kent was found there.
>
> For deep inside of me there is this irrational need to believe that Kent will someday come back from his great adventure full of amazing stories and incredible photographs, and that he will dismiss my concerns with an easy smile.
>
> I live in hope of some day receiving a phone call that begins, "Hey, Mart, I just got in from Katmandu."

Afterword

Nor was the story yet finished. . . .

In late 2002, CILHI formally closed Case 2062 with a "circumstantial group identification," a procedure used to resolve cases in which multiple victims are known but remains are too meager to be identified by forensic means. Without such action in "inconclusive" cases, said our Hawaii informant, "the remains will sit on the shelf at CILHI forever."

The final steps would then be notification of next of kin, followed by a "ceremonial group burial" of crash artifacts and bone fragments at a time and place to be determined.

That location itself posed a dilemma. While most circumstantial ID cases concerned only Americans, this one involved eleven people from five countries, of which one—South Vietnam—no longer existed.

In such a situation, United States soil seemed the nearest thing to common ground. All four photographers worked for American news organizations, and given the exodus after Saigon's fall, it was possible, even likely, that some of the Vietnamese victims had relatives in the United States.

We felt strongly that any final accounting of the dead should include those seven Vietnamese. We knew the names of three—colonels Nhat and Vi, and photographer Tu Vu—but with records of the defunct Vietnam Air Force lost, destroyed, in private hands—or perhaps locked in some file cabinet in Hanoi—our only clue to the identity of the flight crew was the military dog tag bearing the apparent name of Le Trung Hat.

Through an Internet website run by former VNAF members, CILHI case investigator Robert C. Maves learned that the unit involved was the 213th Helicopter Squadron, and that the crew of one helicopter included 2nd Lieutenant Ta Hoa, commander; 2nd Lieutenant Nguyen Dieu, copilot, and Sergeants Nguyen Hoang Anh and Tran Minh Cong as crew chief and gunner.

But if these were the crew members, who was Le Trung Hat? All evidence from 1971 to the present pointed to eleven aboard. Now we had to wonder if there were twelve—a radio operator, perhaps, or an aide to the colonels?

Again, help came from out of the blue. Tom Pho, an aerospace engineer in Orlando, Florida, was scanning the VNAF website when he found our request for information, and offered his services.

Tom, real name Pho Thai Thong, had first-hand knowledge. As a nineteen-year-old Huey crew chief in 1971, he had flown in Laos and survived being shot down over Firebase Hotel 2 on February 26. Four years later, he escaped Vietnam by helicopter on the last day of the war.

Networking among VNAF veterans, Tom drew blanks on Le Trung Hat, but discovered that one of the Hueys shot down on February 10 was commanded by a 2nd Lieutenant Le Trung *Hai*. Then, examining his own dog tag—which he had kept as a souvenir—Tom realized the embossed letters T and I could be easily misread, one for the other. We asked CILHI to recheck the dog tag from Site 2062. Bob Maves replied that the name indeed was Le Trung Hai.

Having solved the "Hat" mystery, Tom Pho next used his VNAF contacts to achieve what we had not been able to do—find a living survivor of the February 10, 1971 mission.

Like Hai and Tom himself, Nguyen Xuan Trinh was a member of the 233rd Helicopter Squadron, on loan to the Laos operation. On that day, commanding the fourth helicopter in the group, he saw the double shootdown, and narrowly escaped a similar fate.

In 1975, by then a major, Trinh was captured when Saigon fell to the communists. He spent thirteen years in a "hard labor camp," came to the United States with his family in 1994, and is now the proprietor of a gas station in Oklahoma City.

While Trinh's recollections generally coincide with those of other witnesses, he added new details to the story, and it was a given that his version of events would be at variance with others on some aspects.

Trinh says that in keeping with VNAF orders for Laos, Ta Hoa's 213th Squadron ship led the flight, and Le Trung Hai flew the *second* one, with 2nd Lieutenant Le Uy Tin, who was Trinh's best friend, as copilot. That appears to contradict other witnesses on the order of shootdown, but the finding of Hai's dog tag, cameras and film at the same site removes any doubt which aircraft carried the photographers.

Trinh could not name Hai's other crew members, but Tom Pho says VNAF's policy of keeping squadron mates together makes it "one hundred percent valid" that the crew chief was his 233rd Squadron colleague, Nguyen Hoang Anh, while a Sergeant De, of the 213th Squadron, flew with Ta Hoa. The gunner in Hai's crew remains unidentified.

Trinh recalls the Hueys straying too far west, where they ran into 23mm and 37mm anti-aircraft fire, and hearing one brief radio transmission—Lieutenant Hai saying *"Tao bi ban!"* or "I'm hit!" As one helicopter exploded and the second spun out of control, Trinh says, he "autorotated" to drop below 37mm range, only to be hit by smaller-caliber weapons. The two surviving Hueys reached Ham Nghi, but were total losses from battle and engine damage, he says.

In mid-2003, shortly before it merged with JTF-FA into a new entity called the Joint POW-MIA Accounting Command, CILHI chose the U.S. military cemetery at Punchbowl Crater, near Honolulu, as the site for a ceremonial burial of artifacts from the Laos crash. For families at distant ends of the compass, that seemed as practical and fair a choice as any.

As of this writing at the turn of the year, no date is set for that event. Nor have we located any kin of the Vietnamese who died serving their cause at Site 2062. But it remains our hope that whenever this memorial takes place, it will embrace all who perished there thirty-three years ago.

Bibliography

Arnett, Peter. *Live from the Battlefield: From Vietnam to Baghdad, 35 Years in the World's War Zones.* New York: Simon & Schuster, 1994.

Braestrup, Peter. *Big Story: How the American Press and Television Reported and Interpreted the Crisis of Tet, 1968.* Boulder, CO: Westview Press, 1977.

Browne, Malcolm. *Muddy Boots and Red Socks: A Reporter's Life.* New York: Times Books, 1993.

Butler, David. *The Fall of Saigon.* New York: Simon & Schuster, 1985.

Chong, Denise. *The Girl in the Picture: The Story of Kim Phuc, the Photograph, and the Vietnam War.* New York: Penguin Books, 1999.

DA Pamphlet 500-40. *U.S. Army Area Handbook for Vietnam.* Washington, DC: Headquarters, Department of the Army, 1964.

Doelling, Otto C., editor. *Handbook for International Correspondents.* New York: The Associated Press, 1999.

Don, Tran Van. *Our Endless War: Inside Vietnam.* San Rafael, CA: Presidio Press, 1978.

Dunnigan, James F. *How to Make War.* New York: Quill/William Morrow and Co., 1988.

Dunnigan, James F., and Austin Bay. *A Quick and Dirty Guide to War.* New York: Quill/William Morrow and Co., 1985.

Esper, George, and The Associated Press. *The Eyewitness History of the Vietnam War, 1961–1975*. New York: Villard Books, 1983.

Faas, Horst, and Tim Page, editors. *Requiem, By the Photographers Who Died in Vietnam and Indochina*. New York: Random House, 1997.

Fall, Bernard. *Hell in a Very Small Place: The Siege of Dien Bien Phu*. Philadelphia: J.B. Lippincott & Co., 1967.

_____. *Street Without Joy: Insurgency in Indochina, 1946–63*. Taipei, Taiwan: Literature House, Ltd., 1968.

_____. *Last Reflections on a War*. Mechanicsville, PA: Stackpole Books, 2000.

Fitzgerald, Frances. *Fire in the Lake: The Vietnamese and the Americans in Vietnam*. Boston: Little, Brown, 1972.

Hammond, William M. *The Military and the Media, 1962–68*. Washington, DC: U.S. Army Center of Military History, 1988.

Hay, Lt. Gen. John H. (ret). *Vietnam Studies: Tactical and Material Innovations*. Washington, DC: Department of the Army.

Herring, George C. *America's Longest War: The United States and Vietnam, 1950–1975*. New York: McGraw-Hill, Inc., 1996.

Karnow, Stanley. *Vietnam: A History. Revised edition*. New York: Viking Press, 1991.

Kirk, Donald. *Tell It to the Dead: Memories of a War*. Armonk, NY: M.E. Sharpe, Inc., 1996.

Kissinger, Henry. *The White House Years*. Boston: Little, Brown, 1979.

Lind, Michael. *Vietnam, the Necessary War: A Reinterpretation of America's Most Disastrous Military Conflict*. New York: Touchstone, 1999.

Lunn, Hugh. *Vietnam: A Reporter's War*. Briarcliff Manor, NY: Stein and Day, 1986.

McMaster, H. R. *Dereliction of Duty: Lyndon Johnson, Robert McNamara, the Joint Chiefs of Staff and the Lies That Led to Vietnam*. New York: HarperCollins Publishers, 1997.

Moore, Lt. Gen. Harold G. (ret), and Joseph L. Galloway. *We Were Soldiers Once... And Young*. New York: Random House, 1992.

Ninh, Bao. *The Sorrow of War*. London: Martin Secker & Warburg, Ltd., 1993 (English translation from original, Hanoi: 1991).

Okamura, Akihiko. *He Died in Vietnam*. Tokyo: publisher unknown, circa 1975.

Page, Tim. *Derailed in Uncle Ho's Victory Garden: Return to Vietnam and Cambodia*. London: Simon & Schuster UK, 1999.

Prados, John. *Blood Road: The Ho Chi Minh Trail and the Vietnam War*. New York: John Wiley & Sons, 1999.

Prochnau, William. *Once Upon a Distant War: Young War Correspondents and the Early Vietnam Battles*. New York: Times Books, 1995.

Reporting Vietnam: American Journalism 1959–1975, Part One. New York: Library of America, 1998.

Robbins, Christopher. *The Invisible Air Force.* London: MacMillan London Ltd, 1979.

Rochester, Stuart I., and Frederick Kiley. *Honor Bound: The History of American Prisoners of War in Southeast Asia, 1961–73.* Washington: Historical Office, Office of the Secretary of Defense, 1998.

Sharp, Admiral U.S. Grant, USN (ret). *Strategy for Defeat: Vietnam in Retrospect.* Novato, CA: Presidio Press, Inc. 1978.

Snepp, Frank W. III. *Decent Interval: An Insider's Account of Saigon's Indecent End Told by the CIA's Chief Strategy Analyst in Vietnam.* New York: Vintage, 1978.

Stanton, Shelby. *Vietnam Order of Battle.* New York: Galahad Books, 1987.

Tin, Bui. *Following Ho Chi Minh: Memoirs of a North Vietnamese Colonel.* Bathhurst, NSW, Australia: Crawford House Publishing, 1995.

Trotta, Liz. *Fighting for Air: In the Trenches with Television News.* New York: Simon & Schuster, 1991.

Tucker, Spencer C., editor. *Encyclopedia of the Vietnam War: A Political, Social & Military History.* Oxford: Oxford University Press, 1998.

Volkert, Kurt, and T. Jeff Williams. *A Cambodian Odyssey and the Deaths of 25 Journalists.* San Jose, CA: Writer's Showcase, 2001.

Wyatt, Clarence. *The American Press in the Vietnam War.* New York: W.W. Norton & Co., 1993.

Zaffiri, Samuel. *Hamburger Hill: The Brutal Battle for Dong Ap Bia, May 11–20, 1969.* Novato, CA: Presidio Press, Inc., 1988.

Periodicals and Other Sources

Elegant, Robert, "How To Lose A War," *Encounter,* August 1981.

Joint Task Force-Full Accounting, Web site: http://www.pacom.mil/JTFFA

"Not To Be Forgotten," official pamphlet, U.S. Army Central Identification Laboratory Hawaii; Hickam AFB, HI, undated.

"The Edge of the Sword," The Media: *Newsweek,* Feb. 22, 1971.

The Press: *Time,* Feb. 22, 1971.

Smiley, Brenda, "Special Report: Excavating MIAs," *Archaeology,* New York: March/April 1996.

Summary of Excavation, Case 2062, 10 March–9 April 1998 in Lao People's Democratic Republic: JTF-FA administrative message, Camp H. M. Smith, HI, May 20, 1998.

Glossary

AH-1 (Cobra gunship): U.S. attack helicopter.

Air Cavalry: Helicopter forces used for scouting, hit-and-run attacks.

Arc Light: Raid by B-52s, long-range strategic bombers adapted for tactical use in Indochina.

AP (The Associated Press): New York–based non-profit news cooperative founded in 1848, now world's largest news-gathering organization.

ARVN: Army of Republic of (South) Vietnam.

A Shau Valley: Eighteen-mile long valley along Vietnam-Laos border.

Binh Doan 70: Literally "Task Force 70," Hanoi's forces deployed against Saigon's invasion of Laos. (See: **Lam Son 719**.)

Bo Doi: Northern soldiers; literally "walk group."

Buggery statue: Much-derided military monument in Saigon's main square.

C-130 "Hercules": U.S. cargo plane.

C&C (Command and Control): Field commander's helicopter.

CBU (Cluster bomb unit): U.S.–made bomb canister to scatter "area denial" explosives over specific area. Delayed-action versions still pose hazards in Laos.

CH-47 "Chinook": U.S. Army cargo helicopter.

CILHI: U.S. Army's Central Identification Laboratory Hawaii, which processes U.S. military remains from Indochina, other areas (See: **JTF-FA**.)

Combat assault: Helicopter-borne infantry attack.

Cooper-Church Amendment: 1970 Senate resolution restricting U.S. forces to 18 miles inside Cambodia; later basis for limiting U.S. to a support role in Laos.

COSVN (Central Office for South Vietnam): Main NVA/VC HQ in eastern Cambodia. Eluded U.S. invasion.

Daisy Cutter (BLU-82): 15,000-pound bomb that explodes above ground to create "instant LZs" for helicopters.

Danang Press Center: MACV-run center for media covering I Corps.

DMZ (Demilitarized Zone): Six-mile (10-km) wide zone dividing North and South Vietnam at 17th parallel under 1954 Geneva Accords. Violated by both sides.

Dodge City: GI name for VC/NVA–dominated area near Danang.

DRV (Democratic Republic of Vietnam): North Vietnam. In 1976, the unified country was renamed Socialist Republic of Vietnam.

Embargo: MACV ban on advance reporting of military operations.

Eye Corps: Verbal shorthand for I Corps (See: **Military Region 1.**)

Fast movers: U.S. fighter-bombers.

Fifty Rock: AP headquarters at 50 Rockefeller Plaza, New York.

Firebase: Temporary artillery base.

Five O'Clock Follies: Popular name for MACV's daily Saigon news briefing.

Geneva conferences: 1954 Accords that ended French-Indochina war, divided Vietnam. 1962 fourteen-nation conference created a neutral Laos.

Hac Bao (Black Panthers): ARVN jungle fighters.

Hamburger Hill: Controversial 1969 battle.

Ham Nghi: Forward HQ of Lam Son 719.

Hanoi: Capital of North Vietnam, now of entire country.

Ho Chi Minh Trail: Jungle road network used by North Vietnam to move troops, supplies through Laos and Cambodia to South Vietnam.

Hue: Vietnam's former imperial capital, center of culture. Devastated by 1968 Tet Offensive.

JTF-FA (Joint Task Force-Full Accounting): Military unit created in 1992 to seek some 2,000 Americans "unaccounted for" in Indochina.

JUSPAO (Joint U.S. Public Affairs Office): Combined U.S. government (civilian) and MACV (military) information offices in Saigon. (See: **MACV.**)

Khe Sanh: U.S. Marine base under NVA siege for 77 days in 1968, reopened in 1971 as support base for Lam Son 719.

Khmer Rouge: Cambodian communist guerrillas.

Lam Son 719: Code name for Saigon's invasion of Laos February 8–April 9, 1971.

LOH-6 "Loach," "Little Bird": light observation helicopter.

Long Cheng: Mountain base of Gen. Vang Pao, Laotian warlord who led CIA "secret army" of Hmong tribesmen.

LZ (landing zone) Ranger North, LZ Ranger South: ARVN bases in Laos during Lam Son 719.

MACV: U.S. Military Assistance Command Vietnam, HQ of U.S. forces.

MIA (Missing in action): Official U.S. term is "unaccounted for."

Military Region I (a. k. a I Corps, Eye Corps): South Vietnam's five northern provinces. MR II included Central Highlands and coast; MR III, Saigon region; MR IV, Mekong Delta.

Montagnards: Indochina's highland tribes, ethnically different from Vietnamese.

NLF (National Liberation Front): South Vietnam's Communist insurgency, made up of People's Liberation Armed Front (PLAF), a. k. a. Viet Cong, and Provisional Revolutionary Government (PRG).

NVA (North Vietnamese Army) : After 1968, acronym replaced PAVN, for People's Army of Vietnam. (See: **Bo Doi**.)

Panhandle: Area of southern Laos including Savannakhet province, Ho Chi Minh Trail.

Parrot's Beak: Part of Cambodia jutting into Vietnam northwest of Saigon.

Pathet Lao: Laos communist insurgency. Joined 1962 neutral coalition, withdrew in 1964, remained hostile until taking power in 1975.

Pink team: Army slang for helicopter attack team, OH-6 scout (white) and AH-1 Cobra gunship (red).

Radio Catinat: Saigon's political rumor mill.

Republic of Vietnam: Created by 1954 Geneva Accords, South Vietnam withstood takeover by North for nearly two decades but collapsed in 1975, two years after U.S. withdrawal.

Route 1, Route 9: Parts of French-built highway system in Indochina.

Saigon: South Vietnam's capital. Renamed Ho Chi Minh City in 1975.

Second Tet: second wave of VC/NVA attacks in South Vietnam, May 1968.

Secret War: CIA-run war in northern Laos against Pathet Lao and North Vietnamese.

Sihanouk Trail: Overland supply route from Sihanoukville port to NVA/VC camps in eastern Cambodia.

Site 2062: JTF-FA/CILHI designation of crash site where VNAF helicopter crashed February 10, 1971, killing four foreign photographers, seven Vietnamese soldiers.

Squirrel: French-built Aerospatiale AS350D helicopter.

Tchepone: Laos town 25 miles west of Vietnam border. Final objective of ARVN invasion. Today called Sepone.

37-mm anti-aircraft gun: One of Soviet-origin weapons used by North Vietnam to defend Ho Chi Minh Trail.

UH-1H Huey: Vietnam War's most versatile helicopter. Served as "slick" (troop assault), medevac, cargo carrier, gunship, command ship.

UPI (United Press International): American news agency owned by Scripps-Howard. AP's main rival.

UXO: Unexploded ordnance.

Viet Cong: "Viet Nam Cong San," i.e., Vietnam Communists. Originally a derogatory term.

VNAF (Vietnam Air Force): Saigon's U.S-trained air force that flew helicopters and small attack bombers.

XRay Delta: Map grid square of southern Laos where Lam Son 719 was staged.

Photo Credits

mamoto in Vietnam, undated (bottom, left); photographer unknown, from a private collection. Vietnamese Army photographer Tu Vu, February 1971; photo by Michael Putzel.

Page 6: US Marine Corps CH-46 crashes during a combat assault near the DMZ, July 18, 1966; photo by Horst Faas (Associated Press). Richard Pyle inside helicopter during a combat assault, May 10, 1969; photo by Wally Terry, private collection. Horst Faas during a military operation 1965 (bottom right); photographer unknown, private collection.

Page 7: Flaming CH-46 helicopter loaded with troops heads for crash, July 18, 1966; photo by Horst Faas (Associated Press). Vietcong eyes Horst Faas during the battle for Dong Xai, June 10, 1966; photo by Horst Faas (Associated Press). Medics work to save Horst Faas during battle at Bu Dop, December 7, 1967; photo by John Wheeler, private collection.

Page 8: Horst Faas and Richard Pyle at Site 2062 in March 1998; photo by Captain Roger King, private collection. Nineteen cameras and photographic lens parts found during the 1998 excavation; photo by Ron Zilberman, private collection.

Photo Section 2, following page 52

Page 1: Larry Burrows poses with an Autoflex camera in London, 1946; photographer unknown, courtesy of L. Burrows Collection. Larry Burrows and Horst Faas (standing) at a Saigon roadblock, 1967; photographer unknown, private collection. Larry Burrows with Leica cameras on the morning of February 7, 1971; photo by Roger Mattingly.

Page 2: Larry Burrows photographs Queen Elisabeth II during Royal Tour in Fiji 1963; photo by Edward P. Christensen, courtesy of L. Burrows Collection. Larry Burrows on location for the film *The Ugly American* in Thailand, undated; photographer unknown, courtesy of L. Burrows Collection.

Page 3: Larry Burrows assists evacuation of wounded, Mimot, Cambodia, 1970; photo by Henri Huet (Associated Press). Larry Burrows crosses a stream with U.S. soldiers in Vietnam, undated; photographer unknown, with inscription, courtesy of Tad Bartimus. Larry Burrows attaches a camera to a H21 U.S. Army helicopter, 1966; photographer unknown, courtesy of L. Burrows Collection.

Page 4: NVA trucks move south on the HCM trail in bomb-blasted jungle, Quang Binh province,1968; photo by Hoang Van Sac, courtesy of Requiem Collection. North Vietnamese workers somewhere on the HCM trail, undated; photo by Van Luong, courtesy of Requiem Collection. North Vietnamese ferry goods on bicycles southwards on the HCM trail, 1969; photo by Huu Ngoi, courtesy of Requiem Collection.

Page 5: NVA soldiers push a truck on muddy uphill stretch of the HCM trail, 1969; photo by Huu Ngoi, courtesy of Requiem Collection. Quang Bing province volunteers move rocks for the construction of the HCM trail, 1970; photo by Hoang Van Sac, courtesy of Requiem Collection. NVA Transport Unit soldiers work on steep rock to construct a section of the HCM trail; photo by Hoang Van Sac, courtesy of Requiem Collection.

Page 6: Gilles Pierre Louis Raoul Huet (1876–1958), his Vietnamese wife, (left to right) their daughter Jeanne Marie and sons Yves, Paul and Henri at their Dalat farm, 1932; photographer unknown, courtesy of Yves Huet. Henri Huet in the field in Vietnam, undated; photographer unknown, courtesy of Inger J. Holmboe.

Page 7: Gilles Pierre Louis Raoul Huet, father of Henri Huet at Dalat, 1954; photo by Henri Huet, courtesy of Inger J. Holmboe. Sonja Pietrowski (Henri Huet's divorced wife), their children Joel Alexis Huet (b.1959) and Sandrine Jannick Huet (b.1962), and Henri's fiancée Inger Johanne Holmboe (right) in New Caledonia, October 1970; photo by Henri Huet, courtesy of Inger J. Holmboe. Henri Huet and his fiancée Inger Johanne Holmboe in Bangkok, autumn 1970; photographer unknown, courtesy of Inger J. Holmboe. Henri Huet rides his scooter with his daughter Sandrine Jannick Huet in Saigon, 1965; photographer unknown, courtesy of Inger J. Holmboe. General William C. Westmoreland congratulates Henri Huet on his 1967 Robert Capa Award, looking on are AP board Chairman Paul Miller (center) and AP General Manager Wes Gallagher (right), New York, 1967; photographer unknown, courtesy of Inger J. Holmboe.

Page 8: Henri Huet assists an U.S. medic during military operation in 1966; photographer unknown, courtesy of Inger J. Holmboe. Henri Huet lies wounded in a trench at Con Thien U.S. Marine base, September 22, 1967; photo by Dana Stone, courtesy of Inger J. Holmboe. Inger Johanne Holmboe in her Stockholm apartment with Huet mementos, 1998; photo by Horst Faas, courtesy of Inger J. Holmboe.

Photo Section 3, following page 100

Page 1: The staff of Associated Press in Saigon in June 1970; photo by Detlev Arndt, private collection. Photographer Dang Van Phuoc (Associated Press) on the cover of *The AP World*, 1968; photographer unknown, private collection.

Page 2: Horst Faas (left), George Esper, and Henri Huet (back) in the AP office, undated; photographer unknown, private collection. Henri Huet (left) and Richard Pyle ride bicycles during coverage of a military operation in Cambodia, 1970; photographer unknown, private collection. Henri Huet (right) with Richard Pyle, Major J. D. Coleman, and Richard Merron (left to right), foreground Hugh Van Es. Huet is about to depart for Tokyo; photographer unknown, private collection. "Five O' Clock Follies" briefing in Saigon, with (seated left to right) Father Patrick O'Connor, Pham Xuan An, Neil Sheehan, Keith Beech, Seymour Topping, Malcolm Brown, unidentified correspondent, and Peter Kalischer (head down); photographer unknown, private collection.

Page 3: Vietnamese troops gather to be airlifted into Laos, February 10, 1971; photo by Sergio Ortiz. U.S. Marine helicopters supporting the invasion of Laos at a forward base, February 10, 1971; photo by Sergio Ortiz.

Page 4: South Vietnamese troops on a troop carrier near Lang Vei about to invade Laos, February 9, 1971; photo by Henri Huet (last rolls of film). Heavy self-propelled U.S. Army artillery supports invasion of Laos, Lang Vei, February 9, 1971; photo by Henri Huet (last rolls of film). A woman North Vietnamese radio operator, 33rd Field Battalion, on the HCM trail, undated; photo by Hua Kiem, courtesy of Requiem Collection.

Page 5: U.S. Special Forces and Vietnamese Hoc Bao troops ready to be airlifted into Laos, February 10, 1971; photo by Kent Potter (last photos) (UPI/Corbis). NVA troops of the Truong Son (HCM trail) command fire at U.S. aircraft, undated; photographer unknown, courtesy of Requiem Collection.

Page 6: Lt. General Hoang Xuan Lam, commander of the Laos invasion, February 1971; photo by Michael Putzel. Major Jim Newman, U.S. Army, a.k.a. "Condor Six," February 1971; photographer unknown, courtesy Jim Newman. Akihiko Okamura, photographer friend of Keisaburo Shimamoto, February 1971; photographer unknown, private collection. Michael Putzel, Associated Press correspondent, February 1971; photographer unknown, courtesy Michael Putzel. Sergio Ortiz, USMC photographer, February 1971; photographer unknown, courtesy of Sergio Ortiz. Marine Corps AH-1 Cobra gunship flies a low pass at the Laotian border, February 1971; photo by Sergio Ortiz.

Page 7: Facing Laos, South Vietnamese troops watch the impact of enemy artillery near Lao Bao, February 9, 1971; photo by Sergio Ortiz. USMC Cobra gunships are the target of North Vietnamese artillery, February 1971; photo by Sergio Ortiz.

Page 8: Wounded Vietnamese, evacuated from Laos, arrive on February 10, 1971; photo by Sergio Ortiz. Cameraman Tony Hirashiki and (left to right) correspondent Steve Bell (ABC), Jack Foisie (LA Times), Bob Sullivan (UPI), and Michael Putzel (AP) at Khe Sanh, February 1971; photo courtesy of Doug Roesemann.

Photo Section 4, following page 132

Page 1: Inscribed photo of Kent Potter in Ann Bathgate's school yearbook, undated; photographer unknown, courtesy of Ann Bathgate. Ann Bathgate, art student and friend of Kent Potter, undated; photo by Kent Potter, courtesy of Ann Bathgate.

Page 2: Kent Potter on his motorbike during school days, undated; photographer unknown, courtesy of Ann Walker. Kent Potter (right) and *Life* photographer Dick Swanson in a helicopter in Vietnam, 1970; photographer unknown, courtesy of Dick Swanson.

Page 3: Kent Potter (top row center) at his 1966 high school graduation; photographer unknown, courtesy of Ann Walker. Kent Potter behind a warning sign at Lao Bao, February 9, 1971; photographer unknown, private collection.

Page 4: Four photographers (left to right), Keisaburo Shimamoto, Henri Huet (back), Larry Burrows, and Kent Potter, wait for takeoff of their helicopter February 10, 1971; photo by Sergio Ortiz. Vietnamese helicopters are parked on a knoll at Ham Nghi; photo by Sergio Ortiz. Four photographers (left to right), Keisaburo Shimamoto, Henri Huet (back), Larry Burrows, and Kent Potter, wait for takeoff of their helicopter February 10, 1971, with a Vietnamese member of the helicopter crew (right); photo by Sergio Ortiz. A jeep with lights blazing leaves the foggy helicopter pad where the photographers are waiting, February 10, 1971; photo by Sergio Ortiz.

Page 5: Formation of "Condors" over Laos, (right) a machine gun of the fourth helicopter; photo by Michael Putzel. Gunners of Company 4, NVA Anti Aircraft Co., Quang Trung Command fire a 27-mm AA gun, lethal to helicopters, 1970; photo by Hua Kiem, courtesy of Requiem Collection. An NVA anti-aircraft gunner takes aim along the HCM Trail, undated; photo by Van Bao, courtesy of Requiem Collection.

Page 6: A U.S. Army helicopter takes off, flying at tree top level, February 11, 1971; photo by Michael Putzel. Major Jim Newman (right) and copilot in Newman's C&C ship fly towards Laos, February 11, 1971; photo by Michael Putzel. The door gunner of Newman's C&C helicopter fires a 50-caliber machine gun at a target in the hills at the Lao border, February 11, 1971; photo by Michael Putzel.

Page 7: Crash site of the photographers' helicopter, February 11, 1971; photo by Michael Putzel. Enlargement of a USAF reconnaissance photo showing the crash site of the photographers' helicopter, undated; USAF handout photo, private collection.

Page 8: Hillside near Site 2062, where an anti-aircraft gun position was found, March 1998; photo by Horst Faas.

Photo Section 5, following page 180

Page 1: War wounded Vietnamese children are evacuated in a helicopter to a Soc Trang Field Hospital in the Mekong Delta, April 10, 1968; photo by Kent Potter (UPI/Corbis).

Page 2: The body of a dead U.S. paratrooper dangles from a helicopter being pulled from the jungle, 1966; photo by Henri Huet (Associated Press). Wounded are helped from a road ambush site near Quan Loi, August 14, 1969; photo by Kent Potter (UPI/Corbis).

Page 3: U.S. Marines emerge from their foxholes at dawn near a shot-down helicopter near the DMZ, 1966; photo by Henri Huet (Associated Press). USMC men bring their artillery into position during fighting at the DMZ, undated; photo by Larry Burrows, courtesy of R. Burrows Collection.

Page 4: Destroyed interior of a Catholic church after fighting in Bien Hoa, February 27, 1969; photo by Kent Potter (UPI/Corbis). A woman mourns the dead wrapped in plastic sheets after the 1968 Tet offensive in Saigon; photo by Keisaburo Shimamoto, private collection.

Page 5: 173rd Airborne Brigade troops cross a flooded river in War Zone C near Ben Cat, 1965; photo by Henri Huet (Associated Press). A U.S. infantryman holds his machine gun high as he crosses a canal in the Mekong Delta, 1968; photo by Henri Huet (Associated Press). Photographer Henri Huet, crossing a canal in the Mekong Delta, on the summer 1968 cover of *The AP World;* photographer unknown, courtesy of Inger J. Holmboe.

Page 6: "Yankee Papa 13" photo essay in *Life* magazine, 1965: Crew Chief James Farley realizes that his fellow pilot Marine is dead; photo by Larry Burrows (*Life*).

Page 7: Medic Thomas Cole (1st Cavalry Division) aids a wounded soldier during the battle of An Thi, 1966; photo by Henri Huet (Associated Press).

Page 8: A U.S. advisor to Vietnamese Special Forces on patrol near the Cambodian border, September 1969; photo by Kent Potter (UPI/Corbis). "Yankee Papa 13" photo essay in *Life* magazine, 1965: Crew Chief James Farley breaks down after the day's events; photo by Larry Burrows (*Life*).

Photo Section 6, following page 228

(All photos taken in March 1998)

Page 1: Typical Lao House along Route 9 near Tchepone; photo by Horst Faas. Lao women hired for the excavation collect their tools for clearing the jungle at An Lang airstrip, Laos; photo by Horst Faas.

Page 2: Hired by the Lao Government on behalf of JTF-FA villagers form a bucket line at the excavation site marked out in squares; photo by Horst Faas. Overview of the steep crash site to be excavated; photo by Horst Faas.

Page 3: The authors with members of the JFT-FA team at site 2062. Left to right: Don Anongdeth, Michael Swam, Aaron Carpenter, Ralf Hawkins, Carl Holden, Lisa Hoshower-Leppo, Michael Harsch, Horst Faas, Bill Adams, Jeffrey Price, Richard Pyle; photo by Roger King, private collection. Lisa Hoshower-Leppo examines item found during the dig; photo by Horst Faas. The logo of the JFT-FA on the T-shirt of one of the team members; photo by Horst Faas.

Page 4: Buckets of soil from the excavation site reach the sifting station; photo by Horst Faas. Lao workers crawl over a narrow bamboo bridge to the excavation site; photo by Horst Faas. A JFT-FA team member (Michael Swam) swings a pickax digging up hard ground; photo by Horst Faas. A boy worker holds on to a rope as he works in the bucket line of the steep excavation site; photo by Horst Faas.

Page 5: Lisa Hoshower-Leppo and Lao workers at the sifting station, using methods of archaeology; photo by Horst Faas. On the last day of the excavation the hillside was denuded of jungle; photo by David Harsch (U.S. Army).

Page 6: Jeff Price holds up a Nikon lens and the remains of a roll of film found during the fifth day of the excavation; photo by Horst Faas. Lisa Hoshower-Leppo and Aaron Carpenter examine steel helmets found; photo by Horst Faas. Jeffrey Price inspects debris of a truck on the Ho Chi Minh Trail near the excavation site; photo by Horst Faas. Some of the hundreds of unexploded cluster bomblets found during the excavation; photo by Horst Faas.

Page 7: Bill Forsyth at work in the CILHI lab in Honolulu, 1998; photo by Ronen Zilberman, private collection. Items found at Site 2062—camera parts, film, boot soles—and Johnie Webb (in the background) in the CILHI lab in Honolulu, 1998; photo by Ronen Zilberman, private collection. The Leica body attributed to Larry Burrows at the CILHI lab in Honolulu; photo by Ronen Zilberman, private collection.

Page 8: Yomiuri Shimbun report of the Buddhist ceremony held by Kenro Shimamoto for his brother Keisaburo at Site 2062 "after twenty-seven years."

Photos show Kenro Shimamoto, a 1998 view of the crash site, and photographer Keisaburo Shimamoto; courtesy of Rikio Imajo and permission of Yomiuri Shimbun. The front and back side of a birth medallion reading "Cecile, nee 16–6–1947" is believed to have been with Henri Huet; photo by Ronen Zilberman, private collection.

Index

Photo sections are indexed by their preceding text page number, with a second number denoting the particular photo page on which the subject appears. For example, **228–3** indicates the third page of the photo insert following page 228.

LaVergne, TN USA
20 December 2009

167637LV00002B/14/P